SECOND ISAIAH

THE ANCHOR BIBLE is a fresh approach to the world's greatest classic. Its object is to make the Bible accessible to the modern reader; its method is to arrive at the meaning of biblical literature through exact translation and extended exposition, and to reconstruct the ancient setting of the biblical story, as well as the circumstances of its transcription and the characteristics of its transcribers.

THE ANCHOR BIBLE is a project of international and interfaith scope. Protestant, Catholic, and Jewish scholars from many countries contribute individual volumes. The project is not sponsored by any ecclesiastical organization and is not intended to reflect any particular theological doctrine. Prepared under our joint supervision, THE ANCHOR BIBLE is an effort to make available all the significant historical and linguistic knowledge which bears on the interpretation of the biblical record.

THE ANCHOR BIBLE is aimed at the general reader with no special formal training in biblical studies; yet, it is written with the most exacting standards of scholarship, reflecting the highest technical accomplishment.

This project marks the beginning of a new era of co-operation among scholars in biblical research, thus forming a common body of knowledge to be shared by all.

William Foxwell Albright
David Noel Freedman
GENERAL EDITORS

Following the death of senior editor W. F. Albright, The Anchor Bible Editorial Board was established to advise and assist David Noel Freedman in his continuing capacity as general editor. The three members of the Editorial Board are among the contributors to The Anchor Bible. They have been associated with the series for a number of years and are familiar with its methods and objectives. Each is a distinguished authority in his area of specialization, and in concert with the others, will provide counsel and judgment as the series continues.

EDITORIAL BOARD

Frank M. Cross, Jr. Old Testament
Raymond E. Brown New Testament
Jonas C. Greenfield Apocrypha

THE ANCHOR BIBLE

SECOND ISAIAH

INTRODUCTION, TRANSLATION, AND NOTES

BY

JOHN L. McKENZIE

Doubleday & Company, Inc.

Garden City, New York

IMPRIMI POTEST
Chicago, April 20, 1967
Ioannes R. Connery, S.I.
Praepositus Provincialis

NIHIL OBSTAT
Donald A. Panella, M.A., S.T.L., S.S.L.
Censor Deputatus

IMPRIMATUR
Terence J. Cooke, D.D.
✠ Auxiliary Bishop of New York
January 18, 1968
New York, New York

PREFACE

Sincere thanks are due to several persons who made the preparation of this work much easier. Acknowledgment is owed in the first place to Dr. David Noel Freedman, whose eighty-four pages of annotations and criticisms have left much more ample traces in the work than one might guess from the few explicit references. Dr. Freedman's suggestions were especially valuable in the criticism of the text. Miss Susan Burchardt, formerly of Doubleday, handled the editing of the manuscript up to the printing of the galley proofs; her diligence is responsible for the discovery and correction of several errors and the removal of some obscurities. Miss Judith Dollenmayer of Doubleday carried the work from the galleys to the bound book. The manuscript was typed by Mrs. James Nicely of South Bend, Indiana; the writing was done at the University of Chicago and at San Francisco Theological Seminary, San Anselmo, California. I had full use of the libraries at Swift Hall and at the Seminary, and without these resources the work could not have been done. To all of these I express my gratitude, as well as to those who expressed their interest in the work and their encouragement.

John L. McKenzie

University of Notre Dame

CONTENTS

III. ZION POEMS

IV. THIRD ISAIAH

PRINCIPAL ABBREVIATIONS

1. PUBLICATIONS

ANEP	The Ancient Near East in Pictures, ed. J. B. Pritchard
ANET	Ancient Near Eastern Texts Relating to the Old Testament, ed. J. B. Pritchard, 2d ed., 1955
BASOR	Bulletin of the American Schools of Oriental Research
BH³	Biblia Hebraica, ed. R. Kittel, 3d edition
BJRL	Bulletin of the John Rylands Library
BWANT	Beiträge zur Wissenschaft vom Alten und Neuen Testaments
BZA	Beihefte zur Zeitschrift für die alttestamentliche Wissenschaft
ET	Expository Times
FRLANT	Forschungen zur Religion und Literatur des Alten und des Neuen Testaments
GHK	Göttingen Handkommentar
GKC	Gesenius' Hebrew Grammar, ed. E. Kautzsch, revised by A. E. Cowley, 2d Eng. edition, 1910
NKZ	Neue Kirchliche Zeitschrift
IQIs	Qumran Isaiah
IQIsa	The St. Mark's Isaiah Scroll, ed. M. Burrows
ZAW	Zeitschrift für die alttestamentliche Wissenschaft

2. VERSIONS

LXX	The Septuagint
MT	Masoretic Text
Syr.	Syriac version, the Peshitta
Targ.	Aramaic translations or paraphrases
Vulg.	The Vulgate

3. OTHER ABBREVIATIONS

Akk.	Akkadian
Gk.	Greek
Heb.	Hebrew
NT	New Testament
OT	Old Testament

INTRODUCTION

CRITICAL QUESTIONS

Some doubt concerning the unity of the Book of Isaiah was first expressed in the twelfth century by Rabbi ibn Ezra. In modern scholarship the theory that Isa xl–lxvi were written later than the prophecies of Isaiah of Jerusalem (Isa i–xxxix) was proposed by two German scholars, Eichhorn in 1783 and Döderlein in 1789. The anonymous author was called Deutero-Isaiah (often in English Second Isaiah). Bernhard Duhm suggested in 1892 that Isa lvi–lxvi is still later than Second Isaiah; and this second anonymous author was called Trito-Isaiah (often in English Third Isaiah).[1] The distinction between First Isaiah and Second Isaiah is so widely accepted in modern scholarship that the argument against it need not be examined at length. The distinction between Second Isaiah and Third Isaiah is almost as widely accepted, and here again the opposite argument need not be studied in itself. More explicit and longer discussions can be found in the works cited in the Selected Bibliography. C. C. Torrey proposed an elaborate theory of the unity of chapters xl–lxvi (+chs. xxxiv–xxxv) in which he argued that the whole work must come from the period in which other scholars place Third Isaiah.[2] More recently, J. D. Smart also argues for the unity of the work, but advances Third Isaiah to the date of Second Isaiah.[3]

Duhm also isolated the four pieces called the Servant Songs (xlii 1–4, xlix 1–6, l 4–9, lii 13 – liii 12; Secs. 8, 25, 28, 30 in this volume) and attributed them to still another author.[4] This opinion has been and still is vigorously contested; both the critical problems and the interpretation of the Servant Songs are discussed below in a

[1] The first edition of Duhm's commentary is a rare book. The theory of Third Isaiah is set forth in the third edition, *Das Buch Jesaja*, GHK (Göttingen, 1914), pp. xx, 389–90.

[2] *The Second Isaiah* (New York, 1928).

[3] *History and Theology of Second Isaiah* (Philadelphia, 1965).

[4] *Das Buch Jesaja*, pp. xv, xx, 284.

separate section. These Songs are the most obscurely understood
and the most disputed passages of the entire book.

The division of Isaiah into these three portions does not solve all
the critical problems. These include the question of the unity of both
Second Isaiah and Third Isaiah, the relation of the Servant Songs
to Second Isaiah, the relation of the three parts to each other, the
date of the collections of Second Isaiah and Third Isaiah and of the
separate pieces within the collections. To most of these questions no
precise and assured answer can be given.

The distinction between First Isaiah and Second Isaiah has been
made on the basis of vocabulary, style, and thought. The most
striking feature of Second Isaiah is the two occurrences of the name
of Cyrus (xliv 28, xlv 1). That Isaiah of Jerusalem (First Isaiah)
could use the name of a king, in a language unknown to him, who
ruled in a kingdom which did not exist in the eighth century B.C.,
taxes probability too far. It is not a question of placing limits to the
vision of prophecy but of the limits of intelligibility; even if the
name were by hypothesis meaningful to the prophet, it could not be
meaningful to his readers or listeners. Yet Cyrus is introduced without any explanation of his identity, or of why he should be an anchor
of hope to the Israelites whom the prophet addresses. If the prophecy
is to be attributed to Isaiah of Jerusalem, then these passages must
be regarded as later expansions.

But if they are so regarded, other questions remain unanswered.
The reader of Second Isaiah becomes convinced that the work has
a style and vocabulary of its own. In an unpublished dissertation
at the University of Chicago, Mrs. Judith Reinken has made a
vocabulary study according to modern statistical methods which
goes beyond any previous study in depth and breadth. This study
simply does not support the thesis of different authorship; nor does
it support the thesis of unity of authorship. This is to say that the
vocabulary alone is not decisive. Nor is the style alone any more
decisive. What is decisive—for chapters xl–lxvi as a whole, post-
poning for the moment the consideration of a Third Isaiah—is that
the work moves in a different world of discourse from that of First
Isaiah. This can be perceived, even though there are literary con-
nections between First and Second Isaiah, to be discussed below.

What are the elements of this world of discourse? We may first
notice some characteristic themes of First Isaiah which are missing
in Second Isaiah. These themes include the kingship of the Davidic

dynasty, the prophetic rebukes against certain political maneuvers, and the prominence of Assyria. To these, two other themes can be added which are found in both First and Third Isaiah, but not in Second Isaiah: threats of judgment and the rebuke of economic and judicial oppression of the poor. But the treatment of these themes in Third Isaiah differs from their treatment in First Isaiah, as we shall point out below. The audience addressed by Second and Third Isaiah is a non-political audience. There is no mention of involvement in foreign affairs, of war and peace, of trust in men and horses. The community of "Jacob-Israel" in Second Isaiah is politically inactive; it has no power of self-determination. This accords with the absence of the Davidic kingship, either as an existing historical force or as a future reality. Neither in the present nor in the future does Second Isaiah see the monarchy as a component of Israel. Where a foreign power is mentioned, it is Babylon, not Assyria.

As we shall see in more detail when we examine the message of the prophet, the community addressed in Second Isaiah is a community which has experienced a major disaster from which it still suffers. It is this disaster, we can assume, which has reduced the community to political impotence. One constantly meets the motif of helplessness in Second Isaiah. The prophet addresses the people with a message of hope; he promises early deliverance, which will be fulfilled in the restoration of Judah and Jerusalem. A comparison of the description of disaster in Second Isaiah (xlii 22, xlix 19–21, li 17–20) with that in First Isaiah (ch. i) shows that the two accounts are not speaking of the same occasion. Furthermore, unless one excises certain passages, the community addressed in Second Isaiah is not resident in Palestine. It is invited to go out from Babylon (xlviii 20, li 11–12). It is being prepared for a new Exodus and a new march through the desert, themes which recur so frequently and so obviously that no citations are necessary here. In the Zion poems (xlix 14 – lii 12, so called because of the style of address), Jerusalem is ruined and abandoned, awaiting the ingathering of its children from afar (xlix 14 – lii 12). Yahweh comes to Zion, bringing his people with him (xl 9–11).

There is no period of Israelite history known to us which offers a suitable background in which such a community could exist except the period between the fall of Jerusalem to the Babylonians in 587 B.C. and the surrender of Babylon to Cyrus of Persia in 539

B.C. In the discussion of the historical background below, reasons will appear why Second Isaiah must fall not only in this period, but more precisely between 550 and 540 B.C. These reasons rest upon the occurrences of the name of Cyrus in the prophecies. The exiled community in Babylon fits the audience that can be discerned; a Palestinian community of this period or any other period, earlier or later, does not fit it. Some efforts to place the prophet and his listeners in Palestine have not been received by scholars; the rejection is not decisive, and the probabilities after these discussions remain unchanged. To this exiled community the prophet addresses a message (see the section on "The Message," below) which is altogether distinctive within the prophetic canon, easily recognized as different from the message of Isaiah of Jerusalem. The form of the discourses (see the discussion of form, below) also is distinctive as compared to the discourses of the earlier prophets. The prophecies read intelligibly as addressed to the Babylonian community in exile; if they are read as addressed to any one else, a number of insoluble problems of interpretation arises. This is ultimately the reason why scholars adhere to the exilic date and the Babylonian location of Second Isaiah.

A similar line of argument supports the distinction between Second Isaiah and Third Isaiah. Here also style and vocabulary and statistics are less significant than the impression that one has moved into still another world of thought. To some degree the reader can test for himself whether the general judgment of critics that the level of composition and thought falls in Third Isaiah is accurate. He should have no trouble recognizing the introduction of a number of new themes in Third Isaiah and the absence of some characteristic themes of Second Isaiah. The community addressed is not a community in exile; there are no references to the new Exodus and the new desert march. Third Isaiah knows the temple and the cult of the temple; these do not occur in Second Isaiah, and on the hypothesis of the Babylonian community we should not expect them to occur. It is worthy of note that the new Zion of Second Isaiah has no temple (see COMMENT on xliv 24–28). Third Isaiah feels the need of explaining why the promised salvation has been delayed (chs. lix, lxiii–lxiv). Furthermore, his idea of salvation differs from the idea seen in Second Isaiah. It is joined with an apocalyptic judgment (lxvi 15–24). The community is rebuked for social evils and for its superstitious cult, neither of which is included in the rebukes of Second Isaiah (chs. lvii–lix, lxv–lxvi). Second Isaiah rebukes the community for weakness in faith, but not for apostasy. There is a resemblance between the Zion poems of chapters xlix–lii (Second Isaiah) and lx–lxii (Third Isaiah), but critics find that the second poems imitate the first group; for some details of these differences, see the section on "The Message," below, and the NOTES and COMMENT.

The most striking new theme in Third Isaiah is the dualism between the two elements of the community, the genuine Israel and the spurious Israel; see especially NOTES and COMMENT on chapters lxv–lxvi and "The Message," below. This dualism means a revision in the idea of salvation and of the new Israel. All these are notable differences both in the scene and in the message, and they establish a presumption that the works are the products of different authors.

Third Isaiah cannot be dated as exactly as Second Isaiah, but there are certain limits within which it seems the work must be placed. A judgment is rendered difficult here by the lack of extensive information concerning the history of the post-exilic Palestinian community. Duhm dated the work about 450 B.C.[5] The work as a whole must be later than 537 B.C., if the hypothesis concerning the character of the community addressed sketched above is correct. At least some passages seem to presuppose that the temple of Jerusalem has been rebuilt, or is expected to be rebuilt (lvi 7, lx 13, lxvi 1, 6, 20). The second temple was dedicated in 515 B.C. As a terminal date, one may look to the reforms of Nehemiah and Ezra. Nehemiah can be dated 445–432 B.C. The chronology of Ezra is still in dispute; but he was no earlier than Nehemiah, nor by any hypothesis later than 397 B.C. The conditions described in Ezra-Nehemiah are not explicitly echoed in Third Isaiah, nor does the community of the Law established by Ezra's reforms appear. The argument from silence is not convincing, but it permits the hypothesis that Third Isaiah was composed between 537 and 445 B.C. The history of the community during this period, as we have said, is not known; but the Books of Ezra-Nehemiah suggest that the community in Palestine was poor and spiritually disorganized. This is the condition which is reflected in Third Isaiah; in fact, the dualism of the community in Third Isaiah reflects a schism, which was dissolving the community as such. One cannot be more precise

[5] *Das Buch Jesaja,* pp. xv, xx, 389.

than this in the hypothesis that Third Isaiah is not a literary unity; this is the hypothesis we adopt below.

Chapters xxxiv–xxxv are included in this volume with Second Isaiah and Third Isaiah. The NOTES and COMMENT on these chapters show in greater detail why they are included here. Their affiliations in style and content are all with Second and Third Isaiah, not with the prophecies of Isaiah of Jerusalem. They are not the only pieces of later material found in Isa i–xxxix; but chapter xxxv is so much in harmony with Second Isaiah that no particular defense of its inclusion is necessary. Chapter xxxiv does not have the same affiliations to Second Isaiah, nor indeed very obviously to the material of Third Isaiah, except lxiii 1–6.

The unity of authorship of Second Isaiah has been denied by some scholars, but the prevailing opinion still favors unity. In the NOTES and COMMENT we treat the section as a unity with the exception of a few verses, most of which deal with anti-idolatrous polemic (see xliv 9–20). The major problem here is the four Servant Songs (xlii 1–4, xlix 1–6, l 4–9, lii 13 – liii 12), which are discussed below. The rest of the work manifests a unity of style, mood, and tone which is not easily associated with diversity of authorship. But the work is divided into two major sections, which can be distinguished by the typical form of address: Jacob/Israel in xl 12 – xlviii 22, and the Zion poems of xlix 14 – lii 12. Chapter liv continues the address to Zion, and chapter lv is not addressed to anyone by name. It has often been noticed that chapter lv is an *inclusio* which returns to the themes of xl 1–11, indicating unity of editorship, if not of authorship. The differences of language and conception in the two parts are minimal, and do not support the thesis of different authors. They do indicate what no one has ever doubted, that Second Isaiah was an author rich in imagination and in language. He alters his perspective from the historical community he addresses in the Jacob/Israel poems to the ideal community whose restoration he has promised; but in so doing, he neither abandons his basic themes nor introduces anything essentially new. The thesis of diversity of authorship is not required; but if it is maintained, it means that the Zion poems were written by a very clever imitator who, unlike most imitators, successfully concealed the imitation.

The contrast between Second and Third Isaiah itself discloses why the unity of Second Isaiah and the diversity of Third Isaiah are both so easily presumed. There are passages of Third Isaiah so obviously different in content and style that defenders of the most rigorous unity must treat them as secondary; such are the passages concerning the eunuchs and foreigners (lvi 1–8) and the apocalyptic judgment (lxvi 15–24). Within the same collection we have imitations of the Zion poems (chs. lx–lxii), explicit repudiation of superstitious cult practices (lvii 3–13, lxv 1–7), and nearly despairing descriptions of the community (lix 1–15, lxiii 15 – lxiv 12); it is very difficult to combine the rebukes and the lamentations with the triumphal tone of the Zion poems of Third Isaiah. Together with allusions to the temple we have what seems to be a rejection of the temple in lxvi 1–4. It is equally difficult to combine the Zion poems with the dualism of the genuine and the spurious Israel. It may seem as if it is the Zion poems which cause the problem; but if one were to solve the problem by dividing Third Isaiah between two authors, other problems hardly less acute would remain. The hypothesis which raises fewest problems is the hypothesis that Third Isaiah is a collection of poems and discourses from a single period, composed by different authors.

This leaves a problem we have not treated, and that is the community of thought and to some extent of language not only between Second and Third Isaiah, but also throughout the entire Book of Isaiah. Those scholars who maintained the unity of the entire book drew up lists of phrases echoed in the separate parts of the book. The echoes are there, and many of them are mentioned in the NOTES and COMMENT. These echoes are not sufficient to show identity of authorship against the historical and critical problems involved, but neither should they be explained as the result of coincidental allusions. In proposing some theories about the origin of Second Isaiah and Third Isaiah, we must also say something about the origin of the Book of Isaiah as we have it.

Without entering into details about the composition of Isa i–xxxix (for which the reader is referred to the proper volume in this series, the forthcoming *First Isaiah* by H. L. Ginsberg [The Anchor Bible, vol. 19]), the presence of material in these chapters, which, by critical consensus, is later than Second Isaiah, makes it impossible that Second Isaiah should have known this collection in its present form. But relationships in vocabulary and in thought make us conclude that Second Isaiah not only knew the oracles of Isaiah of Jerusalem, but also that he thought of himself as the continuator of Isaiah of Jerusalem. Scholars now frequently explain the preservation of prophetic oracles by postulating a group of disciples and scribes who copied, studied, and interpreted the oracles of the prophets. It does not detract from the originality of Second Isaiah that he was moved by a number of the themes which appear in Isaiah of Jerusalem, or in the collection which went by that name. There is no pre-exilic prophet who gives Jerusalem the position which Isaiah of Jerusalem gives it. Second Isaiah resumes this theology by his references to the restored Jerusalem as the work of Yahweh's salvation. There are other themes of Isaiah (see p. XVI) which Second Isaiah does not resume. The restored Israel of Second Isaiah was not conceived under the external form of the pre-exilic monarchy. But it was an Israel centered on Zion. It is surely not by accident that the historical appendix of First Isaiah concludes (xxxix 7) with a prediction of the exile in Babylon. This conjunction need not be the work of Second Isaiah himself, but of the compiler whose purpose was to arrange the collection to relate it to subsequent historical events which make First Isaiah more meaningful. Second Isaiah could have known at least some of the oracles of promises in First Isaiah, in particular those found in the collection of chapters xxviii–xxxiii (xxviii 5–6, xxix 17–24, xxx 19–33, xxxii 15–20, xxxiii 17–24). These oracles are not all certainly from First Isaiah, and the date of a number of them must be judged uncertain.[6] The oracles of promise are curiously alternated in these chapters with threats against Israel, and the arrangement must be deliberate; but neither the text itself nor the arrangement reflects any awareness of the disaster of the fall of the kingdom of Judah. They may be included in the literary and theological framework within which Second Isaiah speaks.

Similarly, the authors and compilers of Third Isaiah thought of themselves as the custodians and the continuators of the Isaiah tradition, now expanded by the work of Second Isaiah. The echoes of Second Isaiah in Third Isaiah are numerous, and many of them are noted in the NOTES and COMMENT. These authors likewise do not lack originality; as we have already noticed, and shall notice further (see section on "The Message," below), they have introduced some notable modifications into the theology of the school of Isaiah. In a number of passages Third Isaiah is obviously writing a commentary on the sayings of Second Isaiah, as in the Zion poems and

[6] See Otto Eissfeldt, *The Old Testament: An Introduction* (New York, 1965), pp. 315–17.

the discourses on the delay of salvation. It must have been from this prophetic school that the final compilation of the Book of Isaiah in its present form came. By the time this happened, prophecy was no longer spoken and written in Judaism; it was compiled and studied. Third Isaiah is intelligible in precisely the way the name indicates, a final collection of prophetic utterances in the spirit and thought which began with Isaiah of Jerusalem and was maintained by his editors and successors, of whom Second Isaiah was the greatest. We have not yet penetrated fully into the mind of these prophetic scribes, or we would understand how they could collect all these sayings under the one name of Isaiah with the honest conviction that Isaiah of Jerusalem spoke through his school and his successors.

HISTORICAL BACKGROUND

The period within which the literature of Isa xl–lxvi was composed begins with the fall of Jerusalem to the Babylonians under Nebuchadnezzar in 587 B.C. In this defeat the city was destroyed and the kingdom of Judah was reduced to a Babylonian province. Some thousands of the inhabitants were removed to Babylonia, to be added to the exiled group which had been taken there in 597 B.C. It is impossible to get accurate figures for the population removed to Babylon or for the proportion of the total population which this group comprised. It is very likely that the majority of the population was left in the land, probably the peasants and the craftsmen who lived in the towns and villages. But there can be no doubt, on the basis both of the literary evidence and of archaeology, that the defeat was a shattering disaster for Judah. Not only Jerusalem but most of the fortified cities were laid in ruins, and some of the cities were abandoned for generations after the war, a few permanently. The population was diminished both by the deportation and by the loss of life in the war, and the economy of the country must have been completely overturned for at least some years. Still a third deportation is mentioned in Jer lii 30, which occurred in 582 B.C.; but neither the occasion of this action nor details are furnished in any source. D. N. Freedman has suggested that this was a retaliation for the assassination of Gedaliah (Jer xli).

The sources give no information about the life of the people either in Palestine or in Babylon during this period. The early exilic community is reflected in Ezekiel (Ezek viii 1, xii 21–28, xiv 5, xx 1), and some episodes which occurred shortly after the defeat are related in Jer xl–xliii. The narrative of Jeremiah reveals an extremely disorganized and lawless country. Nothing is known of the Babylonian administration of the territory; it could scarcely have been neglected, in view of the military activity of Nebuchadnezzar in Syria during the years after 587 B.C.; see below, pp. xxv–xxvii.

For our purpose, it would be of interest to know how much of their ethnic and religious identity the Palestinian survivors of the disaster retained. Most post-exilic literature is written by members and descendants of the group which returned from Babylon from 537 B.C. onward, and from their point of view; they write as if the group which returned moved into a vacuum, in much the same way as early Israel, in the theory of the Deuteronomic history, moved into Canaan after it was emptied of Canaanites. This can scarcely have been the actual condition. But the attitude of the group which returned shows that it was much more conscious of its continuity with pre-exilic Israel than the Palestinian residents were.

This consciousness of continuity is the most astonishing feature of the exilic community. We know of no other ethnic or religious group of the Assyrian and Babylonian period which was able to maintain its identity after such a series of disasters as Israel and Judah experienced in the eighth and seventh and early sixth centuries B.C. Obviously the exilic community must have found a form and structure in which it could survive, but we have no information concerning it. The destruction of the temple of Jerusalem ended the public official cult; historians believe that the synagogue, a form of cultic assembly without sacrifice, appeared in its earliest form during the Exile. We can postulate some type of regular cultic reunion, and it seems that in these reunions it was the prophetic element in Israelite religion which nourished the hope of Israel. It is very probable, as we shall discuss again below (see "Literary Form and Structure"), that the discourses of Second Isaiah were delivered in such cultic assemblies. It was the exilic group, as far as we know, which preserved the literary traditions of Israel; as we have seen Second Isaiah must have been in possession of the collection of Isaiah of Jerusalem. But Second Isaiah did not create the community of the Exile, nor did he assemble the literary traditions which he knows so well; here he depended on the work of others who were before him.

The history of the Neo-Babylonian Empire is almost the history of Nebuchadnezzar (605–562 B.C.). After his death the dissolution of the empire was rapid. Documents for the reign of Nebuchadnezzar after 587 B.C. are few (see *Ancient Near Eastern Texts Relating to the Old Testament* [abbr. ANET], ed. James B. Pritchard, 2d ed., Princeton University Press, 1955, pp. 307–8). His siege of Tyre for thirteen years is mentioned in Ezek xxix 17–20; this passage suggests that the siege was not successful, and it suggests also that Nebuchadnezzar invaded Egypt. This campaign (568 B.C.) is mentioned in a fragmentary tablet.[7] The siege of Tyre (585–572 B.C.) is probably the background for the deportation of some of the people of Judah in 582 B.C., mentioned above; and it is probable that Egypt, which had attempted to resist Nebuchadnezzar in the campaign of 589–587 B.C., was also involved in this campaign. During his reign Nebuchadnezzar maintained friendly relations with the Medes, the allies of his father Nabopolassar in the overthrow of the Assyrian Empire. Nebuchadnezzar himself was married to a Median princess. The traditional spheres of influence of the Mesopotamian powers did not extend to the Iranian plateau, although the Assyrians had fought frontier wars on its borders. The expansion of Iranian power into areas of Mesopotamian concern did not occur until after the death of Nebuchadnezzar in 562 B.C.

Nebuchadnezzar was succeeded by his son Amel-Marduk, who was assassinated in a palace revolution in 560 B.C. This is the Evil-merodach of II Kings xxv 27–30 and Jer lii 31–34 who released Jehoiachin, former king of Judah, from confinement and made him a royal pensioner; it is no doubt Jehoiachin who appears as Iaukin in a Babylonian list of royal pensioners.[8] Amel-Marduk was succeeded by Nergal-shar-usur, often referred to by the Grecized form of his name, Neriglissor. In 556 B.C. Nergal-shar-usur undertook a campaign in Cilicia, possibly to counteract the moves of the Medes toward Asia Minor (see below); he was initially successful, but suffered a defeat and was forced to return, and died shortly thereafter. His son and successor, Labashi-Marduk, still a minor, was removed by the cabinet officers, and Nabonidus reigned as king from 556 B.C. to the surrender of Babylon to Cyrus in 539 B.C.

The documents for the reign of Nabonidus are more abundant than they are for his predecessors[9]; but the last king of Babylon remains an intriguing and enigmatic figure. A document found at Qumran shows that the dream of Nebuchadnezzar (Dan iv) was a story originally told of Nabonidus, who is not mentioned in Daniel. He was not of the royal line and not from Babylon proper but from Harran, a region in northwest Mesopotamia; his mother was a priestess of the moon-god Sin. He appears as an officer of Nebuchad-

[7] ANET, p. 308.
[8] ANET, p. 308.
[9] See ANET, pp. 309–15.

nezzar in 585 B.C., so he could scarcely have been a young man at his accession. On the basis of such texts as ANET, pp. 309–12, he has been called an antiquarian and a religious fanatic, who neglected the affairs of state for temple-building and cult; in fact such inscriptions are common for Assyrian and Babylonian kings, and if nothing but such texts were preserved for figures like Ashur-nasir-pal and Tiglath-pileser III, they too could be called antiquarian and religious fanatics. Campaigns of Nabonidus in Cilicia (554) and Syria (553) are recorded (ANET, p. 305); for what purpose and with what results we do not know. Strangely most of his reign was spent not in Babylon but at the remote oasis of Teima in Arabia (ANET, p. 306); he did not even return to Babylon for the "taking of the hands of Marduk" at the New Year (the rite signifying the annual renewal of kingship), but left his son Bel-shar-usur (the Bel-shazzar of Dan v) as regent in Babylon. This rather inexplicable absence during the very years when Persian power was expanding rapidly has been a puzzle to historians, many of whom have thought that it was due to some desire to conduct archaeological research. R. P. Dougherty argued powerfully that Nabonidus was concerned with strengthening his kingdom through allies and trade in order to meet the threat of Persian power.[10] Whether this absence was connected with his alienation of the priesthood of Marduk is not clear; that he did alienate them is clear from the text of ANET, pp. 312–15. For these priests, the fall of Babylon was simply a transfer of rule by Marduk from Nabonidus to Cyrus. It is altogether probable that the easy victory of Cyrus was due partly to this; the history of the succession after Nebuchadnezzar shows that the government of Babylon had been unstable since the death of the great king.

Compared to the Babylonians, the Medes and the Persians were newcomers on the stage of ancient Near Eastern history. Both tribes are first mentioned by the Assyrian king Shalmaneser III (858–824 B.C.). Herodotus relates that the Median tribes were first united into a kingdom by Deioces about 715 B.C., whose royal city was Ecbatana. This kingdom included the northern part of the Iranian plateau; the Persians lived in the southern part of the plateau, and from the beginnings of recorded history they appear as subject to the Medes. The Persians expanded their territory after the middle of the seventh century B.C. by annexing Anshan, a portion of the ancient kingdom of Elam, which had been destroyed by

[10] *Nabonidus and Belshazzar* (New Haven, 1929).

the Assyrians in the reign of Ashurbanipal (668–630 B.C.). An-shan lay east of the Persian Gulf and received the name of Parsa; it was the seat of the Persians.

Cyaxares, king of the Medes, was allied with Nabopolassar of Babylon in the wars that destroyed the Assyrian kingdom between 625 and 609 B.C. The Babylonian interests, as we have noted, did not extend east of the Zagros Mountains, and the Median power was consolidated as a result of the war. In 559 B.C., Cyrus II, son of Cambyses I of Persia, succeeded to the throne and almost immediately rebelled against his Median overlord, Astyages. The revolt was successful, and the Persian domination was established, which was to endure until the conquests of Alexander the Great. Relations between Medes and Persians remained amicable, and the new kingdom was usually called the kingdom of the Medes and the Persians. This first victory of Cyrus manifested the character he showed during the rest of his career: in comparison with the Assyrian and Babylonian conquerors, he was easy in his treatment of the vanquished; and he incorporated numerous peoples into his empire with little resistance.

The Medes had shown interest in the territories of Asia Minor, and the later Babylonian kings had responded to this interest by moving themselves in this direction. But here Cyrus achieved a success which no earlier power had achieved. In 546 B.C. he attacked and conquered Lydia in Asia Minor, ruled by Croesus; the gold deposits of Lydia made Croesus a king of legendary wealth. This pushed Persian power to the shores of the Aegean Sea. It was evident that a new and mighty power had arisen in the Near East; and it was evident also that Babylon was no longer able to compete with this power. The oracles of Deutero-Isaiah are very probably to be dated at or shortly after the date of Cyrus' conquest of Lydia, when the magnitude of Persian power and Persian ambitions had become apparent.

The next object of Cyrus' conquest was Babylon itself; we have seen that the sojourn of Nabonidus in Arabia may have been an effort to move his base to a more remote and less vulnerable location. Cyrus' armies moved gradually into possession of Mesopotamia; the instability of the kingdom of Nabonidus is manifest from the documents, and many in the kingdom were sympathetic to the invader. Babylonian troops deserted to Cyrus in considerable numbers; and when Cyrus forced a crossing of the Tigris north of Babylonia, the only real engagement of the campaign, Babylon surrendered without further resistance.[11] Cyrus treated the defeated king and the city benevolently; he took the hands of Marduk and succeeded to the kingship of Babylon with no opposition. In this action the oracles of Second Isaiah were vindicated, although there was no literal fulfillment of Isa xlvi–xlvii.

With this victory Cyrus obtained the vast Neo-Babylonian Empire, which included Syria and Palestine. In 538 B.C. he issued a decree permiting the resettlement of a Jewish community in Palestine and the restoration of the cult (Ezra i 1–11, vi 3–5). This decree could hardly have been issued except as a response to a petition from the community in exile. It is in harmony with the generally humane policy of Cyrus, and of most of the Persian kings after him; Persian rule respected local autonomy and religion, while it retained political control. But the Persians left much of the local administration of the provinces in the hands of local authorities. The first company of exiles to return was led by Sheshbazzar in 537 B.C.; he disappears from the narrative of Ezra without any explanation and is replaced by Zerubbabel. The difficulty of explaining the activities of these two men has led some historians to suppose that there are two names of one and the same man. Both Sheshbazzar and Zerubbabel are given the title of "governor," which indicates that they were appointed political administrators of the new community by the king. The rebuilding of the temple was begun very shortly after the return but it was not dedicated until 515 B.C. Everything suggests, as we have noticed, that the community was small and impoverished. It is in this early post-exilic community that we place the collection of Third Isaiah. If this dating is correct, we learn something about the problems of the community from Third Isaiah, which we do not find in other sources.

The character given to Cyrus by the Greek historians Herodotus and Xenophon (in his idealized and romantic biography, the *Cyropaedia*) has traits of legendary glamor. Yet there is some basis in fact for the humanity attributed to him in the legend. More sober cuneiform records attest that there was a vast difference between Cyrus and the kings of Assyria and Babylon in the treatment of conquered peoples. The glowing terms in which Second Isaiah speaks

[11] ANET, p. 306.

of Cyrus attest not only to the fact that the legend had begun in the life of Cyrus, but also that a new type of conqueror had appeared. In a certain way Cyrus lent himself to the conception of a "messianic" figure in the broad sense of the term, a savior-hero sent by Yahweh at a time when the people of Yahweh could not hope for a savior figure drawn from themselves. The Israelite prophet could see in a man of such stature one on whom the spirit of Yahweh had fallen. The empire of Cyrus foreshadowed the reign of Yahweh over all nations.

LITERARY FORM AND STRUCTURE

Second Isaiah differs sufficiently in its form and structure from the books of earlier prophets to raise a number of questions. The collection exhibits a unity which is in evident contrast to the disarrangement characteristic of most prophetic books. The unity of themes and the progression of thought is not as strict as we find in modern writings of comparable length; but the reader recognizes in Second Isaiah a single work of a type which is not usual in the Bible. It is not merely a collection of detached oracles arranged according to such extrinsic principles as the catchword, that is, the connection of two passages by recurrence of the same word, especially at the end and beginning of the passages.[12] How was this unity achieved? How much of it is due to the author, and how much to his editors?

Within this unity, critics distinguish separate utterances; but there is no general agreement on their number nor on the points of division. Either in the original composition or in the editing the sayings have been arranged so that one flows into another. There are, it is true, repetitions of themes and returns to points already made; the unity is sometimes jerky. But the arrangement makes it more difficult to isolate separate sayings than it is in Amos, Hosea, or Isaiah. Most critics now count about fifty to seventy separate sayings in Second Isaiah. In this translation the collection is divided into two major parts, chapters xl–xlviii and chapters xlix–lv, prefaced by two poems in chapters xxxiv–xxxv. In the first major part we have arranged the sayings in twenty-two poems of varying lengths, of which two are a Servant Song and its response. In the second major part there are eight different poems, including three Servant Songs and two responses; but one of these poems is the long poem of

[12] This is substantially the arrangement proposed by Sigmund Mowinckel in "Die Komposition des deuterojesajanischen Buches," ZAW 49 (1931), 87–112, 242–60.

li 1 – lii 12, which is subdivided into ten parts. This arrangement is made for the convenience of the reader and to indicate changes in theme and topic; it does not pretend to isolate each of the original sayings, nor does any modern commentary succeed in doing this.[13]

This division into two major parts is recommended by the content and character of the writings. The poems of the first part are addressed to a group most frequently addressed as Jacob or Israel; this group is most easily identified with the exilic community of Babylon. The themes of these poems are varied, but the promise of return and restoration is the dominant one. The prophet elaborates a presentation of Yahweh as the one God, the Lord of creation and the Lord of history, which is original (see section on "The Message," below). The second part consists of the Zion poems, together with the three Servant Songs. It is Jerusalem or Zion which is addressed; the city is ruined and abandoned, but it awaits a glorious restoration. This is not a real change of theme and still less of basic theological thinking, but it is a change of perspective; and critics have good reason for supposing that the Zion poems, with their vivid imagery and note of taut expectation, are later than the Jacob/Israel addresses and reflect the heightened expectation which was excited by the victories of Cyrus.[14] They may indeed represent two collections, as they certainly represent two series of utterances; but critics are very widely agreed that they do not represent two authors.

Otto Eissfeldt notes that the prophet uses the typical forms of prophetic utterance:[15] the vision and hearing narrative, the word of comfort, the promise, the rebuke, the admonition, the speech of the messenger, the taunt-song. Of particular interest is the prophet's use of the plea or charge (see xli 20–29, for ex-

---

[13] Sidney Smith remarks, perhaps too vigorously, that to speak of strophes in Israelite poetry is to abuse the term strophe. He admits that one may detect stanzas, but that no scheme of balance can be found (*Isaiah XL–LV* [London, 1944], pp. 3–4).

[14] Begrich, however, places the Zion poems early in the prophet's career, before Cyrus' conquest of Lydia (*Studien zu Deuterojesaia*, BZANW 77 [1938], 67–74). The principal reason for this thesis is that the eschatological conception of the restoration of Jerusalem must be earlier than the "historical" expectation of the Jacob/Israel poems; the ideal gives place to the practical, when the practical appears to be within realization. Since Begrich finds the number of historical texts to be small, he places very little of the work of Second Isaiah after 546 B.C., the year of the conquest of Lydia.

[15] *The Old Testament: An Introduction*, p. 339.

ample) and the fragments of hymns scattered through the work (xlii 10–13, xliv 23, for example). These echo the forms of earlier prophets, but they are given a personal turn by Second Isaiah; his style and transitions are generally smooth compared to Amos or First Isaiah. The weaving of separate sayings into a single move-ment of discourse can be seen easily in xl 1–11, which we have en-titled "The Call of the Prophet." There are three speakers (Yahweh and two voices) in verses 1–8, and three separate sayings; and in verses 9–12 the prophet addresses "the messenger," another say-ing. But all these sayings are concerned with the call of the prophet, and in each saying his message is developed from an announcement of forgiveness in the first saying to the coming of Yahweh in the final saying. This introduction is followed by the poem of crea-tion (xl 12–31), which can scarcely be subdivided into separate sayings; it is a literary unity in conception and in execution.

We notice in the comments that the mood and tone change, at times rather sharply, from one poem to another. Thus a pleasing alternation of promise and rebuke is maintained; and these two themes are merged in the final chapter (xlviii) of the first part in a way which makes it almost impossible to handle this chapter in any other way than as a single poem. As each theme is brought to a climax, it elicits the next theme in response. There is more conscious art here than one is accustomed to find in materials assembled by compilers. The alternation of themes in this poem can be contrasted with the three poems of chapter xliii, in which two utterances of promise are followed by a rebuke; the rebuke in turn is followed by another poem of promise.

The Zion poems have an even more evident structure, and we have not broken them down into separate sayings. Here the tone is almost entirely a tone of promise; the flow of the poem is sus-tained by the brilliance of the imagery, the allusions to past his-tory, and the frequent use of dialogue and apostrophe. These de-vices give the poem an intense tone, almost breathless in its urgency; as the promised salvation approaches, the poet creates an atmosphere of excitement. We have already noted that the final Zion poem (ch. lv) resumes the themes of the introduction; the prophet merges hope and fulfillment. The poetry here creates a theological problem (see "The Message," below).

The unity of Second Isaiah led Paul Volz to suggest that Second Isaiah himself was the collector and editor of his discourses.[16] This is connected with another question, whether Second Isaiah was primarily a speaker or a writer, which we discuss below. Karl Elliger suggested that it was Third Isaiah, a single author, who edited the writings of Second Isaiah and added his own contributions.[17] This opinion is not widely accepted; if it were true, it is remarkable that Third Isaiah produced a much more unified work in his edition of Second Isaiah than he did in his own writings. Furthermore, as we have seen, the existence of Third Isaiah as a single author is highly doubtful. Volz's opinion does give an explanation of the remarkable unity of Second Isaiah; if the collection was made by an editor, the editor had a better understanding of his material than any other editor whom we encounter in the Old Testament. It seems we should presuppose at least that Second Isaiah left his writings in a more organized condition than any other writer known to us in the Old Testament.

But does this suggest that Second Isaiah was a writer rather than a speaker? The earlier prophetic books are almost entirely collections of oral utterances, spoken before they were put in writing, and sometimes written in a summary form. These oracles are collected without any context and arranged according to principles which we sometimes find impossible to discover. The polish of Second Isaiah was not achieved by the usual means of collection and edition. Eissfeldt thinks that he wrote his discourses to be circulated in copies. This would be not only a different manner of publishing the prophetic word, it would also be a different conception of the prophetic mission.

If Second Isaiah was a prophetic speaker, in what situation did he speak? The same question can be asked about the pre-exilic prophets, and it is not always easy to answer. We know that prophets spoke in sanctuaries, and the existence of the cultic prophet, who pronounced oracles in the cult, is fairly well assured. Prophets spoke in the audience halls of kings and in the market places of the cities and towns. Actually we can hardly think of many other places in which the prophet could have assembled a sufficient number of people to make it worth his trouble to speak. Second

---

[16] *Jesaia II* (Leipzig, 1932), p. xxxv.
[17] Karl Elliger, "Deuterojesaja in seinem Verhältnis zu Tritojesaja," BWANT IV, 11 (1933).

Isaiah could have spoken in the market places of the towns of Babylonia; but a number of interpreters have suggested that his discourses were spoken in cultic assemblies. Some have even suggested that they can identify the festivals which were appropriate for his discourses. The themes of creation and the kingship of Yahweh, for example, would have been appropriate to the New Year festival. A New Year festival of Yahweh king and creator in pre-exilic Israel has been postulated by a number of scholars, although there is no direct evidence for this festival. The exiles may have commemorated the anniversary of the fall of Jerusalem by a day of lamentation; in this case, the oracles of promise of Second Isaiah would have been the liturgical response to the lamentation. Of these suggestions one can say only that they are not without probability. It is not necessary to identify the utterances of Second Isaiah with any particular festivals in order to accept the view that he spoke in the cultic assembly. One has to suppose that prayer for the restoration of Jerusalem and the temple must have been a part of the cult of the exilic community; Second Isaiah delivers what would be oracular responses to such prayers. He does not reflect to any notable degree a ritual of lamentation and repentance; his theme is that the judgment was merited, but that the time of forgiveness and liberation has arrived. He proclaims the rise of a new Israel through a new Exodus. If one thinks of festivals at which he might have spoken in the cult, Passover is one such festival which comes to mind.

It seems probable that Second Isaiah, like his predecessors in prophecy, was a speaker first and a writer second; and as a speaker he is best located in the cultic assembly, and perhaps as an officer of the cult. If this is correct, then we must suppose that his discourses were more carefully written and revised before they reached their present form than the discourses of other prophets. There must have been a rising tension in the Israelite community as they watched the career of Cyrus moving toward the salvation Second Isaiah promised; but the progress of thought and feeling in the composition is the result not only of the movement of history but of literary craftsmanship. Thus one is inclined to accept the hypothesis of Volz that Second Isaiah himself revised and collected his discourses. The collection was a striking witness that the prophetic word had not lost its power in the fall of Israel; and Second Isaiah himself was the last in the series of prophetic witnesses he invokes in his discourses (see xli 21–29).

One cannot speak of literary structure in Third Isaiah in the same sense in which it appears in Second Isaiah; Third Isaiah, we have seen, is best understood as a compilation of different works by different authors. We have arranged the works in fifteen poems; the analysis of the separate poems is generally in harmony with the analysis proposed by most critics. The poems have not been arranged in what appears to be their chronological order, nor does any other principle appear as governing the arrangement. The three poems in chapters lx–lxii belong together; they imitate the Zion poems of Second Isaiah with some modifications, which have already been discussed; see also the NOTES and COMMENT. As suggested in the first section above, the pieces were collected as the continuation of the prophetic tradition which stemmed from Isaiah of Jerusalem.

As in Second Isaiah, the traditional prophetic literary forms are found; the two forms which predominate are the rebuke and the oracle of promise. Third Isaiah does not employ the dialogue as frequently as it appears in Second Isaiah; the charge or plea appears only in chapter lviii, and there in a somewhat stylized form. The lamentation appears in parts of chapters lix and lxiii–lxiv, although not in the metrical form traditionally associated with this theme. The poem in chapters lxiii–lxiv resembles many of the Psalms in structure, and with many others we have entitled it a "Psalm of Lamentation."

The situation of the oracles of Third Isaiah is obscure. We are dealing again, it seems, with speakers and not with writers. Very possibly lvi 1–8, lvii 3–13, and lviii 1–14 have cultic situations, and not merely because they are concerned with cultic practices. The situation of those oracles which deal with the division in the community (see "The Message," below and COMMENT on chs. lxv–lxvi), must be as singular as their theme. They are addressed to a group within the community; and this indicates that the group which came to be called "the poor" had formed itself into a distinct unity. It seems a farfetched hypothesis to suppose that this group felt it could not take part in the regular cultic assemblies; but Qumran has taught us that the phenomenon of withdrawal was not unknown in Judaism. We have already noticed that the conditions of the post-exilic community before Nehemiah and Ezra suggest that disunity was one of its problems. Other poems are addressed to a wider audience, the community as a whole. This is doubtful for lvii 3–13, which seems to single out a particular group for rebuke; but see COMMENT. The Zion poems show a relationship to Second Isaiah which indicates a literary relationship and not merely memories of something heard or read.

Third Isaiah contains some prose portions which are expansions of the original poems. Besides these we have treated lxvi 22–24 as an expansion of the original poem. The whole of the apocalypse (after lxvi 15) does not appear to be such an expansion; it fills out the balance by carrying out the antithesis of the pious and the wicked in the community. A long prose insertion in lxvi 18–21 contains one of the most remarkable universalist statements in the entire book.

THE SERVANT SONGS

"The Servant Songs" is a title used to designate the following group of passages: xlii 1–4, xlix 1–6, l 4–9, lii 13 – liii 12. Bernhard Duhm in 1892 was the first to isolate this group of texts. He proposed that they were not from Second Isaiah but from a later author, about 450 B.C., more or less the same period as Third Isaiah (also identified by Duhm; see the first section above). It is accepted by almost all modern critics that the Servant Songs form a literary unit by themselves; but apart from this, there is no consensus about their origin and interpretation, and scarcely any passage of the Old Testament is so widely and so divergently discussed as the Servant Songs. The major problems can be thus listed: Are the Songs the work of Second Isaiah? What is their relation to the context and to each other? Who is the Servant? What is the relation of the Servant in the Songs to other "servants" mentioned in Second Isaiah? What is the mission of the Servant?

In each of the Songs a figure called the Servant of Yahweh appears, although the word is not used in the third Song. The title "servant" is not peculiar to the Songs. In Second Isaiah the title is applied to the people of Israel. Elsewhere in the Old Testament it is applied to kings and to prophets, to Moses and to a few others. The "servant" or "slave" of the king in the Old Testament was a high-level court officer. Originally this officer was no doubt the personal slave of the king, one who dealt with the king on an intimate basis and was entrusted with business of unusual importance and delicacy. "Your slave" was a polite form of address used in conversation with the king both by his officers and by his subjects. This usage is clearly the background of the term "the slave of Yahweh." As a title which designates a peculiar relationship and not merely a polite form of self-deprecation, it designates one who has a peculiar commision from Yahweh. This is certainly the meaning of the title in the Songs.

The Servant as he appears in the Songs can be summarized as follows: (a) xlii 1–4: Yahweh is the speaker. He has chosen the Servant and given him his spirit in order that he may bring judgment and teaching to the nations; the Servant will accomplish this without violence. (b) xlix 1-6: the Servant is the speaker. Yahweh has chosen him to restore Israel and to bring light and salvation to the nations. (c) l 4–9: the Servant is the speaker. He is a teacher; he has encountered opposition in his mission, but he is assured of success because Yahweh is with him. (d) lii 13 – liii 12: the speaker is unidentified (see COMMENT). The Servant, a figure of affliction, has died. His death has had an atoning value for "the many," with whom the speaker is identified. The Servant was regarded as guilty, but he will see his own vindication and the fruit of his atoning death.

In the commentary we have adopted the position that the Songs are not related to the context except for the response which follows the first three Songs (xlii 5–9, xlix 7–13, l 10–11). That the Songs and the responses can be removed from the context without any interruption is suggestive, but it is not convincing; several passages in Second Isaiah could be removed or rearranged without violence. The unity of Second Isaiah is not so rigorously organized that one passage always flows from and leads to another. But the Songs are more of an interruption than any other passage which might be placed elsewhere. It would be extremely difficult to find another four scattered passages which, when put together, would exhibit such a close community of topic and tone as the Servant Songs. Here the judgment of the great majority of modern scholars seems to be accurate. Yet it should be noticed that the four Songs do not form a single literary unit. They cannot be read together. They are detached not only from the context but even more obviously from each other. One can ask whether any of the Songs presupposes any one or all of the others; and no such presupposition appears. One can trace a progression in the four, and most interpreters do; but each Song is intelligible (or difficult) in itself.

The three responses, on the other hand, presuppose the preceding Songs. There are literary relationships between the responses, and between the responses and the Songs. This does not show that the responses were written by the author of the Songs; we take the position that they were not. But the author of the responses was in possession of the Songs. Simply as an abstract possibility, it would have to be admitted that the author of any one of the Songs need not have known the other Songs. This leads to the suggestion that the Songs, if they all come from one author, represent prophetic insights and reflections which came at separate points in the writer's career, perhaps widely separated points.

We take the responses, as noted above, as the work of a different hand (or hands). This opinion is ultimately a critical judgment based on subjective taste, and it cannot be made into anything stronger. The most persuasive argument is that these passages are what we have called them, responses. The differences in vocabulary and style are not sufficient to prove diversity of origin beyond all doubt. In the third response in particular, there are echoes of the language and themes of Third Isaiah. There is a clear community of language and thought between the first and second responses. The third response is most easily understood of Israel, and it reflects the duality of Israel, which is characteristic of Third Isaiah. The responses do furnish something of a context for the Songs; and it seems most probable that they come from the person who inserted the Songs into the works of Second Isaiah.

Was this person Second Isaiah himself? To detach the Songs from the context is certainly to suggest that Second Isaiah is not the author; but we have noticed that the literary unity is not so rigorous that it is impossible. The possibilities are these: (a) Second Isaiah inserted them from an earlier writer; (b) They are the work of Second Isaiah, but inserted by a later editor; (c) They are the work of a later writer who inserted them himself; (d) They are the work of a later writer inserted by an editor. We may seem to place too much importance on the work of the editor; but it is significant that if the Songs are the work of a later writer, they were woven into the context of Second Isaiah and not into the context of Third Isaiah. Clearly the editor either thought that they were the work of Second Isaiah or that the Servant himself was Second Isaiah. If the second hypothesis is true, the editor was the first to propose an identification of the Servant. This is not unrelated to the views of Sellin and Elliger, who propose that Second Isaiah wrote the first three Songs and that a disciple (whom Elliger identifies with Third Isaiah, see the first section above) added the fourth Song referring it to Second Isaiah.[18] In

[18] Ernst Sellin, "Tritojesaja, Deuterojesaja und das Gottesknechtsproblem," NKZ 41 (1930), 73–93, 145–73; "Die Lösung des deuterojesajanischen Gottesknechtsrätsels," ZAW 55 (1937), 177–217; Karl Elliger, "Deuterojesaja in seinem Verhältnis zu Tritojesaja," BWANT IV, 11 (1933).

fact I believe that the editor placed them where they are because he thought that Second Isaiah was the Servant; but I am not sure that the editor grasped the meaning of the author of the Songs.

Whether Second Isaiah was the author is treated by Mowinckel as an unimportant question.[19] It is more important than that, but the solution of the problem cannot be detached from the problem of the identity of the Servant (see pp. XLII–LV). Of the options given above, the first has never been seriously defended—mostly, no doubt, because Second Isaiah never to our knowledge incorporates the work of any one. If they are the work of Second Isaiah, one must answer two questions: Why have they no relation to the context? Why is the idea of the Servant found in the Songs reflected in no other passage of Second Isaiah? Neither of these questions defies an answer, but they turn the probabilities against the authorship of Second Isaiah. I say the probabilities, because the possibility must be accepted that Second Isaiah pursued in the Songs a religious insight which differed in scope and character from the oracles of the rest of the collection in chapters xl–lv. Modern critics have not pursued this possibility; those who maintain the authorship of Second Isaiah have given themselves the impossible task of integrating the Songs into the context of Second Isaiah. With all respect to their efforts, it seems that this cannot be done.

The very controversy concerning the identity of the Servant (see pp. XLII–LV) is enough to make Second Isaiah's authorship doubtful. There is never any ambiguity about the "servants" mentioned elsewhere in Second Isaiah. Even if the Servant should be identified with Israel, the mission of the Servant in the fourth Song is reflected in nothing of what Second Isaiah says about Israel. These considerations raise doubts and not certainties; it is theoretically possible, as noted above, that Second Isaiah entered into a new line of thought, which he did not integrate into his discourses. But the collection contains no other examples of such free-standing columns; that Second Isaiah himself should have written them and placed them in their present context is alien to all we know about his style.

We assume as most probable the hypothesis that they were written by a disciple, and that therefore they belong to "Third Isaiah" in the sense in which we use this term in this volume. We assume also as most probable that they have their present position because the

19 *He That Cometh* (Oxford, 1956), p. 188.

editor of Second Isaiah either meant to refer them to Second Isaiah the man, or thought that the author had intended this reference. We also assume that the four Songs are all from one author; there are no convincing reasons for dividing them among more than one. Obviously the responses are also from someone other than Second Isaiah; and the most likely candidate for authorship is the editor who placed the Songs in their present position. He did not write a response to the fourth Song; or if he did, criticism has failed to recover it in the text.

The question of the mission of the Servant cannot be discussed apart from the question of his identity. In the COMMENT we have pointed out what appear to be the most obvious features of his mission, features which any interpretation must incorporate. As the discussion which follows will show, the view one takes of who the Servant is has much to do with one's view of what the Servant does, although the arguments would move with more conviction if the process were reversed. But it must be admitted that the mission of the Servant does not emerge from the Songs with the desired clarity; were there not some ambiguity in the mission itself, the divergent views on the identity of the Servant could not be seriously maintained. These views, it seems, will be most clearly set forth if they are classified, although classification does some injustice to the very carefully elaborated theories of scholars who go to considerable pains to present a distinctive opinion. But the scope of this work does not permit a fair treatment of all the nuances of the various opinions; the reader is referred to the works cited in the Selected Bibliography for fuller treatment of the question in general and of particular opinions. The difficulty of identifying the Servant has led some scholars to deny that the Servant is consistently one figure in the poems. C. C. Torrey traced the Servant theme through the entire collection of chapters xl–lxvi (which he affirmed is the work of one author) and found the Servant to be at times Abraham, at other times Israel personified, at other times the King-Messiah. Some of these variations he found in a single poem.[20]

[20] *The Second Isaiah,* pp. 135–50.

COLLECTIVE INTERPRETATIONS

These interpretations have in common that the Servant is understood to be not an individual person but the personification of a group. The oldest form of this interpretation saw in the Servant a personification of the people of Israel. In modern scholarship since the early nineteenth century this was the prevailing opinion. Most of the works written since 1920 have abandoned the collective interpretation or have modified it but several recent views have not rejected it entirely. There is indeed much to be said for the collective interpretation, although it presents problems its defenders have not solved.

The most obvious argument for the Servant as Israel rests on the fact that Israel is called the servant of Yahweh several times in the text of Second Isaiah. If, however, the Servant Songs are detached from Second Isaiah, this argument loses much of its force. The Servant is called Israel in xlix 3 (see NOTES and COMMENT); the reading is doubted by many critics, but without convincing reasons. Any individual interpretation must take account of this designation. On the other hand, if the Songs are detached from Second Isaiah the opposing argument that the character of the Servant differs notably from the character of Israel in Second Isaiah also loses much of its force. It must be conceded that Israel as the Servant goes considerably beyond the Israel of Second Isaiah; yet the development of the Servant is not a violent departure from this Israel. In the collective interpretation Israel has a mission to proclaim judgment and teaching to the nations (xlii 1–4); it is a light of the nations and a means of salvation (xlix 6); it has suffered (1 4–9, lii 13 – liii 12). If Israel is the Servant of the fourth poem, the death and resurrection of the Servant are much easier to explain; see, for example, Ezek xxxvii 1–14. It is quite true that Second Isaiah does not see the sufferings of Israel as atoning; they are the result of righteous judgment. But another prophet might have reached this level of interpretation.

In spite of the superficial attractiveness of the Servant-Israel theory, the theory raises more problems than it solves. The first Song offers no serious difficulty; but the second Song, in spite of some textual problems (see NOTES and COMMENT) rather clearly makes the

Servant an agent of the restoration of Israel. The third Song, which presents the Servant as a prophet and teacher, becomes forced if Israel is the Servant; and if verse 6 refers to the sufferings of historical Israel, the prophet is being frivolous. If Israel is the Servant of the fourth Song, then the speaker can only be a spokesman for the nations. Nothing in the Song suggests this, and no spokesman for the nations utters anything like this in the entire collection of chapters xl–lxvi. In view of these problems, some interpreters have modified the collective interpretation in various ways. The Servant is not historic Israel but the core of genuine Israelites, who are the prophets and teachers, and who suffer for the whole Israel. This would make the Servant identical with the pious devout group which in Third Isaiah is set against the faithless Israelites. It is not a convincing argument against this that Third Isaiah expresses deep loathing for the faithless and threatens them with certain judgment; we are not of necessity dealing with the writings of the same author, and the insights of the Servant Songs are without parallel in most instances.

These problems have suggested another modification: the Servant is not historic Israel, neither the whole of Israel nor its faithful core, but Israel idealized, an Israel aware of its mission and dedicated to it. The Servant so conceived can exist only in the future; and there is no need to relate anything which is said of the Servant to history. The vision of such an Israel could easily arise from passages like xli 21–29 and xlv 14–25, in which Israel is the witness to the sole divinity of Yahweh and the means through which the nations recognize him. It could have roots in Isa ii 1–4 (=Mic iv 1–3), assuming that this passage is earlier than the Servant Songs. This conception suits the idea of the Servant's mission we adopt in the COMMENT. The Servant appears as a prophet and a teacher. The "judgment" and the "law" he brings to the nations (xlii 1–4) represent the revelation of Yahweh, and the Servant is a covenant bond between Yahweh and the nations. In this hypothesis Israel's relations to the nations are patterned somewhat after the relation of Moses to Israel. This appears to be the proper conception of the Servant's mission; but is it the mission of Israel? And how is it related to the suffering of the Servant in the fourth Song? That the ideal Israel of the future should experience such an ignominious death is in open contradiction to the themes of restoration found in the Zion poems, and in the passages where Israel is the witness and the herald of Yahweh.

Here the difference is too profound to be solved by appeal to different authors. Israel is a witness precisely because it is an object of salvation; Yahweh will demonstrate his saving power by restoring Israel and conferring upon it a grandeur far in excess of anything it had ever known. The ideal Israel of the future as a community which suffers and dies deviates sharply from this conception. There is indeed obscurity in the Servant poems, enough of it so that it should be unnecessary to create any additional obscurity. And it may be added that the conception of an "ideal" Israel is not really a typical pattern of Old Testament thought. The Israel of the future, however "idealized" its conditions, remains always a concrete historical group, the blood descendants of the existing Israel dwelling in the land of Israel.

These considerations show some of the reasons why contemporary scholarship has moved away from the collective interpretation. Yet it has, as we have said, certain attractive features.[21] In the interpretation we shall suggest, some elements of the collective interpretation must be retained. The relation of the Servant to historical Israel whether of the past or of the future as seen by the prophet is more than simple membership in the Israelite community.

INDIVIDUAL INTERPRETATIONS

If the Servant is not the personification of a group, then he must be an individual person. He could be either a fictitious person created by the imagination of the prophet or he could be a historical person. As a historical person he could either be a figure of the past or of the future from the prophet's point of view; the second of these is not the same as the fictitious character. The fictitious character does not exist, has never existed, and is not expected to exist; the historical person is expected to exist, and when we search for the meaning of the prophet it is irrelevant whether his expectations were ever fulfilled. All these variations on the individual interpretation have in fact been suggested.

[21] These attractive features are set forth by Otto Kaiser in his monograph, *Der königliche Knecht* (Göttingen, 1959). Kaiser accepts a number of royal features in the Servant, but explains them as expressions of the prophet's belief that the new Israel as a people has the power and mission given to the monarchy of David.

(1) *The Servant as a Historical Person of the Past*

If one seeks a historical person who can be identified with the Servant, one would think first of Second Isaiah himself. The question was asked in the apostolic church (Acts viii 34). This would place the Songs in their context; it explains the use of the third person; and the progression of the Songs is very easily understood as reflecting the experiences of the prophet's career.[22] The mission of the Servant does not differ so sharply from the mission implied in the discourses of Second Isaiah that the two cannot be taken together. But the identification of the Servant with Second Isaiah falls flat in the fourth Song.[23] The scholars who have defended this theory with erudition and skill have proposed, not without probability, that Second Isaiah wrote the first three Songs and that his disciples wrote the fourth. That the disciples should have described him in terms such as those used in the songs would be at the worst exaggerated admiration. If he died a violent death—a hypothesis that cannot be antecedently excluded—his followers may very well have thought that this was the crowning act of a dedicated life, and have seen in this tragedy the fulfillment of the mysterious ways of Yahweh. Even their belief in his resurrection does not present a serious argument; the belief in the resurrection arose at some time in the post-exilic period, and if the disciples thought of the prophet as an extraordinary man, they may well have thought that he demanded an extraordinary vindication. The lines do not imply a belief in a general resurrection.

With these considerations in favor of the prophet, it is remarkable that Sigmund Mowinckel, whose monograph of 1921 was the most solid plea for this interpretation, abandoned his own opinion in 1931.[24] There are several difficulties, which are not completely

[22] Volz (*Jesaia II,* pp. 164–67) calls the first three poems an autobiographical fragment of Second Isaiah. But he treats the fourth poem as an independent piece by a later author, and understands the Suffering Servant as an ideal individual figure of the eschatological period (pp. 189–95).

[23] Not, however, for Begrich (*Studien zu Deuterojesaja,* pp. 145–51). Since the resurrection of Second Isaiah did not occur, Begrich thinks it is far more reasonable that Second Isaiah himself should have expected it than that a disciple should have described something that did not happen. In Begrich's theory Second Isaiah was sure of being killed by his unbelieving fellow Israelites, and was equally sure that Yahweh would confirm his word by raising him from the dead.

[24] Sigmund Mowinckel, *Der Knecht Jahwäs* (Giessen, 1921); "Die Komposition des deuterojesajanischen Buches," ZAW 49 (1931), 87–112, 242–60.

solved. The mission of the Servant is not the mission of Second Isaiah as we can formulate it from his discourses. The discourses are not really addressed to the nations, but to Israel and to Jerusalem. The horizon of Second Isaiah's vision is limited by the restoration of Jerusalem. He is among the least autobiographical of the prophets. If his self-revelation is compared with that of Isaiah of Jerusalem, Jeremiah, Ezekiel, Amos, or Hosea, it is next to nothing at all— unless it appears in the Servant Songs. It seems unlikely that a prophet who elsewhere hides himself so completely behind his message should in these Songs have become intensely personal. Again, the prophets mentioned above never leave any doubt that it is themselves they are revealing; if the Songs are autobiographical, the prophet left considerable doubt.

A number of other historical persons have been suggested, but none of the suggestions have convinced any scholars besides those who made the suggestions. Duhm himself, who first identified the Servant Songs as such, identified the Servant as an otherwise unknown teacher of the Law who died a violent death; this teacher was not much earlier than Second Isaiah or contemporary with him.[25] The opinion has never been accepted; effectively, to say that the Servant is an unknown historical person is to say that we do not know who the Servant is, and no elaborate theory is required to say this. Ernst Sellin, in his long career of scholarship, identified the Servant at different times with Zerubbabel (1898), Jehoiachin (1901), Moses (1922), and finally (1930) with Second Isaiah.[26] The suggestion of Moses curiously fits well the use of the Exodus themes in Second Isaiah, and we note in the COMMENT on xlii 1–4 that the Servant appears with some of the traits of a new Moses. Sellin derived from the fourth Song a theory that Moses was killed by the Israelites, an event suppressed in Israelite traditions. This and a few other elaborate theories must be regarded as curiosities in the museum of exegesis rather than as permanent contributions to the solution of the problem.

In his last treatment of the problem Sigmund Mowinckel aban-

25 Das Buch Jesaja, p. 284.
26 Ernst Sellin, Serubbabel. Ein Beitrag zur Geschichte der messianischen Erwartung und der Entstehung des Judentums (Leipzig, 1898); Der Knecht Gottes bei Deuterojesaja (Leipzig, 1901); Mose und seine Bedeutung für die israelitisch-jüdische Religionsgeschichte (Leipzig, 1922); "Tritojesaja, Deuterojesaja und das Gottesknechtsproblem," NKZ 41 (1930), 73–93, 145–73.

doned Second Isaiah himself and identified the Servant as a prophet of the school of Second Isaiah who conceived his mission in terms of the Servant Songs and died a violent death.[27] This prophet may have been, Mowinckel thinks, the author of the Songs in which the first person is used. His principal reason for abandoning his earlier view is that the Songs go beyond Second Isaiah in their conception of the mission of the Servant. This opinion does not differ in principle from his earlier view; it simply applies the same methods and arrives at a different identification. The figure of the Servant, he maintains, is not rigorously historical; it is idealized. In this view, it seems, it is just the elements of "idealization" which make the Servant significant.

Mowinckel and Haller have also pointed out some relationships between the Servant Songs and Cyrus in Second Isaiah.[28] Both are called by name (xlv 3, xlix 1); and the response to the first Song in xlii 6–7 bears a close resemblance to xlv 1, 13. These scholars suggest that the Servant is a kind of anti-Cyrus figure. Cyrus was a disappointment in the terms of Second Isaiah; he was a confirmed worshiper of false gods who took the hands of Marduk when he became king of Babylon. The author of the Songs then conceived another savior figure who accomplishes his work by entirely opposite means: by prophetic proclamation, by teaching, and finally by atoning suffering and death. The antithesis between Cyrus and the Servant seems to be well taken. Cyrus is indeed a savior figure in Second Isaiah with some traits which are nearly messianic. In any hypothesis concerning the Servant, the Servant Songs make it clear that the salvation of Israel is not to be achieved on the political plane and by political and military means. Israel is not "saved" merely by being re-established as a community, or even as a kingdom. Its destiny goes much farther than this.

In summary, then, one must judge the efforts to identify the Servant with a historical figure of the past unsuccessful. It is impossible to eliminate the possibility altogether; but no solution to the problem has been found on this assumption.

[27] He That Cometh, pp. 187–257.
[28] Max Haller, "Die Kyros-Lieder Deuterojesajas," FRLANT 36 (1923), 261–77.

(2) *The Servant as a Historical Figure of the Future*

As we have remarked above, this classification refers to those theories which identify the Servant with a historical figure expected to appear, whether the figure actually appeared or not. Under this heading there are only two theories to be considered.

The first is the venerable belief in the Christian church that the Servant poems, in particular the fourth, are predictions of Jesus Christ. In this form the opinion is defended by no one today except in a few fundamentalist circles. This type of predictive prophecy does not appear in the Old Testament. It is another question whether the person and mission of Jesus Christ are interpreted in the New Testament in terms of the Servant poems: that is, whether Jesus or his disciples or both identified him with the Servant of Yahweh. This problem lies outside the scope of this volume; but it is my personal opinion that Jesus was identified with the Servant in the primitive church, and that this identification goes back to Jesus himself. But this does not imply that the poems are a prediction of Jesus Christ in the literal sense of the term.

The second theory identifies the Servant with the Messiah.[29] By the Messiah (not an Old Testament term) is meant the descendant of David who re-establishes the Davidic kingdom and dynasty as the realization of the reign of Yahweh on earth. Such a figure clearly appears in Isa ix 1–6, xi 1–9; Jer xxiii 5–6, and elsewhere. The king as a savior figure is frequent in the Old Testament and in other ancient Near Eastern literature. Whether the Servant exhibits royal features is a question connected with the Servant as an ideal mythological figure, to be discussed below.

In fact the Servant exhibits no clearly royal trait, and the antithesis between the Servant and Cyrus pointed out above is equally valid when the Servant is compared with the Messiah. No royal trait can be ascribed to him except the proclamation of "judgment" and "law" in xlii 1–4, and these terms more obviously have another meaning here; see the NOTES and COMMENT. The same Song emphasizes the absence of force and violence in the mission of the Servant. The Servant is not the same figure as the Messiah, but a parallel figure

---

[29] See J. van der Ploeg, *Les Chants du Serviteur de Jahvé* (Paris, 1936), pp. 149–60, 190–200, who calls the Servant Songs a spiritualization of the work of the Messiah.

which as it stands, cannot be reconciled with the messianic king. A higher synthesis of the two figures, such as Christians believe was fulfilled in Jesus Christ, was not within the vision of the prophets of the Old Testament. Each figure, it seems, reflects the period of Israelite history in which it arose; the king was the savior figure under the monarchy, but during and after the disaster of the Exile no such savior figure could be devised unless it were a *David redivivus* or an eschatological king. This does not imply that the Servant is simply a response of a prophet to the disaster of his times; the insight goes far beyond what the situation elicited. But such a national catastrophe as Israel experienced would open the eyes of at least some to other ways of salvation than the way of the messianic king. In this sense, again, the Servant reflects the people of Israel as a whole.

(3) *The Servant as an Ideal Figure*

As we have explained above, the interpretation of the Servant as an ideal figure is not altogether the same as the interpretation of the Servant as a future historical figure. An ideal figure is not expected to appear as a historical person, although it may be expected that some or several future historical persons may approach or even realize the ideal. It must be admitted that this type of imagination may be judged too subtle for Old Testament literature; yet the Servant Songs are among the most subtle parts of the Old Testament and the failure to find a satisfactory explanation in more conventional terms suggests that we should investigate the unconventional. Under this heading two interpretations come under consideration.

The mythological interpretation finds a connection between the suffering of the Servant and the ritual part played by the Babylonian king in the New Year festival.[30] The New Year festival was the ritual recital and re-enactment of the death and resurrection of the god of vegetation. At one point in the festival there was a ritual portrayal of the death of vegetation as the end of the world; all life and activity ceased, and the king for a while was no longer on his throne. Creation returned to original chaos. Order was restored by the victory of the rising god over the monster of chaos and a new creation. The Babylonian ritual contains ceremonial humiliation of

---

[30] Lorenz Dürr, *Ursprung und Aufbau der israelitisch-jüdischen Heilandserwartung* (Berlin, 1925); Ivan Engnell, "The Ebed-Yahweh Songs and the Suffering Messiah in 'Deutero-Isaiah,'" BJRL 31 (1948), 54–93 (ET).

the king to signify the loss of kingship; kingship was restored when the king took the hands of Marduk. It is suggested that the king was the representative of the people in this ceremony of humiliation and repentance; and this he almost certainly was. In this sense his performance was vicarious. It is further suggested that the king was the representative of the god in the ritual, and that he experienced a ritual death and resurrection. It is suggested that the description of the Servant in the fourth Song is derived from this ritual as a source; the prophet could find there the ideas of a vicarious suffering and death followed by a victorious resurrection. The Servant, then, must be conceived as a royal figure, and therefore he is the Messiah.

The argument is substantially an argument from analogy. The vicarious suffering of the Servant has no real parallel elsewhere in the Old Testament, nor does anything resembling it appear in ancient extrabiblical sources except the ritual suffering of the king. That the two conceptions are only coincidentally similar is not a legitimate assumption. The argument can proceed no further than this. But other scholars ask whether the resemblance is close enough to demand an explanation. Given the hostile attitude of the school of Second and Third Isaiah toward Mesopotamian religion, it is improbable that they would borrow a theme directly from the Babylonian New Year ritual. It seems hardly more likely that they would borrow it from a Canaanite source; and the ceremonial humiliation of the king is not attested in Canaanite ritual, admitting that it is not excluded either. It is an altogether gratuitous assumption that the liturgy was used in Israelite cult, and it cannot be assumed that this was the source. Furthermore, it is not attested that the Mesopotamian king represented the god precisely in a ritual death and resurrection; and the absence of this element removes the principal support of the theory. This view does attempt to explain the third and fourth Songs, but it contributes nothing to the explanation of the first two. We have noticed that the Servant is nowhere presented as a royal figure; and if this is reflected in no other way, the allusions to royal suffering remain obscure.[31] There

[31] Otto Kaiser notices a number of traits of the Servant which he believes are derived from royal titles of the Davidic king as these are found in the Psalms and the historical books (*Der königliche Knecht*, pp. 18–31). These titles are explained in another sense in the NOTES and COMMENT; but it is relevant to the point here to remark that Kaiser does not find these royal traits in the fourth Song.

is no such uncertainty about the royal character of the figure who appears in messianic passages such as Isa ix 1–6.

Yet the problem of identifying the Servant, as the preceding summary shows, is not solved by appealing to a real historical figure, whether present or future, collective or individual. To seek an ideal figure in the Servant is therefore recommended. Such a figure, as we have remarked, does not belong to history; in presenting an ideal figure the prophet need not mean that such a person is expected to appear as a concrete reality. An ideal figure lies neither in the past nor in the future but in both; the figure represents something which is metahistorical. Nor is the ideal figure an individual person in the sense that Cyrus or the Messiah are individual persons. The actions of an ideal figure are not historical actions; they are traits in the portrayal of the idea. The ideal figure gathers together the history of the past and the hopes of the future.

The interpretation we now present is closer to the interpretation of H. H. Rowley than to the views of any other scholar. Rowley begins with H. Wheeler Robinson's theory of the corporate personality in the Old Testament, although he does not apply the theory to the Servant Songs in quite the same way that Robinson did.[32] Robinson pointed out that throughout the Old Testament we encounter individual persons who head or represent a group. Such persons were the patriarchs, and such were the kings of Israel and Judah. There is nothing peculiarly Israelite about the idea of the king as the incorporation of a people; this was found in all ancient Near Eastern monarchies, and indeed in more recent monarchies, when kings identified themselves and each other as "England" and "France." But there is something peculiar about the Israelite patriarchs, who are corporate personalities in another way. The people bore the name of an individual, Jacob/Israel. Throughout the patriarchal stories one meets episodes which show in the person or character of the patriarch or in his adventures traits which echo the people of Israel, either as they were or as they thought themselves to be. Thus Abraham is in Canaan as a stranger, and from there he goes to Egypt; and Jacob has the same experience. The relations of Jacob and Esau are the relations of Israel and Edom. The entrance of Jacob into Canaan and his encounter with the mysterious being at

---

[32] H. H. Rowley, *The Servant of the Lord* (Oxford, 1964), pp. 3–60; H. Wheeler Robinson, "The Hebrew Conception of Corporate Personality," BZAW 66 (1936), 49–62.

the ford of the Jabbok suggest the entrance of Israel into Canaan; there he wins the right of free entry into the land for his descendants. The patriarchs move about the land and associate themselves with towns like Hebron, Shechem, and Bethel, which later become Israelite and Judahite communities, and erect sanctuaries at which their descendants worship Yahweh. They receive and transmit the promises of the land, the covenant, and numerous progeny. The patriarchs are not presented as simple historical individuals. In them the people of Israel lives before it exists as a people, and one can discern the association of the people with its ancestors.

Similarly, the King-Messiah is not conceived simply as the culmination of the dynasty of David nor as another David. He is the fullness of the dynasty, possessing all the qualities of a king and achieving all the deeds which befit a king. Each succeeding descendant is a Messiah and can be addressed in messianic terms, because the Messiah is present in hope and in anticipation in each member of the dynasty. The separate members reign in virtue of the promise of an eternal dynasty to be fulfilled in the Messiah; and the Messiah fulfills the hopes which repose in each member. He recapitulates in himself the entire dynasty without any of its faults and failures. And thus he incorporates Israel, saved and triumphant, "righteous" in the full Old Testament sense of the word.

In discussing the separate interpretations we have remarked of each one that it exhibits some feature which should be preserved in the interpretation of the Servant. In particular, the corporate personality resolves the tension between the individual and the collective traits. The Servant is conceived as an individual figure, but he is the figure who recapitulates in himself all the religious gifts and the religious mission of Israel. He has no secular traits; it is true that the king was not a purely secular figure in Judah, but the Servant is not a warrior. He is a victor, but his victory is achieved in an entirely different way, a way which causes kings to shut their mouths (lii 15). He is the fullness of Israel; in him the history of Israel reaches its achievement. He incorporates the dominant features of Israel's past; he has some of the traits of a new Moses, he is the spokesman of divine revelation, he is the witness of the divinity of Yahweh to Israel and to the nations, he is a prophet. This conception of Israel is the conception of Second Isaiah. For the author of the Servant Songs, as for Second Isaiah, Israel has no future in the world of politics and war. Israel is to reach its proper place among the nations by other means. The Servant is clearly not the King-Messiah; his mission is not conceived in this way, and the images are not the same. Whether the prophet meant to replace the King-Messiah by the Servant is not explicit, but it is hinted. Israel would have to think of its destiny in different terms from those of the past, and its leader in the future could not be another David.

Such a figure is not exactly a "fluid" type, as the Servant is sometimes called. The Servant remains an individual, but an ideal who reflects the genuine character of all Israel. This is not to deny, as some scholars have suggested, a development in the mind of the writer. But the development is not clearly of a kind which permits us to say that the Servant is more clearly individual in some poems and more clearly a collective figure in others. The corporate personality is a consistent reality throughout, although the emphasis may vary. But he cannot be understood except as an incorporation of Israel, and the collective features are never entirely absent. The Israel which perseveres has the features of the Servant.

The corporate personality does not explain the most mysterious of the Songs, the fourth, in which the idea of vicarious atonement and a resurrection are expressed. It does not seem necessary to appeal to a liturgical source for this idea. It is far more probable that the author found the idea of vicarious atonement in the history of Israel. Israel had been the object of judgment, and a remnant had survived the judgment. It was recognized by Second Isaiah that the remnant of Israel had not been preserved for its own sake, but as a witness of the righteousness of Yahweh. Israel could now attest the righteousness of the judgments and the saving acts of Yahweh. Had Israel not been preserved through a judgment, Yahweh would have no witness, and righteousness could not be proclaimed to the nations. Thus Israel through its suffering had become a medium of salvation. This experience is transferred to the individual figure of the Servant. The author does not think that the experience of judgment and salvation has been completed. Through judgment Israel has learned its mission; but the process of judgment is not complete, either for Israel or for the nations. Yet more suffering must come before salvation can issue from judgment; but an innocent one can sustain the judgment which will save others. If salvation is to reach its fulfillment, it must reach it by the means which the history of Israel shows are necessary. The innocent must suffer in order that the guilty may repent and escape judgment. The Servant has the mission of proclaiming this and of being the victim of judgment.

Does this mission reach Israel as well as the nations? The author certainly thought so. In his mind, Israel had not recognized the mysterious ways of Yahweh's judgment and salvation. There must be other prophets who will proclaim this, and the Servant is the climactic figure in the prophetic line, who will proclaim the way of salvation and be himself the medium of salvation. It is not to be doubted that the Servant reflects the traits of Jeremiah; for this prophet more than any other prophet in the canon illustrated the prophet whose proclamation is authenticated by his life. But the Servant will have a wider scope in his mission than Jeremiah had. His success, like the success of Jeremiah, will not appear during his mission; he will be vindicated by events. If the Servant is conceived as an ideal figure, his victory and resurrection need not be taken as anything else but ideal also. The mission of service will never die and never fail in Israel; for Israel must become the Servant, its corporate personality, if it is to survive as the people of Yahweh.

The Servant belongs to the future, for he is what Israel must become. But he also belongs to the past, for his character is formed by reflection on Israel's history and on the character of her leaders. As we have noticed, future figures are expected to approach the ideal or to realize it; but we are not compelled to think that the author conceived the Servant as a definite individual who would arise in the future of Israel. The Servant poems are not "predictions" of the future in the simple sense. They are rather insights into the future, into the ways of God with men, a projection of how judgment and salvation must be realized if they are to be realized at all. For the community to whom the Songs were addressed, they are a challenge to a commitment, to a faith in a future which is revealed in the figure of the Servant. Unless Israel accepts the Servant as its incorporation, it cannot keep faith with Yahweh.

THE MESSAGE

SECOND ISAIAH

The message of Second Isaiah must, it seems, be understood in the historical context established by criticism (see the first section above). If the work is set in some other time and place, the message becomes ambiguous and murky. The prophecies are surely an announcment of salvation addressed to Israel, with interlocutions of rebuke and allusions to Israel's earliest history; but if these cannot be set in some definite series of events, they become broad bland generalities. We notice in the following section and in the NOTES and COMMENT that our understanding of Third Isaiah suffers from the uncertainty of the date and situation of the discourses. There is no reason why Second Isaiah should have more clarity than Third Isaiah; but the discourses suit the period and the situation so well that it seems useless to look elsewhere. If one does, as C. C. Torrey did, then new problems are created and none of the old problems are solved.

What is the dominant theme of Second Isaiah, or can a dominant theme be identified? One is tempted to say that the dominant theme is salvation, long promised and on the eve of fulfillment. But behind this dominant theme is another question: Why is Israel saved, and for what is it saved? Why is Israel the only people which survived the political revolutions of the seventh and sixth centuries, and what is the future toward which Israel looks? If the prophet promised no more than that Israel would, by a cosmic stroke of the power of Yahweh, move into the throne of world empire formerly held by Assyria, at the moment held by Babylon, and soon to be held by Persia, his words would be so irrelevant to reality that they would scarcely deserve even brief comment. If the future he opened for Israel were entirely apocalyptic and eschatological, we would give his words the same treatment we give other apocalyptic literature; such literature can be interesting as an episode in the history of belief but not urgent to us. It is our belief that Second Isaiah presented to Israel a real future into which it could move and find itself as well as Yahweh, that he described for Israel a national existence which Israel as it was could accept as practical. This national existence to him was the fulfillment of the history of Israel and the supreme moment of its encounter with Yahweh.

The dominant theme of Second Isaiah is not salvation, but the mission of Israel for which the nation is saved. Israel is the servant of Yahweh (xli 8–9, xlii 19, xliv 1–2, 21) and the witness of Yahweh (xliii 10, xliv 8, xlviii 6, 20). This office it shares with the Servant (see "The Servant Songs," above). The entire people of Israel receives the prophetic office. When foreign peoples pass over to Israel and acknowledge its leadership, it is to confess that Israel alone knows Yahweh (xlv 14). Because of Yahweh peoples will run to Israel (lv 5). Yahweh's revelation and righteousness will go forth as a light to peoples (li 4). Yahweh has made Israel for his glory (xliii 7), that they may declare his praise (xliii 21); through Israel his holiness will be manifested, and the nations shall recognize that Yahweh alone is God. The same thought is expressed in terms of the submission of the nations to Israel (xlix 22–23); in this latter passage the imagery is more triumphal in tone, but the context does not suggest conquest and domination. The nations submit to Israel not in the manner in which they submitted to the Assyrians or the Babylonians, but in acknowledgment of the supremacy of Yahweh. It is through Israel that the nations must learn the law and the cult of Yahweh.

The idea of the mission of Israel is proposed not bluntly but subtly, and it underlies most of the themes we identify as dominant in Second Isaiah. The prophet often lets his work be done by implication. This is apparent in his reflections on the past of Israel. The deliverance of Israel from Babylon is described several times in terms of the Exodus from Egypt and the passage through the desert (xxxv 5–7, xliii 15–17, xlviii 21, li 9–10). Paradoxically the prophet urges his hearers not to remember the past, for the wonder of the saving act which is near will exceed by far the wonders of the past (xliii 18). But apart from these allusions, the prophet's reflections on the past dwell on the past failures of Israel. Israel's blindness and deafness to the revealed word of Yahweh has hidden from them the true meaning of the judgment which fell upon the people; Israel did not recognize that its disasters were the judgments of Yahweh for its sins (xlii 18–25). It has not even been faithful in its cultic duties (xliii 22–24; see COMMENT), and if it challenged Yahweh in a legal process, Yahweh would prove a history of guilt which goes back to Israel's first father (xliii 26–28). Israel's invocation of the name of Yahweh has been insincere (xlviii 1–2); and in spite of the threats of Yahweh, now long realized in history, Israel has never relaxed its inflexible obstinacy (xlviii 3–6, 8–10). This judgment was necessary in order that Yahweh could maintain his glory, the recognition of his authentic divinity; for his divinity would not be authentic unless his judgments were righteous. He could not let such obstinacy pass unchallenged without manifesting moral weakness or co-operating with evil. The tone of the reflections becomes more charged with emotion when Yahweh in a sorrowful exclamation thinks of what might have been had Israel listened to his revelation (xlviii 17–18). The prophet points to the faith and the fidelity of Abraham and Sarah, which brought them the blessings of Yahweh (li 1–2); the contrast between Abraham and his descendants is implicit but clear. Surely the present generation has no greater obstacles to faith than Abraham experienced; but the present generation should have the assurance which comes from their history.

Second Isaiah was not the first of the prophets to appeal to the traditions of Israel. Brief appeals are found in Amos and Hosea and First Isaiah. The reflections become more extensive in Jeremiah, and still more extensive in Ezekiel; Ezekiel's view of the past of Israel was more pessimistic than the view of Second Isaiah. In both Jeremiah and Ezekiel one senses a feeling of despair, a conviction that the past of Israel reaches its due fullness in the disaster which breaks upon Judah. For both Jeremiah and Ezekiel the past seems irreversible, and no action either of Yahweh or of Israel can be expected to alter the course of events. For both prophets the expected restoration of Israel lies in a dim and distant future. Second Isaiah shares much of their pessimism about the past, but his promises deal with the immediate future. The judgment of Yahweh has been accomplished, and there is now room for his compassion. Second Isaiah finds, in the past, traditions of saving acts which present a pattern for the future. Israel has failed; it is given a new opportunity, and a recognition of its past failures will perhaps keep it from repeating them. For the past of Israel shows that it is a people of destiny, a destiny which clearly it has not yet realized.

But Second Isaiah goes back beyond the Exodus to found his

statement of the saving power of Yahweh. He is, according to the most widely accepted critical views of the composition of the Old Testament books, the first writer to consider creation extensively, and to draw theological conclusions from the belief in Yahweh as creator. This does not imply that belief in Yahweh as creator did not exist in Israel before Second Isaiah; but he seems to be the first to have made this belief meaningful in the whole context of Israelite faith. Passages in books which generally come from prophets and poets earlier than Second Isaiah are regarded by critics as later expansions of these books on grounds other than the theological and homiletic use of the belief in creation. If critics are correct in attributing this development to Second Isaiah, then we should be able to suggest some elements in the world of belief and thought of the prophet, which would help to explain it.

An easy and rather obvious hypothesis would be the encounter of the Israelites with the cosmic myths of Mesopotamia celebrated in the cult of Babylon. But this could scarcely have been the first encounter of the Israelites with these myths. Nor would this have been the first encounter of the Israelites with national gods whose power was so tangibly reflected in the power of the peoples who worshiped them; Assyria had been a stronger power than Babylon. It may be suggested that the monotheistic and the universalistic outlook of Second Isaiah (see below, pp. LXIV–LXVI) led him to seek a statement of the cosmic supremacy of Yahweh in a form in which traditional belief had not stated it. The Israelites knew and used mythological imagery to describe Yahweh's creation; indeed, Second Isaiah himself uses this imagery (li 9–10). But the mythological imagery did not clearly affirm the absolute supremacy of Yahweh. The creation account of Genesis i is best understood as a piece of anti-mythological polemic; and it is highly probable that this account and Second Isaiah were formed in the same world of thought.

We find at the very opening of the discourses a long poem on creation (xl 12–26). The purpose of the poem is to show that the power of the nations—and in particular Babylon, the power of the moment—is so slight as to be inconsiderable. The nations can offer no serious threat; he who creates the world and its inhabitants is also the lord of the history of the world and its inhabitants. Nor does the creator give way to fatigue and weakness; the world itself is the witness of his unfailing power, which he communicates to those who wait for him (xl 28–31). Second Isaiah refers to creation in later poems. The creator is superior to diviners and wise men, and sends his shepherd to accomplish his purpose (xliv 24–28, xlv 12–13). His creation of earth as a place for human habitation assures men that his purpose is to save men by revealing himself to them through Israel (xlv 18–19). The creative power is once more associated with the coming of Cyrus in xlviii 12–15; it is clear that Second Isaiah likes this association. With the appearance of Cyrus the historical horizon of the Israelites was broadened beyond anything they had known previously; and the cosmic scope of Yahweh's power is almost forced upon the vision of the prophet. No God who lacked supreme creative power could direct history over such a vast area. The prophet associates creation with Israelite history by describing the events of the Exodus in terms which echo the imagery of the cosmic myths of creation (li 9–10). Yahweh's victory over his adversaries is seen not in his conquest of some monstrous demon of chaos, but in the ease with which he overcomes the obstacles placed by nature in the way of the salvation of his people. Here he is truly revealed as creator in the historical experience of Israel; the belief in creation does not repose only on a mythological recital of events which lie outside history.

Several passages suggest that Second Isaiah knew that he was presenting something novel in his allusions to creation, or was at least recasting and making explicit a traditional belief not grasped in its fullness (xl 21, 28, xlv 11–12, xlviii 12). In the belief in creation the Israelites could perceive the reality of Yahweh in a way in which they had not noticed it before. This returns us to the idea of mission. They were to proclaim Yahweh to the men of the whole world, a world in which all belonged equally to Yahweh and in which his power was nowhere restricted. He has no competitor; the nations must hear of him not so much as the God of Israel as the God of the world. Israel's horizons, the prophet seems to say, have been narrow even when their belief has been substantially what it ought to be; now they must learn that Yahweh goes beyond his own people, and they must be ready to go with him.

We have noted that the most obvious theme of Second Isaiah, in the sense that no other theme is mentioned so many times, is the theme of salvation. In subordinating this theme to the idea of mission we do not mean to imply that it is less important. Israel must know and proclaim Yahweh primarily as a God who saves; and the Israel which the prophet addressed had not understood this quality

in its profundity. The prophet begins the discourses with a proclamation of salvation (xl 1–2), and indeed of the most grateful
and unexpected salvation, forgiveness and deliverance after the
execution of judgment. This salvation is described as a theophany, an
ancient image in Israel (xl 9–11); Yahweh comes as a shepherd, an
image suggesting tender kindness. Thus the presentation of salvation
begins with a picture which is the antithesis of judgment. The
prophet does not refrain from rebuke, as we have noted above; but
the rebuke is not uttered in a context of threat.

The Israel which is saved is the continuation of the Israel which suffered judgment (xliii 5–7; see COMMENT). Israel is dear to Yahweh,
and he will give peoples as its price (xliii 3–4; see COMMENT). This
passage should be read in conjunction with the theme of mission;
without this theme it would be an expression of national and religious
narrowness, as the theme of universalism makes clear (see below
pp. LXV–LXVII). Israel is precious because it has a destiny no other
people has. The power to save is proved by Yahweh's salvation of
Israel (xliii 8–13); and no other god has demonstrated his power to
save in such an incredible manner, for he brought back to life a
people which had perished. Israel is the witness to Yahweh's saving
power by its very existence, whether it proclaims his salvation in
word or not. Israel attests Yahweh's salvation as it attests his creation, not from hearsay but from experience.

The theme of forgiveness, mentioned in xl 1–2, is repeated in
xliv 22. We shall return to this under the theme of the renewal of
Israel; but forgiveness is an essential component of salvation. Israel
would not be truly saved if it had to drag into the new era a chain
of guilt. Second Isaiah and his contemporaries were heirs of the
ancient Israelite belief that Yahweh visited guilt upon descendants
to the third and fourth generation (Exod xx 4), and it could well
be conceived that the colossal guilt of pre-exilic Israel would endure
as an eternal stain, which could not be burned out (Ezek xxiv 6–14).
The statement of total forgiveness is necessary if the salvation was
to deserve the name. It is the first step without which no other step
was possible.

The quality of salvation is determined by Yahweh, not by the
Israelites. The sovereign independence of Yahweh must be affirmed
in his saving acts, and it is compared to the independence of the
potter over the vessels of his manufacture (xlv 9–13). It is not
fanciful to think that the Israelite dream included the restoration

of Israel to glory through such deeds as those by which David established his monarchy. But instead of that, Israel is to be re-established in a quite different condition through the power of an alien conqueror. Behind this lies the idea of mission once more; Israel's way of salvation is determined by what Yahweh wills that Israel should become. This purpose is not submitted to questioning. The metaphor of carrying (xlvi 3–4), while it does suggest the man carrying the child, may also imply that Israel is to be carried in the direction in which Yahweh wishes it to go.

Salvation is clearly the theme of the Zion poems to such an extent that it is scarcely possible to select single lines which illustrate the theme. We have noted that Jerusalem is an important element of the theme of salvation in both First and Second Isaiah. The revelation of Yahweh and his cult cannot be detached from the place where his name should dwell. Second Isaiah has not reached the vision of an Israel restored without Zion restored. We have noticed that he sees a continuity between the restored Israel and the old Israel. This continuity does not touch such things as king and temple, which have no place in his vision. The continuity appears in the restoration of the historic political and religious center of Israel. Would it indeed be a restored Israel unless Yahweh blessed the place which had fallen under his judgment? This is a concrete token of forgiveness, and allusions to forgiveness are numerous in the Zion poems (xlix 14–16, l 1–3, li 17–23, liv 1–10, lv 6–9). If Israel is to be a witness to Yahweh's salvation, there must be evidence which all the world can see; and the restored Zion is such evidence.

The salvation of Zion is described in somewhat extravagant terms (see the NOTES and COMMENT on the Zion poems). The prophet allows his imagination a free reign; yet the images are closely related to the realities—the restoration of the city, the return of exiles, security in the covenant of Yahweh, the righteousness the restored community should exhibit. Compared to the Zion poems of Third Isaiah (lx–lxii) the writing of Second Isaiah is restrained. The new Zion is not an image of the secular city; it is a new Zion, not another Nineveh or Babylon. It is an ideal community, for the prophet supposes ideal relations between the community and Yahweh. In a city of "righteousness," in the pregnant sense of the Hebrew word, there cannot be unrighteousness; and unrighteousness includes not only sin but poverty, defeat and disaster. This is the true nature of salvation, that Israel and Zion are established in righteousness.

The salvation of Israel is gratuitous; it is not granted because of the merits of Israel. Yahweh has chosen Israel, he loves Israel, and he saves Israel on his own account and for his glory (xliv 25, xlviii 9, 11). He is ready with forgiveness before Israel acknowledges its guilt. This too echoes the theme of mission. By his reflections on the past the prophet makes it clear that Israel has not been faithful to its election and has been a rebellious servant. But Yahweh's purpose, which is revealed as a wider salvation than Israel has seen, is not to be frustrated by his servant. Even though Israel is blind and stubborn, it has not lost its mission, and Yahweh saves Israel that it may fulfill its mission.

The Israel which is saved is a renewed Israel. It is renewed in strength (xl 28–31), which does not mean political or military power; it is renewed in the strength of hope and courage to walk in the path Yahweh opens—again the idea of mission is implicit. It is superior to any obstacle (xli 15–16; see the NOTES and COMMENT). Israel is able with the providence of Yahweh to march through the desert (xli 17–20, xlii 15–16). The regeneration of the desert becomes a figure of the regeneration of Israel (xliv 1–5); Yahweh pours his spirit and blessing on Israel (xliv 3). The Zion poems sing of the renewal of Zion after its desolation and abandonment. Zion will be repopulated (xlix 19–23). The city and the wasted land will once more be beautiful (lii 1–2, 9–10). The new Zion will be larger than the old Zion (liv 1–3) and will be built with a magnificence greater than anything in its past (liv 11–12). There will be no lack of food and drink (lv 1–3). The covenant which bound Israel to Yahweh will be renewed (lv 3).

What is the significance of this renewal? Most of the language, especially in the Zion poems, seems to have a material character. The renewal of Israel is much less explicitly moral and religious than it is in Jer xxxi 31–34 or Ezek xxxvi 26–27. But behind the imagery is the love and kindness of Yahweh, expressed in his forgiveness and in his protection, and in his announcement of the restoration of Zion and Judah. This renewal of Yahweh's favor means that the blindness, deafness and obstinacy for which the prophet rebukes Israel have disappeared. Israel is now awake to Yahweh's revelation and submissive to his law. The restored Israel is fit and equipped for the mission Yahweh lays upon it.

Second Isaiah has often been called the most explicit spokesman of monotheism up to his time. This description is somewhat exaggerated, but no earlier prophet so often confronts Yahweh and false gods. The allusions to creation (see above, pp. LIX–LXI) are insistent that Yahweh alone creates; there is none comparable to him (xl 18, 25). Yahweh challenges the nations and their gods to produce prophecies which, like his prophecies, have been verified (xli 21–24, 26–29, xliii 12, xliv 6–8). The nations shall be brought to confess that Yahweh alone is God (xlv 14, 20–21, 24–25). Second Isaiah scoffs at idols (xlvi 6–7), a theme that has been expanded by commentators (see NOTES and COMMENT on xl 29–30, xli 6–7, xliv 9–20). Yahweh is the only God who saves (xliii 10–13, xliv 24–28, xlv 20–25, xlviii 12–15, li 4–6, 12), and no one can hinder his saving action. He and he alone governs the course of events (xli 1–4, 25–26, xliii 14, xliv 24–28, xlv 1–7, 8–13, xlvi 8–11, xlviii 14–15, liv 15–17). It is Yahweh who accomplished the judgment on Israel (xli 18–25, xliii 28, xlviii 9–11, 17–18, li 7–23, liv 7–8), and it is Yahweh who delivers and restores Israel. Other nations, which do not worship him, are no less subject to his sovereignty, even though they do not know it; but history and the witness of Israel will reveal it. A summary of these passages shows that Second Isaiah's statements of monotheism are based on the actions of Yahweh in history and in creation and on prophecy, and not on an abstract consideration of the divine essence. The unique divinity of Yahweh is a fact of experience—this puts his thesis rather boldly. No other god makes the claims Yahweh makes in prophecy, and the claims are vindicated in the history of Israel. When Israel takes up the mission of proclaiming Yahweh, it has ample evidence for him whom it proclaims.

Here also we may look for some elements in the situation of Second Isaiah which contribute to this development. It is not a tenable position that Israel before Second Isaiah or even before Amos was not monotheistic in a proper sense. But what is the proper sense? There are no speculative statements of monotheism in the Old Testament before Second Isaiah, but neither are there speculative statements in Second Isaiah; as we have seen, he argues from history and prophecy. Israel was monotheistic in the sense not only that it worshiped no god but Yahweh, but that it took no account of any other god. Earlier books of the Old Testament do not reflect an idea of Yahweh as a god who is stronger than his competitors;

Yahweh has no competitors. The absence of any explicit denials of the reality of other gods implies that their reality was not accepted even as a working hypothesis. The cult of other gods is rejected in the Old Testament not only as an offense to Yahweh, but as an irrational action. In spite of this attitude of historical Israel, the Israel known from history, we have a candor in Second Isaiah which does not appear earlier.

Second Isaiah himself hints rather broadly that he addressed a community suffering from some degree of doubt (xl 18, 25, 27, xli 18–25, xliii 10–13, xlv 9–12, xlvi 5, 12, xlviii 5, li 12–13). It is easy to understand that there should have been doubt. The judgment on Israel could more easily be understood as a failure of Yahweh than as a righteous judgment. The Israelites had known mighty nations and their gods before Babylon, but for the first time they knew a people and gods who had defeated Judah utterly. Second Isaiah addressed those who had been transported to a foreign country, where the wealth and success of the nation was attributed to the gods whose temples they could see and whose cult they could observe. Nor was there any hope of restoration except that presented by Second Isaiah. The Israelites of Babylon could well have said, in a modern phrase, that Yahweh was dead. In this atmosphere of doubt a mere restatement of earlier belief was not enough. In his monotheism Second Isaiah met the challenge of history without evasion.

The affirmation of Yahweh as the one God has as its correlative the recognition of Yahweh by all peoples. This universalism of outlook in Second Isaiah is another element of the prophet's discourses, which has no real antecedent in earlier books of the Old Testament. The number of passages in which universalism is explicit is not large, but the theme is unambiguous where it occurs. The great statement of it appears in the poem of xlv 14–25 (see NOTES and COMMENT). This poem begins with lines which suggest a triumphant conquering Israel, but it becomes immediately apparent that the surrender to Israel, which the prophet describes, is a surrender to Yahweh with a confession of explicit monotheism (xlv 14). Yahweh then declares that this has been his purpose from creation, that all men should recognize him. They are invited to turn to him as the only God who saves; indeed, he has sworn that this shall happen. When it happens it is the supreme glory of Israel (xlv 25), for Israel is his witness. Yahweh promises to the nations the same things he has given Israel (li 4–5); the key words here, "teaching," "judgment,"

"victory," and "deliverance," are words which Second Isaiah elsewhere associates with Israel. The position of Israel does not mean
that it receives blessings Yahweh does not give to other peoples;
its position is that of mediator of blessings. Universalism is also
evident in the Servant Songs (discussed above), which we do not
attribute to Second Isaiah.

Second Isaiah's theology of history appears in his treatment of
the rise of Cyrus and the fall of Babylon, the two events which
alter the course of Israel's history. He announces several times that
the rise of Cyrus is the work of Yahweh (xli 1–4, 25, xliv 28 – xlv
7, xlv 13, xlvi 11, xlviii 15). These announcements, we have noted,
are associated with statements of the creative power of Yahweh.
One may ask whether this is not a narrow Israelite interpretation of
history; but one may also ask whether the re-establishment of a
Jewish community in Palestine was not the most enduring achievement of Cyrus of Persia. Titles which must have been strange to
Israelite ears were attached to a foreign conqueror; he is the elect
and the anointed of Yahweh, the man of Yahweh's purpose. This is
not limited to the restoration of Jerusalem. For his own purpose
Yahweh delivers kingdoms to Cyrus. Such a view of conquest does
not differ notably from Isaiah's recognition that Assyria was the rod
of Yahweh's anger (Isa x 5–6) or Jeremiah's admission that
Yahweh has delivered the kingdoms of the earth to Nebuchadnezzar
(Jer xxv 8–28, xxvii 1–22). The difference is in the saving purpose
of Yahweh; Assyria and Babylon were instruments of judgment on
Israel, but the judgment of which Cyrus is the instrument falls on
Babylon. The deliverance of Israel through Cyrus seems to have
created problems for the Israelite community (xlv 9–13); but
Yahweh does not allow his ways to be questioned. As we have
noted, the quality and the way of salvation are determined by
Yahweh, not by Israel. The work of Cyrus did not restore to Israel
its independence, still less any of the glory of the monarchy of
David and Solomon, and Second Isaiah does not promise that it
will. It will suit the purpose of Yahweh, who will through Cyrus re-
create an Israel which will be a more suitable instrument than the
old Israel was.

The fall of Babylon was a necessary step in the theology of
history. Jeremiah had predicted the fall of Babylon in the same
passages in which he declared that Yahweh has delivered the kingdoms of the earth to Nebuchadnezzar (Jer xxv 12–14, 26). Babylon

had contemned the power and righteousness of Yahweh, and had exceeded its mission of judgment. In two poems (Isa xlvi–xlvii), Yahweh's judgment falls on the gods of Babylon and on the city. The fatal faults of Babylon were pride and confidence in superstitious worship. Such worldly and unbelieving power cannot survive beyond the time of its usefulness. The righteousness of Yahweh demanded that Babylon be judged as Israel was; and the poem is couched in terms which suit the punishment to the crime. There is no similar hostile judgment of Cyrus and the Persians, for they had not yet manifested the qualities which would draw judgment. As an instrument of judgment Babylon had advanced the purpose of Yahweh; as a mere conqueror it retarded his purpose, and had to be removed. The rise and fall of kingdoms and empires, in the mind of Second Isaiah, must not be attributed to the forces of politics and war; none of these things happen except when they serve Yahweh's purpose in creation and history, and the focus of his purpose is Israel. It is from Israel that history becomes intelligible.

Third Isaiah

We have identified Third Isaiah as a collection of pieces from different authors, united as a continuation of Isaiah and exhibiting a community of theme and situation. The message of Third Isaiah, however, does not exhibit the unity which appears in Second Isaiah, and it is perhaps not altogether accurate to speak of the "message" of these chapters. Nevertheless, the collection is composed of more than scattered pieces assembled at random; and some effort to synthesize the common elements will help to render the oracles intelligible. It will also illustrate the differences between chapters xl–lv and lvi–lxvi which lead us to distribute these collections among different authors.

The cult was not included among the themes of Second Isaiah because it does not appear. In Third Isaiah, on the contrary, a cultic interest is seen in lvi 1–2, lviii 1–12, 13–14, lxvi 1–4. The interest is not the same in all these passages. Observance of the Sabbath is recommended as a vital observance in lvi 1–2 and lviii 13–14. But the poem of lviii 1–12 is an echo of such passages as Isa l 10–17; Jer vii 1–15; Hos vi 4–6; Amos v 21–24. These prophetic oracles attack the vanity of cultic observances maintained without attention to the law of Yahweh, and in particular those laws which govern the relation between man and man. It is on the observance of these laws, and not on fidelity to cultic observances, that the fulfillment of salvation depends. It is a theme of much of the collection, as we note below (pp. LXIX–LXX) that salvation is delayed.

Other oracles attack certain superstitious rites difficult to identify (lvii 3–13, lxvi 1–7, 11–12, 17; see the NOTES and COMMENT). These oracles also echo the pre-exilic prophets who charged the Israelites with accepting the gods and the ritual of Canaanite cults. These cults, however, we can identify better than the superstitions mentioned in Third Isaiah. On the assumption that we have dated these passages correctly, these oracles reveal the religious conditions of the Palestinian Jewish community of the sixth and fifth centuries; for there are almost no other allusions to religious corruption in this community. To the writers of Third Isaiah, as to the earlier prophets, such rites are infidelity to Yahweh. To accept superstition was to deny the reality of Yahweh, even if those who practiced these rites meant them to be a supplementary form of devotion.

In some poems of Third Isaiah the attitude toward the Gentiles is remarkably broad. Foreigners and eunuchs are admitted to the community of Israel (lvi 3–7). Foreign peoples will come to worship at Zion, and some will be admitted to serve as priests and Levites (lxvi 18–21, 22–23). The striking feature of these passages is the admission of foreigners and other ineligibles to full cultic standing; the temple is their house of prayer, and they offer sacrifice with the Israelites. These lines, if the critical dating of the passages is correct, come from a period when purity of blood became a rigorous test for admission to the Israelite community, and was applied with particular rigor to admission to the priestly and Levitical classes. The writer does not move against this practice directly, but he certainly treats it as a temporary dispensation, which must yield in the day when Yahweh is recognized by the nations. No Old Testament writer says more clearly that the difference between Israelites and Gentiles must disappear in the fullness of Israel. The triumphal passages of the Zion poems of Third Isaiah (lx 2, 6–16, lxi 5, lxii 2) do not affirm this as clearly, but they should be read in conjunction with the passages cited above. The foreigners of the Zion poems will serve the sanctuary of Yahweh by their contributions; but this poet draws a distinction between their service and the privileged priesthood of the Israelites (lxi 5–6).

The theme of salvation is prominent in Third Isaiah, as it is in Second Isaiah. Salvation is light and healing (lviii 8) and the sure protection of Yahweh (lviii 8–9). It is the provision of food in abundance and the restoration of the ruins of Judah (lviii 10–12). It is the resettlement of Israel in a prosperous land (lxv 8–10), a life of peace and joy, a life long and full of abundance (lxv 17–25). Salvation will come suddenly (lxvi 7–9) and will be the result of the tender care of Yahweh (lxvi 10–14). Salvation is the particular theme of the Zion poems (chs. lx–lxii). Here the wealth acquired from the contribution of the nations which submit to Yahweh is emphasized. Salvation is the peace and security created by the dwelling of Yahweh, joy and honor, and a restoration of Israel as the spouse of Yahweh. In these poems (see NOTES and COMMENT) the material element of salvation is even more prominent than it is in the Zion poems of Second Isaiah, and readers sometimes feel that the material element is overemphasized. This may be granted; this prophet does indeed see a restored and renewed Israel, which fulfills its mission of proclaiming Yahweh to the nations, but he sees it much more directly from the point of view of Israel, which is secured in its blessings by the accomplishment of the saving plans of Yahweh.

The theme of salvation in Third Isaiah has an element which is not found in Second Isaiah; salvation is promised but has been delayed, and the prophets ask why. The discourse on fasting (lviii 1–12) implies clearly that salvation is delayed because the community, or a part of it (see below, p. LXX) is satisfied with the performance of ritual observances and is not concerned with the cultivation of good human relations within the community. If the genuine fast of compassion and generosity is instituted, then salvation will break forth like the sudden dawn of Palestine. The poem of lix 1–20 asks the question bluntly, and gives the answer: salvation is delayed not by the weakness of Yahweh but because of the failure of the community to regenerate itself morally. This prophet does not mention cultic lapses; he is concerned entirely with the sins of man against man. Indeed, he seems to believe that only a theophany, an inbreak of the divine power and righteousness, will remove the barrier to salvation. This theophany must be a judgment against those who delay the arrival of salvation. These are Israelites; and we meet here another new theme in Third Isaiah.

The discourses of Third Isaiah exhibit that feature of post-exilic Judaism called "the piety of the poor." This is explicit in lvii 15, lxi 1–3, lxvi 2 (see the NOTES and COMMENT). It is implicit in the poems of lvi 9–lvii 2, 3–13, lviii 1–12, lix 1–20, lxv 1–7, 11–16, lxvi 5, 15–16, 24 (see the NOTES and COMMENT). The obstacle to salvation must be removed; and it is the unfaithful Israelites who constitute the obstacle. Judgment falls upon them as it fell upon the nations and upon the whole of Israel in the Exile. But there cannot be another such sweeping judgment upon the whole people; and the coming judgment will be selective. Not only the passages which exhibit the piety of the poor, but also the threatening oracles, identify the faithless in Israel with the wealthy ruling class; in this respect Third Isaiah continues the tradition of the pre-exilic prophets. But the pre-exilic prophets saw the ruling classes as dragging the entire nation down to ruin. Third Isaiah had learned the lesson of the indestructibility of Israel, but he had also learned the lesson of judgment. Israel could not survive as it was; the Israel of destiny had to be purified of those elements which kept salvation out of its reach. This is the way in which the writers of Third Isaiah met the problem of rebellious Israel, and it differs from the way in which their predecessors met the problem. There is a true Israel and a false Israel, and the false Israel must be rooted out.

The judgment by which this is accomplished takes on eschatological, even apocalyptic features. The writers apparently conceive of this judgment, which winnows out the spurious Israelites, as final; and indeed even the most undisciplined prophetic imagination could scarcely conceive of such a judgment as accomplished through instruments like Assyria and Babylon. The Israel which is purged by the process of lxv 13–16 remains purged; the judgment is followed by a new act of creation (lxv 17), which has features derived from Paradise and from First Isaiah (see NOTES and COMMENT). The death which strikes the faithless Israelites is a kind of prolonged death; they remain as monuments to the judgment of Yahweh (lxvi 15, 24). In this note the tragic duality of the genuine and the spurious Israel is ended. The modern reader finds the note not altogether pleasing, but it is a development of the prophetic theology of salvation and judgment. It is also an effort to solve the problem of personal responsibility as opposed to collective responsibility, a problem which was not solved in the preaching of the pre-exilic prophets. Perhaps it was not solved by Third Isaiah either, and it may not have been solved by subsequent thinkers. But Third Isaiah faces it, and attempts to affirm a solution which will not compromise either the righteousness of Yahweh or the dignity of the human person. Collective responsibility cannot mean that the individual person becomes meaningless. If Israel can find its destiny, then the individual Israelite should be able to find it too; at least he should not be prevented from finding it by those of his fellow Israelites who refuse it.

SELECTED BIBLIOGRAPHY

Begrich, Joachim, *Studien zu Deuterojesaja* (BZANW 77 [1938]). Reprinted by Chr. Kaiser Verlag: Munich, 1963.

Duhm, Bernhard, *Das Buch Jesaja* (Handkommentar zum Alten Testament).

Eissfeldt, Otto, *The Old Testament: An Introduction.* Translated by P. R. Ackroyd. New York: Harper & Row, 1965.

Elliger, Karl, *Die Einheit des Tritojesaja* (BWANT III, 9). Stuttgart: W. Kohlhammer, 1928.

Elliger, Karl, *Deuterojesaja in seinem Verhältnis zu Tritojesaja* (BWANT IV, 11). Stuttgart: W. Kohlhammer, 1933.

Haller, Max, *Das Judentum* (Die Schriften des Alten Testaments). Göttingen: Vandenhoeck & Ruprecht, 1914.

Kaiser, Otto, *Der königliche Knecht* (FRLANT N.F. 52). Göttingen: Vandenhoeck & Ruprecht, 1959.

Knight, George A. F., *Deutero-Isaiah; A Theological Commentary on Isaiah 40–55.* New York: Abingdon, 1965.

Lindblom, J., *The Servant Songs in Deutero-Isaiah.* Lund: 1965.

Mowinckel, Sigmund, *He That Cometh.* Translated by G. W. Anderson. Oxford: Basil Blackwell, 1956.

Muilenburg, James, *The Interpreter's Bible,* V, pp. 381–773. New York: Abingdon, 1956.

North, Christopher, *The Second Isaiah.* London: Oxford University, 1964.

North, Christopher, *The Suffering Servant in Deutero-Isaiah.* London: Oxford University, 2d ed., 1956.

Ploeg, J. van der, *Les Chants du Serviteur de Jahvé.* Paris: J. Gabalda, 1936.

Rignell, L. G., *A Study of Isaiah Ch. 40–55.* Lund: C. W. K. Gleerup, 1956.

Rowley, H. H., *The Servant of the Lord and Other Essays on the Old Testament,* pp. 1–93. Oxford: Basil Blackwell, 2d ed., 1965.

Smart, James D., *History and Theology of Second Isaiah*. Philadelphia: Westminster, 1965.

Smith, Sidney, *Isaiah XL–LV*. London: Humphrey Milford, 1944.

Torrey, C. C., *The Second Isaiah; A New Interpretation*. New York: Charles Scribner's Sons, 1928.

Volz, Paul, *Jesaia II* (Kommentar zum Alten Testament). Leipzig: Werner Scholl, 1932.

I. SCATTERED POEMS

1. YAHWEH'S VENGEANCE ON EDOM
(xxxiv 1–17)

XXXIV

1 Come here, nations, to listen; and peoples, pay attention;
Let the earth hear, and all that it contains; the world, and
all that it produces.

2 For Yahweh is angry at all nations, and is furious at all
their hosts;
He has devoted them to destruction, he has delivered them
to slaughter.

3 Their dead lie scattered, the stench of their corpses arises;
The mountains are wet with their blood.

4 All the host of the heavens rots;
The heavens are rolled up like a scroll, and all their host
withers,
As leaves wither on the vine, as they wither on the fig tree.

5 For my sword appears[a] in the heavens;
See, it comes down upon Edom, for judgment on the
people whom I have condemned.

6 Yahweh has a sword, dripping blood, smeared with fat,
With the blood of lambs and goats, with the fat of rams'
kidneys;
For Yahweh has a sacrifice in Bozrah, a great slaughter in
the land of Edom.

7 Wild oxen will perish with them, and young bulls with
wild bulls;
Their land will be drunk with blood, their dust steeped in
fat.

[a] Read "appears" with 1QIs[a]; Heb. "is drunk" probably arose from the following verses.

8   For Yahweh has a day of vengeance, a year of retribution for the cause of Zion.

9   Its streams will be turned to pitch, its dust to brimstone; And its land will become flaming pitch.

10   Night and day it will never be quenched, its smoke will rise perpetually;
It will lie a waste for generations to come; no one will pass through it for ever and ever.

11   But the owl and the jackdaw shall possess it, the night hawk and the raven shall dwell there;
He will stretch over it the line of desolation and the measure of waste.

12   *b*Satyrs will dwell there, and its nobles will be no more*b*;
They shall call it No-Kingdom-There, and all its princes will vanish.

13   Thorns will grow in its palaces, nettles and brambles in its fortresses;
It will be the haunt of jackals, the pasture of ostriches.

14   Demons shall meet with fiends, and one satyr will call to another;
Yes, the night hag will alight there and find her nesting place.

15   There*c* the snake will nest and lay and brood and hatch her eggs*d*;
Yes, the vultures will assemble there; *e*none shall miss her mate.*e*

16   Look in Yahweh's book and read; not one of these things will be lacking*f*;
For his*g* mouth has ordained it, and it is his spirit which assembles them.

---

b–b Supplying a lacuna from LXX; Heb. "Its nobles. . . ."
c The sense suggests "there" rather than Heb. "thither."
d The context suggests "her eggs" rather than Heb. "in her shadow."
e–e Transferring this half line from vs. 16; Heb. "each her mate."
f Transferring "none shall miss her mate" to vs. 15 (see note *e–e*).
g "His mouth" with 1QIs; Heb. "my mouth."

17 For it is he who casts the lot for them, and his hand
apportions for them^h by line;
They shall possess it forever, they shall dwell there for
generations to come.

^h Hebrew reads feminine "them" in the first colon, masculine in the second.
1QIs^a shows a correction of the masculine to the feminine.

NOTES

xxxiv 2. See lxvi 15–16, 24 for similar imagery of the judgment on
the nations.

5. *sword* of Yahweh. Personified as in Ezek xxi 8–17.

6. *Bozrah* is mentioned in prophetic threats against Edom in lxiii 1;
Jer xlix 13, 22; Amos i 12. The city is probably to be located at the
modern Buseira (which preserves the name), about 120 miles south of
Amman.

7. The wild ox has long been extinct in the Near East; it is known
from Assyrian literature and art, in which hunting the wild ox appears
as a royal sport. It is mentioned in eight other passages in the OT besides
this; all are poetic.

8. *vengeance* and *retribution*. Legal terms designating the punishment
of one who does damages and where possible, the recovery of the
damages. "Vindication" and "compensation" would correspond to the
idea. But in Hebrew there are no distinct words for these ideas such as
we have in English. The legal terms go back to the custom of the blood
feud, in which the only vindication or satisfaction or compensation
known was revenge. The lack of refinement of language gives such
passages as this a harsh tone to modern readers.

9–10. The imagery echoes the story of the destruction of Sodom and
Gomorrah (Gen xix 24–28).

11. D. N. Freedman points out that 11b exhibits a common feature of
Hebrew verse only recently noticed, the division of natural pairs in order
to secure poetic variation and balance. *The line* and the stones (plum-
mets, here translated *measure*) go together, as do *desolation* and *waste*
(*tōhû wābōhû;* see Gen i 2). The line in prose would read, "He will
stretch over it the line and plummet of desolation and waste." The line
and plummet were used by builders of walls; here by paradox, Yahweh
uses them to plan destruction.

11–15. The passage imitates and expands the picture of the fall of
Babylon (Isa xiii 20–22). In popular belief ruins were inhabited not
only by wild animals, especially nocturnal predatory beasts and birds,

but also by demons. Animals and demons are interchanged in this passage; and the identification of some of the beasts and birds is uncertain.

12. *satyrs*. Mentioned in Isa xiii 21; the same word much more frequently designates a he-goat, and the satyr (like the Greek demon *satyros*) is a demon with goat features.

13. D. N. Freedman points out that this line illustrates a feature of Hebrew verse; the preposition is used only with the second noun of *palaces* and *fortresses*, but serves for both. It could also stand with the first noun. It is impossible to render this in translation.

14. There is a wordplay in Hebrew with *demons* and *fiends*. "Demon" suggests a desert dweller.

night hag. Heb. *lîlît*, "Lilith," Akk. *lilitu*, found only here in the OT. The night hag was a *succuba* who deceived men by phantom enticements. "Meeting" and "calling" indicate that demons are numerous: the place is entirely given over to them.

15. *eggs*. Heb. *bēṣeyāh*, is very similar in writing to "in her shadow" (*beṣillāh*) and seems to suit the context better.

16. *Yahweh's book*. Could be Isa xiii, to which there are several implicit allusions in the passage; but Isa xiii is concerned with Babylon, not Edom.

17. The line echoes the apportionment of the land of Israel to the tribes (see Josh xvii–xix); by a similar decree Edom is apportioned to the demons.

COMMENT

This poem, and the poem following, belong in style and content with Isa xl–lxvi (SECS. 3–47), although it is not possible to affirm that they are from the same author or authors. A comparison of this poem with the collection of Third Isaiah (lvi–lxvi [SECS. 33–47]) is enough to show that it is akin to this collection and not to Isa i–xxxiii. How the two poems came to have their present location is uncertain. It appears that they did not form a part of the collections of Isa xl–lxvi, and also that they were appended to Isa i–xxxiii before Second and Third Isaiah; for they precede the historical appendix, Isa xxxvi–xxxix, which may be taken as a conclusion of the first edition of the Book of Isaiah.

In character this poem is apocalyptic—a word that generally designates the type of literature which succeeded prophecy in Judaism and viewed the end of history as a judgment of God ex-

ecuted in a world catastrophe. The roots of this idea can be found
in the earlier prophets—for example, in the "Day of Yahweh" of
Amos v 18–20; Isa ii 5–22; the fall of Babylon in Isa xiii 1–22. The
NOTES draw attention to several literary affinities between this poem
and Isa xiii which suggest a dependence of this poem on the earlier
work. But the "Day of Yahweh" of the earlier prophets is not seen
as a world catastrophe and the end of history; it is the judgment
of Yahweh executed in a particular moment of history, even though
the language used is cosmic in scope. Other instances of apocalyptic will be noticed in the collection of Third Isaiah; it is a literary
form not found in Second Isaiah.

The poem begins with an apostrophe to all nations, and it is
against all nations that the judgment is directed in vss. 1–4. No distinction is made between one nation and another; none is spared,
and in these lines no one is singled out for special judgment. In the
development of Israelite belief, this attitude toward the nations which
did not acknowledge the sovereignty of Yahweh was quite logical.
If Israel itself had experienced the destroying judgment of Yahweh
for its rebellion, the peoples which had never accepted his sovereignty at all could hardly expect better treatment. This is not a development of the thesis of Amos iii 2 that the election of Israel imposed upon Israel a greater responsibility. But the events of the fall
of Judah and the Exile acquainted the Israelites with great nations
which blasphemed the name of Yahweh in the sense that they did
not confess that Yahweh is lord and did not confess the lordship
of Yahweh. Yahweh would have to prove his lordship by judgment.

This general view of the nations becomes suddenly quite specific
in vs. 6 to the conclusion of the poem. The transition is so sudden
that one is led to wonder whether the poet did not adapt an earlier
apocalyptic poem of general scope to his particular objective. In
post-exilic literature Edom becomes an object of peculiar hatred
(see Jer xliv 7–22, closely parallel to Obadiah; Ezek xxxv 1–15).
These passages make it clear that after the fall of Judah in 587 B.C.,
the Edomites overran the south of Judah as far north as Hebron.
The Edomite occupation continued after the restoration of Jerusalem.
This occupation of Judahite territory was regarded as an act of
treachery; it was neither forgotten nor forgiven, although there was
a fairly long history of Judahite aggression against Edom going back
to David's time.

The imagery of vss. 6–7 is crude at best. The religious quality of such passages is saved only by the theme of judgment; and the Israelite prophets speak of Yahweh's judgment on the nations in terms no harsher than the terms they use in speaking of Yahweh's judgment of Israel.

The NOTES call attention to OT passages on which vss. 9–16 depend. Even in the exilic period the number of abandoned sites in the ancient Near East was large enough to permit biblical writers to portray such sites with convincing realism; Jerusalem itself was one after the catastrophe of 587 B.C. Such sites were abandoned by the gods, whose cult was no longer carried on there, and they became the haunts of demons. This popular demonology is reflected both in this passage and in Isa xiii, on which this passage depends. The existence of such abandoned cities, we may be sure, gave a certain force to the biblical proclamations of God's judgments. Even now the traveler who sees once populous cities that have been abandoned for centuries can scarcely view these sites without some awe and fear; is his own city any more assured of immortality than these?

2. THE MARCH OF THE REDEEMED
(xxxv 1–10)

XXXV

1   Let the wilderness and the desert rejoice; let the arid land
     be glad and burst into blossoms;

2   Let it bloom continually with daffodils; let it rejoice—
     yes, rejoice and break out in song;
     It shall be given the glory of Lebanon, the splendor of
     Carmel and Sharon;
     These shall see the glory of Yahweh, the splendor of our
     God.

3   Grasp the feeble hands, strengthen the failing knees;

4   Tell the fainthearted: Courage, do not be afraid;
     Look, it is your God; vengeance comes;
     It is God's retribution; he comes to save you.

5   Then the eyes of the blind will be enlightened, and the
     ears of the deaf will be opened;

6   Then the lame will gambol like a stag, and the tongue of
     the dumb will break into song;
     For rivers shall be cleft in the desert, and streams in the
     arid land.

7   The hot sand will become a pool, and the parched ground
     fountains of water;
     In the haunt of jackals her place of rest; *a*grass . . . to reeds
     and papyrus*a*

8   A pure highway*b* will be there; it will be called the Holy
     Way;

a–a The line is so corrupt as to be unintelligible; the translation is literal.

b Reading with LXX; Heb. "a highway and a road," which seems to be an
unnecessary tautology possibly glossing an unintelligible text. The LXX reading
suits the context very well.

No one unclean shall pass over it,[c] nor shall fools wander
in it.

9 No lion will be there, nor shall any rapacious beast enter
it[d];
The redeemed shall travel there.

10 The ransomed of Yahweh will return;
They shall enter Zion in song, with eternal joy upon their
heads;
They will possess gladness and joy, and grief and groaning
will flee.

[c] Omitting "and this for them walking the road" of Heb.

[d] Omitting "it will not be found" of Heb.; the phrase cannot be construed except by taking the "lion" and "rapacious beast" together as the antecedent of the feminine verb (D. N. Freedman). So construed, the line is an unnecessary emphasis added to two very well-balanced lines.

Notes

xxxv 2. *Lebanon* with its cedars and *Carmel and Sharon* (in the coastal plain) with their forests are proverbial examples of rich vegetation. The desert through which redeemed Israel travels is converted into a well-watered land.

5. Quoted loosely in Matt xi 5 and Luke vii 22 as messianic signs.

6. The verse alludes to the miraculous provision of water in the Exodus narratives: Exod xvii 1–7; Num xx 2–13.

8. There is here a very probable allusion to the Sacred Way of Babylon and other Mesopotamian cities. This road connected important temples and was the route of solemn processions in which the images of the gods were borne from one temple to another; A. L. Oppenheim, *Ancient Mesopotamia* (Chicago, 1964), p. 139.

10. *joy upon their heads.* An obvious metaphor which may have a basis in a cultic or festive practice of wearing wreaths or garlands to symbolize rejoicing. The practice is so widespread that the assumption is easy.

COMMENT

The editor of the collection of First Isaiah has matched the grim oracle of judgment with a poem of deliverance. The basic theme is the theme of the journey through the wilderness; the NOTES cite related allusions in the Exodus narratives. In the Exodus Israel was provided in its journey through the desert with water from the rock and manna from the heavens. In the journey of Israel from its Babylonian exile the desert itself will be regenerated. The luxuriant growth of wild flowers in the desert after the winter rains suggests the possibility of a complete transformation of the desert into a land more generously endowed with vegetation than the historic land of Israel to which the exiles were returning. Ancient Israel was well aware of the miracle of water in the desert, even though the transformation which modern methods of irrigation can effect was still unknown. But the desert traveler could see the contrast between the rich and refreshing green of the oasis and the hot dull wilderness of sand and stone in which the oasis lay. Yahweh could transform the entire desert into a vast oasis.

Like the land through which they travel, the people who make the journey are also regenerated. There are no blind, lame, deaf, or dumb among them; for Yahweh has healed them. To the Israelite, "healing" meant more than the cure of disease; likewise in Greek a common word for "healing" is the word which is translated "save." Deliverance from exile was deliverance from guilt, and from the ills of man which are signs of his guilt; for afflictions like blindness and lameness were signs of God's judgment. This work means that Yahweh has come; in the OT his work of judgment and of saving is conceived as a coming, often in the imagery of the theophany.

The pilgrim people of Israel travel upon a road Yahweh has built for them; on the allusion to "the Holy Way," see NOTE on vs. 8. As yet, it seems, the Persians, the first great roadbuilders of the ancient Near East, had not yet begun their work. But there are allusions (see xl 3–4) to the grading and filling of highways, necessary when wheeled vehicles used the road in addition to pedestrian and animal traffic. This is the road on which Yahweh travels for his people, and thus it becomes a processional road, fit for a god and for a king. The tone is entirely one of joy, without the note of triumph which is perceived in some other poems of the return.

The modern reader may sense a harsh contrast between the poems of salvation and judgment. While it is true that Israel has experienced its judgment, salvation as envisaged here is for Israel alone; no attention is given to the nations. This narrowness is not without its compensation in some other passages, which will be noted in the course of the COMMENT. In this area Israel's understanding of the scope of Yahweh's saving will was still developing.

The ideas and the style of this poem are so closely related to the poems of xl–lv (SECS. 3–32) that identity of authorship is very strongly suggested. The NOTES in xl–lv point out some of the community of thought and language. We may suppose that this poem was detached from the other poems of Second Isaiah and by some roundabout way reached the collection of First Isaiah independently.

II. DELIVERANCE FROM BABYLON

3. THE CALL OF THE PROPHET
(xl 1–11)

XL

1   "Comfort, comfort my people," says your God.

2   "Speak kindly to Jerusalem, and proclaim to her,
    That her sentence is served, her penalty is paid,
    That she has received from Yahweh's hand double for all
     her sins."

3   A voice calls:
  "Clear a road in the steppe for Yahweh,
    Grade a highway in the desert for our God.

4   Let every valley be filled, and every mountain and hill
     be leveled;
    Let the ridge become a plain, and the hillocks a prairie.

5   The glory of Yahweh will be revealed, and all flesh will see
     together;
    For the mouth of Yahweh has spoken."

6   A voice said: "Proclaim!" And I said,[a] "What shall I
     proclaim?"
  "All flesh is grass, and its constancy like the blossom of
    the field.

7   The grass withers, the blossom fades,
    When the wind of Yahweh blows on them.
    [b]Surely the people is grass.[b]

8   The grass withers, the blossom fades;
    But the word of our God shall endure forever."

9   Get you up on a high mountain, messenger Zion!

[a] "I said" with LXX and 1QIs[a]; Heb. "he said."
[b-b] This line, which overloads the context, is very probably a gloss.

Lift your voice with power, messenger Jerusalem!
  Lift it, do not fear!
Say to the cities of Judah: See, it is your God!
10   See the Lord Yahweh,
  He comes in strength,*c* and his arm rules for him:
  His reward is with him, and his prize goes before him,
11   Like a shepherd who feeds his flock, who gathers the lambs
    with his arm,
  And takes them to his bosom, and leads the nursing ewes
    to rest.

c Reading *beḥōzek* with LXX and 1QIs*ᵃ*; Heb. *beḥāzāk*, "as a strong one."

NOTES

xl 2. The double penalty is the disaster of 587 B.C., in which the kingdom of Judah was overturned by the Babylonians and Jerusalem was destroyed and abandoned. Jerusalem is personified as a woman throughout Second Isaiah.

3. In ancient oriental monarchies roads were cleared for the passage of the king; see xxxv 8–10.

6. *constancy*. Follows the Heb., but the textual tradition is not altogether certain. The word is more frequently translated by such words as "loving-kindness." It designates that relationship which unites kinship or social groups; it is fidelity to mutual obligations.

7. *the wind of Yahweh*. The hot east wind from the desert, the *khamsin*, which withers vegetation.

9. The *messenger* is Zion-Jerusalem, usually personified as feminine.

10–11. This is the theme of theophany. Yahweh usually appears in the storm (see Ps xviii 7–15; Hab iii), but violence is not suggested here.

COMMENT

The first poem is best understood as a prologue to the entire composition. It is the announcement of good news, and the good news is the coming of Yahweh. It is only in the later poems that it becomes clear that Yahweh comes to liberate and restore Israel. The opening words have given the Book of Second Isaiah the title of "Book of

Consolation." Second Isaiah is much more than a book of consolation, but this is certainly a dominant theme. The poem employs the form of dialogue, which is usual in Second Isaiah; at times it is difficult to distinguish the speakers. The speakers are the prophet, Yahweh, and two unidentified voices. The suggestion that these are voices of Yahweh's heavenly council (Muilenburg) has some probability. The heavenly council occurs in Job i–ii; I Kings xxii 19–22; Jer xxiii 18, 22. Whether the voices are to be identified with the heavenly council or not, they must be understood as heavenly voices, the voices of Yahweh's messengers. It is from them that the prophet receives his commission.

The poem describes a prophet's vocation, and may be compared to Isa vi; Jer i; Ezek i. Although Second Isaiah is skillful in the use of visual imagery, he does not employ it here; his vocation resembles the vocation of Jeremiah rather than the vocation of Isaiah or Ezekiel. The revelation of Yahweh he conceives as spoken word, in the traditional manner of prophecy. The first words, the words which set the theme of consolation, are the words of Yahweh himself. These are followed by one of the heavenly voices, and only then does the prophet speak. The voices bid him announce his message; and the message—if the prophet, as is most probable, is the speaker in vss. 9–11—goes beyond the words of the voice in 6–8.

There is no certain parallel in earlier books of the OT to the thought in vs. 2 that Jerusalem has served its sentence and paid its penalty. The word rendered "sentence" designates a term of service, whether military or forced labor. Not only has Jerusalem served its sentence, but it has paid double. It is doubtful that the prophet means that Yahweh's judgment has exceeded the bounds of justice. Double payment was imposed upon the thief (Exod xxii 4, 7) and for breach of trust (Exod xxii 9). The goods of Job were restored to him double, including even the years of his life, but not his children (Job xlii 12–16). Even heavier restitution could be imposed by law or by royal decree (Exod xxii 1; II Sam xii 6). The prophet seems to conceive the fall of Jerusalem both as a punishment for crime and a payment of damages. The disintegration of the people and kingdom of Israel was a shattering disaster, and the prophet throughout his poems is awed by the unexpected miracle of survival. Yahweh's judgment could not have been more complete and decisive than it was, yet Israel has survived it. The statement, however, could scarcely have been made by Amos or First Isaiah.

The good news, we noticed, is the coming of Yahweh. The theme of the road appears in xxxv 8–10, where it is the road on which Israel marches. There seems to be no room for a distinction between the road of Yahweh and the road of Israel, for Yahweh travels with his people as he did in the Exodus (xliii 2, 19, xlix 10, lii 12). It is in Israel that his glory, his manifest holiness, appears; he is now seen to be holy in his saving acts as he was seen to be holy in his judgments. Yahweh's glory demands acknowledgment, and this great saving act will impress itself upon all flesh—which means all mankind, not only the people of Israel. The theme of universal recognition is developed in the poems following.

The words of the voice in vss. 6–7 express a kind of sententious wisdom, which is typical of Wisdom literature. Indeed, it seems that the saying of the voice is proposed as a Wisdom "riddle" to which the prophet discerns the answer. The saying was not well understood by the glossator who added the last line of 7; he interpreted the saying as referring to Israel. The voice contrasts the weakness of men with the power of Yahweh. The fierce blast of the desert wind withers vegetation when it is prolonged; the change from life to death is sudden and unexpected, and it is no wonder that biblical writers have so often seen in the desert wind an image of the judgments of God. Man is no more enduring than grass; the only enduring reality is his experience of the word of Yahweh. The "word" here is used in the pregnant sense usual in Hebrew—the word and the deed it signifies are taken as a single reality. It is not only the spoken word of Yahweh, but the deed it accomplishes which has enduring reality. Man cannot annul Yahweh's word.

This is the key to the prophet's message. He was aware of the existence of earlier oracles of promise; several of the poems which follow allude to them. This word must stand, and Israel, which is their object, must stand. At once he translates the generality of vss. 6–7 into the particular moment of history in which it was spoken. Yahweh has spoken, and has announced his coming. He speaks to Jerusalem, the messenger of the cities of Judah. At the time when he spoke Jerusalem and the cities of Judah must have been generally abandoned, or no more than wretched village settlements. He personifies them as already risen from the ruins; for the word of Yahweh begins at once to effect what it signifies. The "reward" and the "prize" which accompany him can only be, it seems, the people of Israel whom he leads back to their own land. He leads them like a shepherd, a title often given to ancient Near Eastern kings, Israelite and others, and to Yahweh himself (Gen xlix 24; Pss xxviii 9, lxxviii 52, lxxx 2; Jer xxiii 3, xxxi 19; and above all Ps xxiii). Yahweh has repossessed that which is his own.

4. YAHWEH CREATOR AND SAVIOR
(xl 12–31)

XL

12   Who has measured the waters of the sea[a] in the hollow of
his hand, and stretched his span across the sky?
Who contained the dust of the earth in a measure, and
weighed the mountains in a scale,
And the hills in a balance?

13   Who has directed the spirit of Yahweh, and what counselor has taught him?

14   Whom has he consulted to gain insight, and who has
instructed him in the path of judgment,
[b]and taught him knowledge[b] and acquainted him with the
way of understanding?

15   See, the nations are a drop from a bucket; they are counted
as dust on the scales;
See, the coastlands are weighed as powder.

16   Lebanon is not enough for burning, nor its wild beasts for
whole burnt offerings.

17   All the nations are as nothing before him; they are
counted as emptiness[c] and a void against him.

18   To whom do you liken El? Or what counterpart will you
set up opposite him?

19   [d]The smelter casts a statue; the goldsmith plates it with
gold,
And casts[e] chains of silver.

[a] Reading with 1QIs[a]; Heb. "waters."
[b–b] These words, missing in LXX, are probably a scribal expansion.
[c] Reading with 1QIs[a]; Heb. "from nothing."
[d–d] Verses 19–20, a fragment of a polemic against idolatry, are a gloss here.
[e] Conjectural emendation suggested by grammar; Heb. "caster."

20   A tree fit for consecration,^f a trunk which will not rot he
      selects;
      The skillful artisan seeks out, to set up an image that will
      not totter.^d

21   Do you not know? Have you not heard? Has it not been
      declared to you from the beginning?
      Have you not understood from the foundation^g of the
      earth?

22   He sits upon the dome of the earth, and its inhabitants
      are as locusts;
      He stretches out the heavens like a veil; he spreads them
      like a tent to dwell in.

23   He reduces rulers to nothing; the judges of the earth he
      obliterates.

24   Hardly are they planted, hardly are they sown,
      Hardly has their stock taken root in the earth—
      He but blows on them, and they wither; and the storm
      bears them away like stubble.

25   "To whom would you liken me, that I should be his equal?"
      says the Holy One.

26   Lift up your eyes on high, and see who created these
      things;
      He who leads out their hosts by number, and calls all of
      them by name;
      So great is his strength, so mighty is he in power, not one
      of them is missing.

27   Why do you say, Jacob—why do you declare, Israel,
      "My way is hidden from Yahweh, and my right is passed
      over by my God"?

28   Do you not know? Have you not heard?
      Yahweh is the eternal God, who has created the ends of
      the earth;
      He does not faint nor grow weary; his mind is inscrutable.

---

f Heb. m^esukkān is probably a kind of tree; literally "a tree of consecration."
g Conjectural emendation suggested by parallelism; Heb. "foundations." But the
preposition in the preceding line may govern both nouns (D. N. Freedman).

29   He strengthens the weary, and to the feeble he gives
      power.

30   Youths faint and grow weary, and young men stumble and
      fall;

31   But those who hope in Yahweh will regain strength; they
      will sprout wings like eagles;
      They will run without weariness; they will walk without
      tiring.

NOTES

xl 15. *the coastlands*. Appears frequently in II Isaiah; this translation
is preferred to the older version "islands." The word designates the
coastal region of Syria and Phoenicia, for the Israelites a remote area,
the limits of the earth.

16. An allusion to the cedar forests of Lebanon. The line is a mild
statement of the relative unimportance of sacrifice; see NOTES on xliii
23–24 and COMMENT (SEC. 15).

18. *El*. An archaic divine title, found also in Canaanite. El was the
father of the gods in Canaanite mythology. The title is found in many
Israelite personal names.

22. The image is that of the sky as a solid dome over the disk of the
earth; this was the usual ancient Near Eastern conception; see Gen i and
the Babylonian creation poem *Enuma elish* (ANET, p. 67). By a mixture
of images the sky is also represented as a veil or a curtain like a tent
(Ps civ 2).

23. Compare with Job xii 18–19.

25. *the Holy One*. This title is an echo of I Isa.

31. The figure makes one wonder whether there is an obscure
mythological allusion to some eternal bird like the phoenix. More
probably the figure is a simple hyperbole. It is not merely a matter of
sustaining strength, but of restoring strength to the feeble. When a person
who is greatly weakened suddenly begins to run, it is as if he sprouts
wings.

COMMENT

The prophet begins with an appeal to the power of Yahweh exhibited in creation. To modern readers it is surprising that this appeal should first appear in such a way so late in OT literature. Critical examination of the OT books indicates that creation was not a prominent theme in pre-exilic literature, and that no one proposed the theme with so much emphasis prior to Second Isaiah. That he should be among the first to treat the idea suits the situation in which he uttered his prophecies. Israel had experienced the power of foreign nations in a way new to its experience. The power of an ancient Near Eastern nation was a testimonial to the power of its gods. Second Isaiah writes apologetics for doubting Israelites who wondered whether the power of Yahweh could be measured against the power that Marduk, the local god of Babylon, and head of the Babylonian pantheon, exhibited in the Neo-Babylonian Empire. Second Isaiah could not have been appealing to an entirely new idea; when we say that the idea of creation is less prominent in pre-exilic literature, we do not mean that it is not found at all. The attribution of creation to various gods was conventional in the religious literature of Mesopotamia; Second Isaiah speaks to those Israelites who thought of Yahweh as creator in the same conventional terms. He recalled to them an ancient article of their faith.

Volz, followed by J. D. Smart (against Duhm), takes the question in vs. 12 as ironical, as is the question in 13; the answer to the question of 12 is not "Yahweh," but "no man"; the interrogative "Who" is the same in both 12 and 13. This interpretation has much in its favor. The lines so interpreted are uttered in the same ironic tone as the questions of Job xxxviii. Verse 12, therefore, is not an imaginative picture of creation. Just as no one has exercised the creative power, so no one has comprehended the spirit of Yahweh, or instructed him how to carry on his providence. The vastness of the creative power reduces all nations and men to nothing; if men wish to worship the creator, they will find that the entire visible universe is not sufficient for a worthy sacrifice. In comparison with Yahweh, no nation is to be reckoned as important. The basis of this argument must be a theology of creation recognized as different from the creation myths of Mesopotamia; see ANET, pp. 60–72. And in fact the OT creation accounts and allusions to creation, even those mythological in character, are quite different from the Mesopotamian myths. For the purposes of Second Isaiah it was sufficient that the claims of Yahweh were unparalleled. Hence no god can be presented as a rival to him. We have treated vss. 19–20 as a gloss; the polemic against idolatry in the crass sense, in the sense of worship of the image, appears elsewhere in Second Isaiah (and some of these passages are likewise doubtfully original); but these two verses do not harmonize with the context.

The prophet declares that Israel has known that Yahweh is the sole creator from the beginning; we have already noticed that he appeals to an ancient article of faith. He is not asking his listeners to adopt a new belief, but simply to maintain the traditional faith. That there were difficulties in so doing was evident, and it is his purpose to meet them; but first he asks his listeners whether they recognize their own beliefs and whether they are willing to stand by them. It may be assumed that they were not ready for an explicit abandonment of Israelite belief, and the prophet counts on this to make his presentation. The picture of the universe (vs. 22) is the common cosmological picture of the ancient Near East, and found also in Gen i. The sky is a dome which overarches the disk of the earth, and above this dome Yahweh sits enthroned. The comparison of the heavens to a tent or a veil is more common; the "firmament" of Gen i 6–7 is unique in the OT. And since Yahweh can roll up the heavens like a curtain or scroll (see xxxiv 4), men are even less able to resist him.

The thought of vss. 23–24 is echoed at greater length by a no less skillful poet in Job xii 16–25. Second Isaiah does not detach the theology of creation from the theology of history; Yahweh made the earth to be inhabited (xlv 18). But since the visible structure of the universe manifestly outlives the individual nation, man placed against the backdrop of the universe becomes utterly insignificant; and this is his point. Babylon is not an enduring reality; neither Babylon nor its gods should be compared to Yahweh. The doubting Israelites would not think of making the comparison explicit; but when they wonder whether the power of Babylon will endure, they are making it equal to Yahweh. Let them look at the stars, which Yahweh knows by number and by name. Job also presents God as leading out the stars to their places (xxxviii 31–33). The mention of the stars was of peculiar interest, for Mesopotamia was the ancient home of astrology and of astral cults. The author of the creation narrative of *P* insists that the sun and moon and stars are merely lights and signs for the reckoning of the calendar (Gen i 14–18).

In vs. 27 the prophet turns to address Israel; vs. 28 (against Volz) connects these lines with the preceding. The appeal is motivated by faith in Yahweh as creator. The complaint which Israel voices is that Yahweh does not attend to it. The "way" and the "right" of Israel designate the position of Israel as a covenant people. For these doubters, the promises and the saving deeds of Yahweh are things of the past; they are not present realities. With fine insight Second Isaiah goes beneath this express doubt of the saving will of Yahweh and identifies it as a doubt of Yahweh's power. To say that Yahweh will not do what he says is equivalent to saying that he cannot do it. In later poems the prophet touches explicitly on the doubt of Yahweh's saving will; but here he touches the radical doubt, the doubt that cannot see the hand of Yahweh in the world of history and experience. The answer to this doubt is the affirmation of Yahweh the creator.

To say that Yahweh is creator does not afford a complete understanding of Yahweh's mind. Second Isaiah knows and often repeats that Yahweh is mysterious. But the mystery must not become an excuse for abandoning faith in him. Yahweh is eternal; he does not weaken with age and fatigue as men do. This is not for the prophet a means of proposing the stale apologetic argument that Yahweh acts in his own good time. Yahweh is always active, and any time is his time. What the prophet means is that Yahweh communicates some of the unfailing strength of his eternity to those who believe in him. As Yahweh always acts with full vigor, so those who trust in him find their vigor renewed to perpetual fullness. They receive the power to do what they must do; they can live in a hope which is as strong as he in whom they hope. Israel must face its future with a conviction that the promises of Yahweh are not dimmed or frustrated. The creator has not yielded his sovereignty to another.

5. THE LIBERATOR COMES
(xli 1–7)

XLI

1 "Be silent before me, coastlands; and let the peoples renew their strength.
Let them draw near, then let them speak; let us come
together for judgment.

2 Who has raised up a righteous one from the east and calls[a]
him to follow?
Who delivers nations to him and subdues kings?[b]
He reduces them[c] to dust with his sword and to driven
stubble with his bow.

3 He pursues them, he advances in security; he does not
travel by foot on the road.

4 Who has wrought, who has done this? He who calls the
generations from the beginning—
I Yahweh am the first, and I shall be at the end.

5 The coastlands see and fear; the ends of the earth tremble;
They draw near, they come."

6 [d]Each man helps his neighbor, and says to his brother,
"Courage!"

7 The smith encourages the smelter, and the polisher encourages the hammerer,
Saying of the soldering, "It is good"; and he fastens it
with nails so that it will not totter.[d]

---

[a] Reading "and called" with 1QIs[a]; Heb. "called."
[b] Reading *yôrîd* with 1QIs[a]; Heb. has *yard*, an anomalous form.
[c] "Them," omitted in Heb., may be supplied by conjecture; but the antecedent
nouns are sufficiently close to allow the omission of the suffix in poetry.
[d-d] These lines, like xli 19–20, are a fragment of a polemic against idolatry
and a gloss here.

Notes

xli 1. *The peoples* will have to gather all their strength to meet the challenge of Yahweh.

2. Hebrew reads "righteousness," here used in the sense of victory; but it is altogether likely that the abstract noun is used for the person (D. N. Freedman). Cyrus the Great of Persia is meant.

3. According to Heb., which is followed here, he does not travel by foot; his course is so rapid and so easy that he seems to fly rather than to walk. 1QIsᵃ reads "They do not discern the path of his feet." This would likewise signify the swiftness of his course, which is so rapid that it cannot be followed, much less predicted.

4. Yahweh *calls the generations from the beginning;* he directs history from the origins of man.

Comment

The prophet has been the speaker in the previous chapter; now Yahweh is the speaker. The change of person occurs with no introductory formula; at times the prophet passes from speech in his own person to speech in the person of Yahweh with no indication of the change. The prophet proceeds in this poem to set forth the manifest grounds for the hope he presents to Israel. As elsewhere in the prophecy, he begins with an apostrophe to the nations. No particular nations are meant; the "coastlands" for the Israelites meant the limits of the earth. The saving act Yahweh will perform is of such magnitude and so unexpected that no people, however remote, can let it pass without notice and without thinking of its significance. If any would dispute the prophet's claim, he challenges them to a legal contest with him; he can prove his case. His question is, "Who has raised up a righteous one from the east?" In the moment of history when the prophet spoke, no one could be uncertain of whom he meant, although the name of Cyrus does not appear until xliv 28 (see Introduction, "Historical Background"). As noted more than once in the Notes and Comment, the word we translate "righteousness" has a breadth of meaning which cannot be captured in a single English word. Here possibly "victory" would be a clearer rendition; but something would be lost in this word. For victory is conceived as the fruit of righteousness; it is the vindication of a legitimate claim. Cyrus is summoned in Righteousness, that attribute of Yahweh which works in such a way that things become as they ought to be. Before Yahweh's righteousness no king and no nation has a claim to power, for they are nothing before him (xl 17). Yahweh awards the kings and nations to Cyrus because Cyrus is the instrument of his will to save, as well as the instrument of his judgment on the arrogance of conquerors. Therefore Yahweh makes Cyrus' journey easy.

Only Yahweh can be doing this; no other god claims to do it. Somewhat serenely the prophet ignores any claim that might have been presented on behalf of the gods of Persia. This he can do because the deliverance of Israel is not in the plans of Cyrus, and obviously not in the plans of the gods of Persia. Cyrus will achieve something for which neither his own plans nor his resources are responsible. He will conquer as none of his predecessors have done, because it is necessary that he conquer the entire world known to the Israelites before Israel can be restored on its own land. This is not the work of Persian gods.

Verses 6–7 appear to be another fragment of polemic against crass idoltary, i.e., the worship of the material image, which has wandered from its original place and cannot be restored. For comment on this type of polemic, see NOTES and COMMENT on xliv 9–20 (SEC. 17).

6. ASSURANCE TO ISRAEL
(xli 8–20)

XLI

8 "But you Israel my servant, Jacob whom I have chosen,
    The seed of Abraham my friend,

9 You whom I have seized from the ends of the earth, whom
    I have called from its remote parts,
    I have said to you, 'You are my servant; I have chosen you,
    I have not rejected you.'

10 Do not fear, for I am with you; do not look about anxiously,
    for I am your God.
    I strengthen you, truly I help you; truly I hold you fast
    with my victorious right hand.

11 See, they are all ashamed and humiliated who were angry
    with you;
    They are reduced to nothing, they perish who sought a
    quarrel with you.

12 If you look for those who contended with you, you will not
    find them;
    They are annihilated, reduced to nothing, those who warred
    with you.

13 For it is I Yahweh, I am your God, I grasp you by your
    right hand;
    I say to you, 'Do not fear,' I help you.

14 Do not fear, Jacob—you worm! Israel—you insect![a]
    I help you—the oracle of Yahweh; your avenger is the
    Holy One of Israel.

15 See, I make you a threshing-sledge,[b] new with double edges;

[a] Conjectural emendation recommended by parallelism; Heb. "men."
[b] Hebrew adds "threshing tool"; omitted.

You will thresh the mountains, you will beat them to
dust; and you will reduce the hills to straw.

16   You will winnow them, and the wind will bear them
away; the whirlwind will scatter them.

But you will rejoice in Yahweh; in the Holy One of Israel
you will exult.

17   The needy and the poor seek water, and there is none;
their tongue is parched with thirst;

I Yahweh will answer them; I the God of Israel will not
abandon them.

18   I will open rivers on bare heights, and springs in the midst
of the valleys;

I will make the steppe a pool of water, and the desert a
fountain.

19   I will put cedars in the steppe—acacias, myrtles, and olive
trees;

I will place the juniper in the desert—the box tree and the
cypress together,

20   That they may see and know, that they may attend and
consider together,

That the hand of Yahweh has done this, the Holy One of
Israel has created it."

NOTES

xli 9. *the ends of the earth . . . remote parts.* Refers to the places in
Mesopotamia to which the people of Judah had been transported by
Nebuchadnezzar of Babylon after the fall of Jerusalem in 587 B.C.,
rather than to the call of Abraham from Mesopotamia (Duhm).

11–12. An allusion in the first place to Babylon, whose fall is im-
minent, but also to the neighboring peoples of Judah such as the Am-
monites and Edomites, who took advantage of the disaster of 587 B.C.

14. *avenger.* The kinsman who avenges the murder of his kinsman. He
is therefore the defender or the vindicator. The title is frequently applied
to Yahweh in the OT, especially in II Isaiah. *Worm* and *insect*
emphasize Israel's smallness and powerlessness.

15–16. The figure of the *threshing-sledge* is directed not to peoples and
nations, but to mountains (Volz). The *mountains* are a symbol of

loftiness and pride and power; nothing will be able to withstand the restored Israel.

17–18. The theme of the watering and the flowering of the desert is repeated; see xxxv 6.

COMMENT

Yahweh is still the speaker (following the misplaced fragment, vss. 6–7); from the nations he turns to address the Israelites. If the question of the identity of the Servant of Yahweh rested upon such verses as xli 8, there would be no problems. Israel is clearly called the Servant of Yahweh more than once. But the idea of "Servant" turns out to be too fluid for a simple identification; this is not to deny that Israel must be included in the definition in some way but a definition must be sought which is wider than Israel. Second Isaiah is perhaps the earliest of the prophets to place the beginnings of Israel's election in Abraham; outside of Second and Third Isaiah, the name of the patriarch occurs only in Mic vii 20; Isa xxix 22; Jer xxxiii 26; Ezek xxxiii 24, and the originality of these passages is questionable. Abraham is given the title "my friend," which survives in the modern Arab name of Hebron, El-Khalil, "the friend." Jacob is used by Second Isaiah as a name of the people and not as the name of the patriarch. The language of vs. 9 is something like the language used of Cyrus in xli 2, 25; and some interpreters, following C. C. Torrey, have referred xli 2 to Abraham. The context seems to make this quite improbable. The reference in vs. 9 is to Israel and alludes to the dispersion of the Israelites during the catastrophes of the Assyrian and Babylonian wars. The prophet believes no region too remote for Yahweh to recover the fugitives of his people.

The saving power and will of Yahweh are seen in his preservation of Israel while other nations perished. The statement in vss. 11–12 is general, and perhaps it is a mistake to attempt to find a particular meaning in this generality. But none of the peoples whom historical Israel had known, whether as friendly or hostile, had survived into the middle of the sixth century B.C. except Babylon; and Babylon's fate was already discernible in the figure of Cyrus. This knowledge lends weight to the prophet's statement in xl 15, 22–24. If all Israel's past enemies have vanished and Yahweh and Israel remain, why should Israel fear? There is nothing they should fear, as the prophet says elsewhere in the poems, except divine judgment.

The people of Yahweh's choice is neither rich nor numerous nor powerful; and after its experiences in the Babylonian wars the terms "worm" and "insect" were all too suitable. But the people of Israel is attached to the power of Yahweh. As we observe in the NOTE on vss. 15–16, the figure of the threshing-sledge is directed to mountains and not to peoples and nations. Mountains may indeed be a figurative designation of nations and peoples, but such a figure would be neither obvious nor apt. The mountains represent something solid and almost as eternal as Yahweh himself, immovable obstacles in the way of man's progress. But Israel, invested with the power of Yahweh, will even wear down mountains on its march toward salvation.

The theme of the renewal of the desert appears again in vss. 17–20; see xxxv 1–2, 7. The march of Israel is not mentioned, but the desert is the scene of the march. The figure is not to be taken literally. Yahweh will bring Israel through the desert on its return to its land as he brought it through the desert on its first entrance. Where Yahweh is present, nature is in the presence of its creator who can transform what he has created. The transformation of a defeated and scattered people into a nation is a wonder no less incredible than the transformation of the desert. It is the reversal of the process of judgment by which Yahweh turns cities and settled land into a desert (xxxiv 8–15; see also Jer iv 23–28).

7. A CHALLENGE TO THE NATIONS
(xli 21–29)

XLI

21 "Bring up your plea," says Yahweh; "produce your arguments," says the king of Jacob.

22 "Let them approach closely*a* and declare to us what will
happen,

Tell us the past, and we will attend.

Or let them announce to us the future, and we shall know
what will be hereafter.

23 Tell us what will happen in the time to come, and we
shall know that you are gods;

Do something, either good or evil, that we may look
anxiously and fear*b* together.

24 See, you are nothing,*c* and your deeds are naught*d*;
An abomination is he who chooses you.

25 I have raised up one from the north, and he came; from
the east *e*I have called him by name*e*;

And he shall tread*f* princes like clay, as a potter tramples
mud.

26 Who has declared this from the beginning, that we may
know? and from former times, that we may say, 'He is
right'?

a Hebrew is retained, but the hiphil is rendered as intensive rather than causa-
tive (D. N. Freedman).

b Reading Kethib of MT rather than Kere, "let us see"; the emphasis is on
fear, not on vision.

c Reading "nothing" instead of Heb. "from nothing"; the initial *mem* could
have arisen by dittography from the preceding word.

d This emendation supposes the same dittography of *mem* as we have in note *c*,
and the correction of *ayin* to *samek*, thus removing a non-word.

e–e A conjectural emendation; Heb. "he called on my name."

f A conjectural emendation; Heb. "he shall come."

    Indeed, there is no one who declares, no one who reveals, no one who listens to your words.

27   In the beginning I spoke*g* to Zion, and to Jerusalem I will send a messenger.

28   I looked, and there was no one; and of these there was none to give counsel,
    That I should ask them and they should answer.

29   See, all of them are nothing,*h* and*i* their works are nothing; Wind and emptiness are their images."

g A conjectural emendation; Heb. "behold, behold them."
h A conjectural emendation, supported by 1QIs*a*; Heb. "vanity."
i The conjunction is missing in Hebrew, but read in 1QIs*a*.

NOTES

    xli 21. *Plea* and *arguments* refer to an imagined legal process. The title "king" is frequently applied to Yahweh in the OT, but "king of Jacob" occurs only here; see "king of Israel," xliv 6; Zeph iii 15.

    24. *abomination.* A common Hebrew epithet for idols, is here transferred to the worshiper.

    25. The emended text secures a better parallel between the two members; Yahweh is the subject in both. For a hypothetical explanation of the variant, see COMMENT.

    27. The text and the meaning of the verse are uncertain; see footnote *g*. If the restoration of the first half of the verse is correct, it is impossible to define what is meant by Yahweh's speaking to Zion in the beginning. The suggested emendation adds the minimum, which is a verb somewhat related to the second member of the line. The Heb. undoubtedly conceals a more specific word, but neither the text nor the versions offer any secure basis for conjecture.

    28. The image of the legal process is continued. Yahweh has summoned his adversaries, but no one has appeared.

COMMENT

    The image of the legal contest occurs again (see SEC. 5), and Yahweh is the speaker; the challenge here is addressed not to the nations but to their gods. This is the confrontation toward which the prophet has been leading, and he returns to it in the following poems. The gods are challenged either to relate the past or to disclose the future; they can do neither. In the collection of Israelite traditions available to Second Isaiah both history and prophecy were contained. No other nation had such a collection of historical memories, all centered upon the saving acts of God. An invitation to produce a comparable recital was quite safe. No such recital existed. Nor could the gods produce documents to demonstrate their prophecy. They can do nothing, they are nothing.

Certainly the mention of "one from the north and . . . the east" (vs. 25) is intended to confirm the preceding declaration. The emendation of "he called my name" (Heb.) to "I have called him by name" is not merely apologetic, intended to waive the obvious historical fact that Cyrus was not a worshiper of Yahweh. To "call by name" is a common Hebrew phrase with reference to one who has a vocation and a mission, and it is far more likely that an overzealous scribe converted Cyrus to a worshiper of Yahweh. The ambiguity of the identity of the "one from the north" is still present because he is not named (see xli 2); but the following line makes it quite probable that it is Cyrus, and not Abraham or restored Israel. From the north and the east is an ambiguity which may not be entirely due to poetic parallelism; historically armies or travelers from the east could enter Palestine only by traveling westward to Syria and southward from there. Both directions are mentioned in the OT as the direction from which movement comes.

The prophet asked who has predicted this; as we see in the NOTE on vs. 27, it is impossible to find in the OT the passages he may have had in mind. He had available, as we have said, history and prophecy; and the prophetic collections include oracles of deliverance and salvation. These furnish a sufficient basis for the claim. It seems superfluous to add that no god was with Yahweh as counselor or helper; and it may be a part of the rigid monotheism of Second Isaiah to insist that the heavenly host or the heavenly council does not include any of the gods of the nations.

8. THE FIRST SERVANT POEM: THE MISSION OF THE SERVANT
(xlii 1–4)

XLII

1 "See my servant whom I hold fast, my chosen one with
    whom I am pleased;
  I set my spirit upon him; he will bring forth judgment to
    the nations.
2 He will not cry out nor raise his voice; he will not shout in
    the streets.
3 The crushed reed he will not break, and the fading wick he
    will not extinguish;
  Faithfully he will pronounce judgment.
4 He will not faint, he will not be crushed,*a* until he es-
    tablishes judgment on the earth;
  And the coastlands shall wait for his instruction."

a Vocalizing passive *yērôṣ* instead of Heb. *yārûṣ.*

NOTES

xlii 1. The *spirit* is the charismatic impulse which moves men to deeds
of strength, courage, and wisdom. When it falls upon the king, it
empowers him to wage war and to judge wisely. It is not a prophetic
charisma in prophecy before Ezekiel. Here the result of the spirit in the
Servant is judgment, a word that means more than the delivery of a
legal verdict. It is the establishment of peace and righteousness.

4. *coastlands.* See NOTE on xl 15.

instruction. Heb. *torah,* traditionally priestly instruction in the cult.
Here the meaning seems to be wider, almost equivalent to "revelation."

COMMENT

This is the first of the four Servant Songs (see INTRODUCTION, "The Servant Songs"). The isolation of these four poems from the rest of Second Isaiah does not of itself imply different authorship, nor in the COMMENT do we take a position on the identity of the Servant. The position which is taken and the reasons for which it is taken are set forth in the INTRODUCTION ("The Servant Songs"). The Servant of this poem is a chosen one. The verb "choose" and the adjective "chosen" are applied in the OT to David, to Israel, to Zion, and to Israelites in the plural. The word is certainly a favorite of Second and Third Isaiah. To be "pleased" perhaps says less than the Heb.; the phrase is parallel to "hold fast." The Servant is chosen for a mission, and the word signifies that Yahweh has decided upon him. As one to whom a mission is committed, the Servant receives the spirit; see NOTE on vs. 1.

"Judgment" (vss. 2, 3, and in the response, 5) is a word too broad for translation by a single English word. Begrich, Sidney Smith, Lindblom, and Muilenburg prefer to understand the word in the judicial sense. This seems inadequate both in the particular context and in the general context of the Servant Songs. The context of this poem and the other Servant poems does not suggest that the Servant will exercise a judicial function toward the nations. Judgment also means a law, or the right way of doing things; it is related to "instruction" (vs. 4), by which we have translated *torah*, conventionally rendered by "law." But "law" is not the original meaning of the word. "Judgment" and "law" together convey the idea of revelation, the revelation which in Israel's history is initiated in the patriarchal period and takes form in the covenant of Sinai. The Servant is the mediator of the revelation of Yahweh, and this is his mission. Verses 2–3 suggest the manner in which the mission is to be fulfilled. Verse 2 stands in striking contrast to lviii 1 (Third Isaiah); and the line can scarcely mean that the Servant will not speak except in quiet personal conversation. The speech of the Servant is rather contrasted to the loud proclamations of public authority and to the shouting of the officers of public authority. The Servant will not impose his words on his listeners. Nor (vs. 3) will he use violence and coercion. "The crushed reed" and "the fading wick" signify the poor and the helpless, so often mentioned in prophetic literature as the victims of oppression by the wealthy and powerful. The figure is unusual, but no other suggested meanings seem superior. The Servant does not employ this type of pressure; he simply "pronounces judgment faithfully"; he delivers accurately the revelation with which he has been entrusted. There is a hint in vs. 5 that he will need strength to persevere in his mission; this becomes more explicit in the third and fourth Servant Songs.

The mission of the Servant is clearly a mission to the nations; a mission to Israel is not mentioned. The scope of revelation and salvation is broadened. This too becomes more explicit in the response to this Song and in the later Servant Songs and responses. The broadening of the scope of revelation is not found in the Servant Songs only; it appears in Second Isaiah, and it is noted as it occurs. On the "coastlands" see xl 15; they are mentioned as one of the most remote areas known to the Israelites at this time.

If the mission of the Servant in this poem is to be summed up in one word, the word would be prophecy. But the word is not used; and in fact the words "judgment" and "law" are associated with priestly revelation rather than with prophetic revelation. But it is never suggested that the Servant is a priest. It seems that we encounter the idea of covenant law, a tradition which went back to the premonarchic period of Israel. Just as Yahweh by the revelation of covenant law established the people of Israel and the Israelite way of life, so the Servant will make Yahweh known beyond Israel. In this poem the Servant, it is suggested, is rather another Moses than another prophet.

9. RESPONSE TO THE POEM
(xlii 5–9)

XLII

5 Thus says the God Yahweh, who created the heavens and
     stretched them out,
     Who spread out the earth with its vegetation, who gives
     breath to the people upon it,
     And spirit to those who walk upon it;

6 "I Yahweh have called you in righteousness, I have taken*a*
     you by the hand;
     I have formed*a* you; I have made*a* you a covenant for a
     people and a light of nations,

7 To open blind eyes, to release the captive from prison,
     And from the dungeon those who sit in darkness.

8 I am Yahweh, that is my name;
     My glory I will not give to another, nor my praise to idols.

9 The former predictions—see, they have come to pass; and
     new things I announce to you;
     Before they sprout forth, I declare them to you."

a Reading with the versions; Heb. future.

Notes

xlii 5. *stretched them out*. Here the heavens are referred to as a tent.

6. *light of nations* is repeated in xlix 6, *covenant for a people* in xlix 8. "Covenant for a people" is literally "covenant of a people," an obscure phrase. But just as "covenant of eternity" means "eternal covenant," so "covenant of people" means "people-covenant," a covenant large enough to encompass peoples. In spite of the singular, "people" here does not refer to the people of Israel.

The second line exhibits an unusual type of poetic structure, retained in the translation; the two verbs are balanced against the two objects. We should expect "I have formed you a covenant for a people, I have made you a light of nations" (D. N. Freedman).

7. See NOTE on xxxv 5.

9. *The former predictions.* It is not possible to cite which predictions the prophet meant here.

COMMENT

This section is called a response to the Servant Song; responses can also be identified after the second and third Songs. The ideas of the Song are repeated and simplified. To attempt to point out differences in language and thought would lose us in inconclusive subtleties; whether the Song and the response are from the same hand or not, the author of the response, if different from the author of the Song, has woven the same ideas and phrases together in a way which makes it extremely difficult to distinguish him. He appeals to creation (see xl 12–31 [SEC. 4]). "Spirit" (vs. 5) is the principle of life both in animals and men (Eccles iii 19–21; Ps civ 29–30). The use of spirit in this sense differs from the use of spirit to signify the charismatic impulse (see NOTE on xlii 1); yet the choice of the word here suggests the growth of spirit in man under the revelation of Yahweh. Verse 6 echoes the words addressed to Cyrus in xli 2, to Israel in xli 10. The providence of Yahweh exhibits a consistency which permits the interchange of such phrases for different objects. The same verse 6 makes much more explicit the universal scope of the mission of the Servant. On the rare phrases used see the NOTE. These phrases really indicate more than a "mission," but it is hard to define them more closely. The Servant is called a covenant; the force of the figure means that the Servant mediates between Yahweh and peoples, that the Servant becomes a bond of union. That he is also a "light" does not refer to his revealing mission; the light is explained in the following verse as the light of joy and deliverance. The blindness and captivity, in view of the general context, must be taken as figurative rather than literal; it is the blindness and captivity of ignorance of Yahweh and service of false gods. Yahweh affirms his identity (vs. 8); the affirmation of the name is a solemn affirmation, for the name discloses the reality of him who bears it. It is a common OT formula to say that one recognizes the reality of Yahweh when one learns or confesses that his name is Yahweh. His glory is the recognition of his holiness; the time has come when he can no longer allow other gods to arrogate to themselves the recognition due to him alone.

As in xli 26–27, the prediction of these events is affirmed. The Israelites should recognize the unique divinity of Yahweh when they see his predictions come to pass. This is a motive for faith in the predictions which are uttered now. The saving event announced is not the end of history but the beginning of a new phase of history. One may say that Yahweh cannot save the nations until he has saved Israel; and Israel could not be saved until it had passed through judgment. The Servant plays a new role as the agent of Yahweh's salvation.

10. A HYMN TO YAHWEH THE REDEEMER
(xlii 10–17)

XLII

10   Sing to Yahweh a new song, his praise from the ends of
the earth!

Let the sea and its fullness thunder,[a] the coastlands and
those who dwell in them!

11   Let the steppe and its cities raise their voices, the settlements where Kedar dwells!

Let the inhabitants of Sela cry out for joy, from the
mountain peaks let them shout!

12   Let them give glory to Yahweh! Let them tell his praise
in the coastlands!

13   Yahweh marches forth like a hero; like a man of war he
arouses his ardor.

He shouts—yes, he raises the war cry; he shows his prowess
against his enemies.

14   "Long have I been silent; I have kept my peace, I have contained myself;

Like a woman in travail, I have groaned and panted, I
have gasped for air.

15   I will dry up mountains and hills; I will wither all their
vegetation.

I will change rivers to deserts,[b] and ponds I will dry up.

16   I will conduct the blind on the road[c]; I will lead them on
the paths,[c]

[a] Reading as in Pss xcvi 11, xcviii 7; Heb. "those who go down to the sea."
The corruption may have arisen from a haplography that has left us parts of
two different lines (D. N. Freedman).
[b] A conjectural emendation; Heb. "islands."
[c] Omitting "which they do not know," found in Heb.

I will turn darkness to light before them, and rough country
   I will level.
These things I will do, and I will not leave off."
17   They are turned back, they are put to shame, those who
   put their trust in carved idols,
Those who say to a molten image, "You are our gods."

NOTES

xlii 10–11. These verses span the territory known to the Israelites,
from the Phoenician and Syrian coasts to the steppes east and south of
Israel.

11. *settlements*. In this verse, unwalled enclosures for permanent dwelling.

Kedar. A nomadic Arabian tribe (Song of Sol i 5; Isa lx 7; Jer xlix
28, et al.).

Sela. An Edomite town (II Kings xiv 7); possibly it was located at
the site of the later Petra.

13. *hero* and *man of war*. These titles are frequently applied to
Yahweh in the prophets and in poetry.

15. Implicit here is the image of the east wind from the desert. The
conversion of the desert into a watered land with rich vegetation is inverted.

16. The two verbs in the last line are translated as future, although
they are grammatically past. Yet the series of future verbs they summarize hardly permits the past in the final line. The temporal force of
Hebrew verbs is loose in poetry.

COMMENT

Here as elsewhere, Second Isaiah interrupts his discourses with
hymns or fragments of hymns; see xliv 23, xlix 13; the refrain (vs.
10) resembles the introduction to Pss xcvi and xcviii. Distant lands
are invited to join the hymn; even the roaring of the sea, so often in
the OT a symbol of chaos, becomes the booming voice of nature
praising its creator. The poet moves not only to the coastlands, mentioned several times previously, but in the other direction toward the
steppes and the desert to the south, the regions of nomadic tribes.
Sela was an Edomite settlement; there is nothing here of the
hostility of xxxiv 5–17 and lxiii 1–6.

Verses 10–12 may be taken as the introduction to the poem that follows, which is not a hymn in form and structure. The presentation of Yahweh as a warrior is not new; see Deut x 17; Zeph iii 17; Pss xxiv 8, lxxviii 65; Exod xv 3. The holy wars of early Israel were wars of Yahweh, and Yahweh himself marched at the head of the host, symbolized in the ark of the covenant. The imagery is retained in post-exilic literature, but its meaning becomes more sophisticated and less primitive. The activity that is ascribed to Yahweh in this context is not military.

By a bold image the prophet compares the restraint of Yahweh to the pangs of a woman in travail; the image is elsewhere applied to those who are suffering fear or pain, but not to Yahweh. The impatience of Yahweh, as seen from the Israelite point of view, is due to the length of time taken to deliver Israel. Once Yahweh satisfies his desire, his activity shows itself in the transformation of nature; see xxxv 1–2, 6–7. Here the activity is reversed; land is transformed into desert. It does not seem that this is a threat directed at any particular object; it is a statement of Yahweh's creative sovereignty, by which he can convert watered land into desert and desert into land rich with vegetation. Nature is indifferent to him; it is no obstacle to his will.

If the preceding context has been interpreted correctly, then the blind of vs. 16 are exiled Israel. They are blind because they see no light—that is, they see no hope of deliverance. Their journey to their land will be rendered easy by Yahweh (xxxv 5–10). The promise concludes with a rejection of idolatry. We have noted (see COMMENT on xl 12–31) that Second Isaiah conducts a subtle polemic against the doubts of the Israelites. He does not accuse them here of worshiping other gods, but simply points out the folly of worshiping other gods. The Israelites, while continuing to worship Yahweh, may have wondered whether the gods of Babylon were not real competing powers, and in this sense "put their trust" in them.

11. ISRAEL THE BLIND SERVANT
(xlii 18–25)

XLII

18 "Listen, you deaf! Look closely, you blind!

19 Who is blind if not my servant? And deaf like my messenger whom I send?
Who is blind like the one whom I send, and blind like the servant of Yahweh?*

20 You have seen much, but you have not observed; your ears are open, but you* have not heard."

21 Yahweh wished, because of his righteousness, to make his teaching great and glorious;

22 But this is a people plundered and spoiled; they are all of them trapped *in caves*;
They are hidden in dungeons.
They have been plundered, and there was no one to deliver—spoiled, and none to say, "Give back!"

23 Who among you has hearkened to this? Who listened attentively to what was to happen?

24 Who surrendered Jacob to spoilers, and Israel to plunderers?
Was it not Yahweh, against whom we sinned, in whose ways we would not walk,
And to whose teaching we would not listen?

a–a This line, which repeats the preceding line, is very probably a gloss.
b A conjectural emendation; Heb. "restitution? reconciliation?"
c The second person is read with the versions and some Heb. manuscripts and is demanded by the sense; Heb. has third person.
d–d A conjectural emendation; Heb. "young men." This change demands a different vocalization with no change in the consonants.

25 He poured out upon him his flaming anger[e] and the fury
   of war;
   It scorched him on all sides, and he did not know it; it
   consumed him, but he paid no attention.

[e] The construct form *ḥᵃmat,* demanded by grammar and the versions, is read
in 1QIsᵃ.

Notes

xlii 19b. We suggest in footnote *ᵃ* that this line is a gloss which repeats
the preceding line, 19a. Possibly the gloss is an early attempt to deal
with the problem of the identity of the Servant; see INTRODUCTION,
"The Message," and COMMENT on the Servant poems. The servant messenger of 19a can scarcely be any other than Israel; 19b identifies Israel
with the Servant of Yahweh of the Servant poems. No satisfactory sense
has been made by commentators of *mᵉšullam.* The suggested emendation
supposes only a slight corruption from *mᵉšullaḥî.*

20. The verb forms are ambiguous. Kere has infinitive absolute *rā'ôt,*
parallel to the infinitive absolute in the second member; kethib, supported
by 1QIsᵃ, has the perfect. The translation is not affected.

21. *teaching.* Heb. *torah,* here again approaches the meaning of revelation. It includes Yahweh's manifestation of himself to Israel in saving
acts and in covenant and law.

22. Because of Israel's infidelity the disasters of the Babylonian war
have fallen upon them.

In the last line, *plundered* and *spoiled* (literally "for plunder" and
"spoil") illustrate the poetic use of a single preposition for two parallel
nouns (D. N. Freedman). 1QIsᵃ, however, has the missing preposition.

24. *spoilers.* Renders an abstract feminine noun parallel to a masculine
participle (D. N. Freedman), a combination found elsewhere in Hebrew
poetry. The last three verbs of the verse, translated in the first person,
in Heb. are first person followed by the third person twice. No change in
the text seems necessary. The speaker slips out of his identification with
the people after the first verb. We retain the first person because this is
what is meant; and a literal rendition would be both obscure and
awkward.

Comment

Yahweh is the speaker in vss. 18–20, and the discourse is continued by the prophet for the remainder of the poem. Again the
Servant addressed is clearly Israel. Second Isaiah again uses words
that were used in a somewhat different sense in a preceding context:
"blind" and "deaf" mean those oppressed and desperate in xxxv 5,
xlii 7, 16. Here it is clear that blindness and deafness mean lack of
insight into the meaning of history as interpreted by prophecy.
Israel is one sent, a messenger, like the Servant of xlii 1–9; but how
is Israel to declare that which it does not perceive nor understand?
It was the intention of Yahweh to make his teaching "great and
glorious"; his revelation of himself was to be universally manifest
and convincing. This purpose has not been achieved, because those
who were to announce it are hiding or imprisoned. The description
of vs. 22, which must apply to the Israelites, seems exaggerated in
view of what is known of the conditions of the Israelite community
in Babylon; it may be less exaggerated if it has reference to life in
Palestine during the sixth century B.C. But the phrases should not be
taken at face value. Israel was effectively destroyed as a people and
a religious community; the survivors lived without the old social and
religious structures and without having developed any new ones. The
messenger has been unable to deliver his message.

But more than this, Israel has not understood what happened
and why their fall happened. The Israelites may even have explained their fall as due to the superiority of other nations and
their gods to Yahweh. This particular kind of infidelity is directly attested only in Jer xliv 15–19; the women of Judah attribute the misfortunes of the country to their abandonment of the worship of the
queen of heaven. It is difficult to deny that the prophetic charge of
the worship of false gods did not sometimes imply a similar confession. This is the height of blindness: not to recognize that Yahweh
is God in judgment as in deliverance, and that nothing happens to
them that is not his will. Yahweh himself delivered them. He judged
them and condemned them because they would not listen to his
revelation, the revelation that was committed to them to be announced to peoples and nations. The prophet draws a paradoxical
picture of a man who stands in the midst of a blazing fire and does

not notice it (vs. 25). So insensible had Israel become that it could not even discern the presence of disaster. The Israelites had not yet perceived the reality of God, and so they are messengers who cannot hear the message nor see where they are going.

Obviously the tone of the "Book of Consolation" is changed in this poem. The discourse of Second Isaiah is not a simple statement that everything is going to be all right now that the worst is over. As Israel was created for a purpose, so it is restored for a purpose. It did not recognize the purpose of its creation; it must recognize the purpose of its restoration. And it will not unless it learns the meaning of the oracles of the pre-exilic prophets, which explained the process of Israel's collapse. Second Isaiah repeats and summarizes these prophecies.

12. PROMISE OF REDEMPTION
(xliii 1–7)

XLIII

1 "And now," thus speaks Yahweh—your creator, Jacob, and
your maker, Israel—
"Do not fear, for I am your avenger; I have called you by
name, you are mine.

2 If you pass through waters,[a] I am with you—through rivers,
they will not drown you.
If you walk through fire, you will not be scorched—through
flame, it will not consume you.

3 For I Yahweh am your God, the Holy One of Israel, your
savior.
I have given Egypt as your ransom, Cush and Seba as your
price.

4 Because I esteem you as precious; you are honorable, and
I love you;
So I give men[b] as your price, and peoples as payment for
you.

5 Do not be afraid, for I am with you;
From the east I will bring your seed, and from the west I
will gather you.

6 I will say to the north, 'Yield,' and to the south, 'Let go;
Bring my sons from afar, and my daughters from the end
of the earth,

7 All who are called by my name, and whom for my glory
I have created—I have formed and made.'"

[a] Hebrew can be read *bᵉmô yam*, "through the sea," instead of "through
waters." This would be an even more explicit allusion to the Exodus
(D. N. Freedman).
[b] "Lands," *'ᵃdāmôt*, has been suggested instead of Heb. *'ādām*. Either word
furnishes a good parallel to "peoples."

NOTES

xliii 1. Yahweh is the creator and maker of Israel by his saving acts in the Exodus and by his covenant. The origin of Israel is not like the origin of other peoples, which in the OT are generally represented as the descendants of eponymous ancestors. Jacob/Israel is the eponymous ancestor, but Israel as a people begins to exist with the covenant.

avenger. See NOTE on xli 14.

2. A remarkable echo of xlii 25, with a complete change in the meaning of the figure of flame. In the second line one preposition serves for both nouns (D. N. Freedman).

3. *the Holy One of Israel.* An echo of I Isaiah.

Egypt, Cush and *Seba* evoke no concrete historical allusion. Cush (Ethiopia) is roughly equivalent with the modern Sudan, the Nile Valley south of the First Cataract; Seba, mentioned in xlv 14 and in only three other passages of the OT, is probably to be located in or near the same region.

5. *east* and *west* suggest a wider dispersion of Israel than is known for the middle of the sixth century B.C., and is probably a poetic hyperbole.

COMMENT

The preceding reference to the judgment is followed by a swift change of tone, and one of the most encouraging passages of the "Book of Consolation" is uttered. The repetition of the personal pronouns is striking; it is "I—you" throughout. Yahweh is Israel's creator, maker, avenger; he has given Israel its name, which signifies that it belongs to him; see xli 25 and COMMENT (SEC. 7). The waters and the fire signify the judgments Israel has experienced; as we have noticed, Yahweh is as much Israel's God in judgment as he is in deliverance. The waters may be an allusion to the passage through the sea in the Exodus. First Isaiah compares the invasion of Assyria to the inundation of a river (viii 7–8). The solemn affirmation of the name of Yahweh is an assurance; see xlii 8 and COMMENT (SEC. 9).

The three countries mentioned in vs. 3 are all in Africa, but this seems to have no significance except that the peoples are remote. D. N. Freedman suggests that the line implies a prediction of the conquest of Egypt in exchange for Judah, as Ezekiel promised Nebuchadnezzar Egypt for Tyre (Ezek xxix 17–20). It would seem strange that Egypt should occur to two different prophets as the object of an exchange. The line does not mean that Yahweh readily sacrifices any people to preserve Israel; Second Isaiah is more subtle than that. It means that whatever price is necessary to redeem Israel, Yahweh is prepared to pay; the sum is a human figure applied to Yahweh. "Honorable" is the usual translation of the word employed; but it is more probable that the element of "wealth" is also implied. Yahweh treasures Israel as an object of value.

Because of this devotion Yahweh will achieve the new creation of Israel by the ingathering of his people. However far they may have been scattered from their land, he will bring them back. It is important that there be continuity between the old Israel and the new, or it would not be a genuine work of salvation and restoration. Deliverance must come to the descendants of those who had passed through the fire and water of judgment. Because the four directions are mentioned, it is not necessary to think that the prophet suddenly changes his view to see an ingathering of all the nations. Though we have noted that Second Isaiah shows breadth in his conception of salvation, he does not show it in every line. This passage stands between the preceding passage in which Israel's failure as a messenger is stated, and the following passage in which Israel's vocation as witness is set forth. The task at hand in the work of salvation is the re-establishment of the people who is messenger and witness. It is Israel that is called by the name of Yahweh, and that Yahweh has created for his glory.

13. ISRAEL THE WITNESS OF
YAHWEH'S FIDELITY
(xliii 8–13)

XLIII

8 "Lead forth the people that are blind but have eyes, that are
   deaf but have ears;

9 Let all the nations assemble, and let the peoples be
   gathered.
   Who among them has*a* announced this? Who predicted*a*
   to us the things that happened in the past?
   Let them produce their witnesses and prove their case; let
   them announce*b* that it may be said, 'It is true.'

10 But you are my witnesses—'the oracle of Yahweh'—and my
   servants*c* whom I have chosen,
   That they*d* may know and believe me, and may understand*d* that it is I.
   Before me no god was formed, and after me there will
   be no other.

11 I, I am Yahweh, and besides me there is no savior.

12 I announce and I save; I proclaim; there is no strange
   (god) among you.

a–a In Heb. the first verb is singular, the second plural; the translation does
not show this. 1QIs*a* reads the plural in both verbs and omits the suffix
"to us" after the second verb. Hebrew could be vocalized as singular with no
change in the consonantal text. D. N. Freedman suggests that Heb. represents
a conflate text made from two traditions, one with the verbs in the singular
and one with the verbs in the plural.
b Reading with 1QIs*a*; Heb. "they will hear."
c Plural by conjectural emendation; Heb. singular.
d Third person by conjectural emendation; Heb. "you."

You are my witnesses"—the oracle of Yahweh—"I am God.
13 Yes, from eternity*e* I am;
    There is no one who delivers from my hands; I act, and no
    one thwarts it."

e "From eternity" with LXX; Heb. "from the day."

NOTES

xliii 8. The people that are blind and deaf must be Israel (see xlii
18–19 and COMMENT [SEC. 11]). Like the nations, they have not seen
the hand of Yahweh at work in history. The text is ambiguous (see footnote *a*): grammatically the prophet must be the speaker but the words
are appropriate to Yahweh.
9. The translation accepts the view that the perfect has a jussive or
precative force (D. N. Freedman), and makes it unnecessary to introduce a commonly accepted emendation.
12. The translation is based on a suggestion of D. N. Freedman.

COMMENT

Yahweh is still the speaker; this poem should possibly be regarded as a continuation of the preceding, although the change of
topic suggests the division which we have placed in the text. Yahweh
again calls for a confrontation with the nations. It is a confrontation
at law, as it was in xli 1, 21–24. Israel is now summoned as
Yahweh's witnesses, a new conception of the function of Israel. Israel
is blind and deaf (xlii 18–20), but they have the capacity of vision
and hearing; and the prophet has called upon them to learn. The
challenge, as in the preceding confrontations, is to match prophecy
with prophecy. Yahweh presents Israel as his evidence. We have
pointed out (see COMMENT on xli 21–29, xlii 18–25 [SECS. 7,
11]) that Second Isaiah knew well Israel's heritage of history and
prophecy; and in the light of xlii 1–4, we should add the heritage
of covenant law. Israel alone among the nations has a true history
and an interpretation of the meaning of history; Israel alone is conscious of its destiny and of the path which it must follow to attain its
destiny. They can bear the witness they are charged to give.
What is the burden of this witness? Here the monotheism of

Second Isaiah emerges in full force. Israel can testify that Yahweh alone is God, that he is eternal. Israel can testify to his power and freedom, because it has experienced his power and freedom in its history. Yahweh alone judges and Yahweh alone saves; and no one, god or man, can hinder his action. Israel is not asked to testify to this by "revelation" in the sense of a document, but to testify to its own experience. Yahweh is recognized as God because he performs the acts of God; Israel is his proof.

14. POEMS OF PROMISE
(xliii 14–21)

XLIII

14 Thus says Yahweh your avenger, the Holy One of Israel:
"For your sake I have sent to Babylon; I have let down the
bars of the prison*ᵃ*;
The Chaldeans are bound in chains.*ᵇ*

15 I Yahweh am your Holy One, the creator of Israel, your
king."

16 Thus says Yahweh, who makes a road in the sea and a path
in the midst of fierce waters,

17 Who leads out chariot and horse, a mighty host together—
They lie down not to rise again; they are quenched, like a
wick they are extinguished.

18 "Do not remember the things that are past; and do not consider bygone events.

19 See, I am doing something new; now it bursts forth—do
you not know it?
Indeed, I lay a road in the steppe, and paths*ᶜ* in the
desert.

20 The wild beasts will pay me honor—the jackals and the
ostriches—

ᵃ "Of the prison" by conjectural emendation suggested by the context; the
omission of two letters in Hebrew is supposed.
ᵇ No reading or emendation of this line is satisfactory. Heb. "on the ships
their cries of joy." The translation follows a reconstruction based on Gr.:
ba'ᵃnākôt ruttᵉḵû. One would expect a third verb in the first person with
Yahweh as the subject, and Heb. permits one to expect that this line had to do
with mourning and cries of joy. Greek is very probably itself rendered from a
corrupt text; but it has an antithesis between the release of the Israelites and
the imprisonment of the Chaldeans.
ᶜ "Paths" with 1QIsᵃ; Heb. "rivers."

Because I produce water in the steppe, and rivers in the
desert,
To give drink to my chosen people.

21   The people whom I have formed for myself will tell my
praises."

NOTES

xliii 14. The deliverance from Babylon is anticipated as actually accomplished. If the restoration of 14c is correct, the fall of Babylon is also
anticipated.

The Chaldeans. The name of the tribe which settled in Lower Mesopotamia during the Assyrian period and established the Neo-Babylonian
kingdom.

16–17. The restoration of Israel is a new exodus in which the wonders
of the first Exodus are re-enacted.

18. Israel is not to forget the saving deeds of Yahweh in the past,
of which they have just been reminded. They are to forget their disasters.
But even the saving deeds of the past are exceeded by the saving act of
the present.

19–20. The passage of Israel through the desert is re-enacted.

COMMENT

Yahweh is still the speaker, but a break is indicated by the introductory line. This poem of promise is a restatement of themes
already employed by Second Isaiah. The opening lines of the speech
of Yahweh present serious textual difficulties. C. C. Torrey (*The
Second Isaiah* [see Selected Bibliography], pp. 39–52), followed by
J. D. Smart, proposed that Babylon and the Chaldeans were introduced into the text to give an interpretation of a line which was
corrupt when the scribe found it. But the lines are still corrupt.
Babylon and the Chaldeans (the name of the tribe that settled in
Lower Mesopotamia during the Assyrian period and established
the Neo-Babylonian kingdom) are both mentioned elsewhere in the
poems of Second Isaiah, and it is extremely difficult to suppose that
they are intruded in all these passages. But it must be conceded
that it is exactly the words which give meaning to the lines which
are restored by conjectural emendation, and the meaning of the line

must be regarded as uncertain. The title Holy One, which occurs in vss. 14 and 15, is an echo of First Isaiah.

The liberation of Israel is clearly presented as a new exodus: the passage through the sea and the destruction of horses and chariots. The prophet does not mean that the same event will be repeated; he states a past achievement of Yahweh as the ground for belief that Yahweh can do what he promises now. We note that the recommendation not to remember the past is directed in the first place to the judgments of the past, but not exclusively; the new wonder Yahweh will achieve is so stupendous that it will make the Israelites forget the wonders of their early history. It is "new," unexpected and unprecedented. What is "new" is the laying of a road in the desert (xxxv 8–10, xl 3–4) and the conversion of the desert into a land of water and rich vegetation (xxxv 6–7, xli 18–19). The prophet knew that the traditions of his people told of their dangers and sufferings in their passage through what is often called in Deuteronomy "the great and terrible desert." Yahweh gave them water from the rock and manna from the sky, but the desert remained. In the new exodus there will be a transformation of the desert of passage. The providence of Yahweh for his people will go far beyond the providence he exhibited toward their fathers.

The question arises as to how the prophet conceived these wonders, and how the modern reader is to conceive them. If we think of them as entirely literal, it is evident that they had no fulfillment; and thus it would appear that the arm of Yahweh was shorter than the prophet thought. In an artist of such craftsmanship and a prophet of more than usual subtlety such a simplistic solution seems unlikely. Whether the desert actually blossomed with roses or not would, in his mind, neither add to the wonder of the restoration nor detract from it. The saving acts of Yahweh were described in the terms of Israelite tradition, terms which themselves did not rigorously conform to the course of events. If we think of the wonders in these terms, then they were fulfilled. Yahweh overcame the desert, that great barrier of travel in the ancient Near East; he did it once in Israel's origins, and he would do it again in Israel's restoration.

15. UNGRATEFUL ISRAEL
(xliii 22–28)

XLIII

22 "But you have not called me, Jacob; you have not[a] wearied
    yourself for me, Israel;

23 You have not brought me your flocks as whole burnt offer-
    ings; you have not honored me with your sacrifices;
    I have not made you serve me with meal offerings; I have
    not wearied you with incense;

24 You have not bought me a reed for a price; you have not
    sated me with the fat of your victims;
    No, you have made me work by your sins; you have wearied
    me with your iniquities.

25 I, I blot out your guilt for my sake, and your sins I will not
    remember.

26 Stir up your memory, and we will enter judgment together;
    you state your case, that you may be proved right.

27 Your first father sinned, and your interpreters have re-
    belled against me;

28 I slew[b] the princes of the sanctuary, and I delivered[c]
    Jacob to the ban, and Israel to reviling."

[a] "Not" with LXX, omitted in Heb. But the one negative may serve for both
verbs (D. N. Freedman).
[b] The translation takes 'ahallēl from ḥālal, "pierce," and involves a change in
vocalization, not in the consonantal text.
[c] Past tense by conjectural emendation; Heb. future.

NOTES

xliii 22–24. The passage is constructed on a play on the word "weary."

23–24. *I have not wearied you with incense* means "I have not wearied you with demands for incense." The phrase is obscure by itself, and the meaning is suggested by the preceding colon. But the preceding colon in 1QIs^a reads "You have not made meal offerings to me." This reading removes some of the ambiguity in the passage (see COMMENT), but it makes the line about incense even more difficult. Prophetic passages such as Amos v 21–25; Hos vi 6; Mic vi 1–8; Isa i 10–17 reject Israelite sacrifices as insincere. Jer vii 21–22 seems to deny that Yahweh imposed any law requiring sacrifices. Here, on the contrary, the prophet accuses the Israelites of not offering sacrifice. The inconsistency is probably no more than the result of rhetorical emphasis. The prophet plays on the words *work* and *serve*.

24. There is a play on the words "buy" (*kānāh*) and "reed" (*kāneh*). The force of the play is elusive, since no cultic use of the reed is known.

26. The line contains the "charge" pattern, in which Yahweh lays a charge against his people after the manner of one who prosecutes a suit at law; see Hos iv 1 ff.; Mic vi 1–5.

27. It is not entirely clear who the *first father* is, or what the sin is. Second Isaiah knew Abraham (see li 2), and it is not merely because the traditions do not contain any sin of Abraham that this identification seems less likely than any other. Jacob/Israel is used constantly as a patronymic title of the people in the first part of Second Isaiah, and thus Jacob is most probably intended. But the Jacob stories of Genesis contain nothing which is there represented as sin; one may think of Jacob's deception of his father (Gen xxvii) and of Esau (Gen xxv 29–34) and of Laban (Gen xxx 25 – xxxi 21), but the narrators of Genesis see these as instances of Yahweh's protection. A more refined moral judgment of Jacob is hinted in Hos xii 2–3, and a similar judgment must lie at the base of this allusion. It is most unlikely that the prophet alludes to Gen iii, of which he shows no knowledge; and Adam is not treated in the OT as the first father of Israel.

The *interpreters* are also difficult to identify. The text is not entirely certain, although we have retained MT. The Syr. suggests "rulers"; but this word, apart from the fact that its meaning is clear, stands no better in parallelism with "first father" than "interpreters." No explanation can be recommended other than that the interpreters are those whose duty it was to interpret the Law: the priests.

28. *the princes of the sanctuary.* The heads of the priestly families.
ban. The practice of complete extermination of a people (Josh vi
16–24).

COMMENT

As in xlii 18–25, there is a reversal of tone; from promise the
discourse turns to recall Israel's iniquitous past. There are certain
obscurities in the passage that defy a satisfactory interpretation.
"You have not called me" (that is, invoked my name in prayer)
probably does not mean that the cult of Yahweh had been abandoned; nowhere in the OT is this most serious charge laid. The phrase
more probably means that the prayer of Israel had been insincere,
the kind of charge which is laid in Isa i 10–17; it recalls also passages
like Isa xxviii 14–15, xxx 1–5, 8–17, xxxi 1–3, where Israel is
accused of placing its security in military and diplomatic means
instead of faith in Yahweh. If the first phrase of the verse is so
interpreted, it seems better to read a negative in the second phrase,
which is difficult to translate as it stands. Israel has simply not
worked very hard at its cultic obligations.

But vss. 23–24 make it difficult to accept the sense just suggested,
if these verses refer to the situation of the Israelites either in
Babylonia or in Palestine. For the sacrificial system had been an-
nulled by the destruction of the temple of Jerusalem in 587 B.C.
It is true that Jer xli 5 mentions men who made a pilgrimage to the
site of the temple to worship; but it should be noted that animals
are not included in the list of their offerings. If this is meant by
23–24, then it is not a charge of anything, but a simple note of
fact that sacrifices could not be offered. And by a somewhat ironical
turn of phrase, verse 23 suggests that Yahweh has relieved the
Israelites of the duty of sacrifice by destroying the temple in which
sacrifice was offered.

It is perhaps simpler to take the verses together as a recital of
Israel's failure to perform its cultic obligations properly both in the
past and in the present. When Israel was free to offer sacrifices, it
offered them without devotion; now that it cannot offer them it still
fails to give Yahweh due worship. We know in fact very little about
the cultic practices followed by Jews resident in Babylon; the passage

suggests that the prophet did not regard them as fulfilling the duty of cult. The charge concludes with the play on the word "weary": Israel has fatigued Yahweh with its sins, it has made him tired of Israel.

Verse 25 is a brief reversal which is almost dramatic in character. The charge, resumed in 26, is interrupted by an exclamation of total forgiveness. Whatever the past, it is over. Not the diction but the startling contrast with what precedes and follows gives the line such impact. The exclamation is followed by a challenge to a legal confrontation; Second Isaiah has employed this figure before (xli 1, 21–24, xliii 8–13), but the challenge was addressed to the nations and their gods; here it is addressed to Israel, as similar challenges were uttered by the pre-exilic prophets; see NOTE on vs. 26. Let Israel state its complaints against Yahweh. That there were complaints is evident from Jer xxxi 29–30; Ezek xviii 2, 25; Isa xl 27. Let these complaints be stated, and Yahweh will respond with a bill of indictment that goes all the way back to the eponymous ancestor of Israel. Yet he has just dismissed this whole bill with the statement that all is blotted out.

Israel has no response. The prophet chooses the leaders of the people, those who were most reponsible, for in ancient society the leaders made the decisions. Similarly Jer v 4–6 expresses the hope that corruption will be found only among "the poor folk without sense" and not among the great; but when the great are corrupted, the people is doomed beyond hope, for the only element that would furnish a basis for hope is gone. The concluding line speaks of Yahweh's judgment as the "ban" (see NOTE); this means total and irremediable destruction. The restoration of Israel is a miracle of a new creation.

16. THE FIDELITY OF YAHWEH
(xliv 1–8)

XLIV

1 "And now listen, Jacob my servant, Israel whom I have chosen:

2 Thus says Yahweh your maker, who formed you from the womb—he will help you;

Do not be afraid, my servant Jacob, Jeshurun whom I have chosen;

3 For I will pour out water on the thirsty soil, streams on the dry ground;

I will pour out my spirit on your race, my blessing on your offspring.

4 And they will sprout like grass *ᵃin the midst of water,ᵃ* like poplars on the banks of streams.

5 One will say, 'I belong to Yahweh,' and another will be called byᵇ the name of Jacob;

Another will write on his hand, 'Belonging to Yahweh,' and will be calledᶜ by the name of Israel."

6 Thus saysᵈ the king of Israel, Yahweh of hosts, its avenger: "I am first and I am last; and there is no god other than I.

7 Who is like me? Let him call out; let him speak up, let him confront me.

ᵉWho has proclaimed from eternity the things to come,ᵉ

ᵃ⁻ᵃ Reading with LXX; missing in Heb. The emendation is partly supported by 1QIsᵃ (kᵉbên).

ᵇ Conjectural emendation; Heb. "will call on."

ᶜ Passive with Targ. and Syr.; Heb. active.

ᵈ Omitting "Yahweh" with LXX; found in Heb.

ᵉ⁻ᵉ Hebrew reads "from my placing an eternal people and things to come," which approaches nonsense. The emendation, *mî hišmîʿa mēʿōlām ʾōtîyōt*, demands that two missing consonants be supplied, one omitted, and a different division of the words.

and declared to us*f* what was to happen?

8 Do not tremble and do not be afraid*g*; have I not proclaimed it and announced it to you*h* long before?
You are my witnesses; is there a god other than I? There
is no rock; I know none."

f Reading with Targ.; Heb. "to them."
g Reading with 1QIs*a*. Heb. *tirhû* not found elsewhere.
h The suffix "to you" follows the first verb in Heb.; like the English suffix in
the translation, it serves both verbs.

NOTES

xliv 2. *Jeshurun*. Appears only here and in Deut xxxii 15, xxxiii 5, 26.
The name is obscure. It is usually interpreted as a derivative from
yašar, "upright."

3. *spirit*. See NOTE on xlii 1. It is only in later literature that the spirit
is diffused upon a whole people; this is an event of the messianic age
(Isa xxxii 15; Ezek xxxix 29; Zech xii 10). Thus the spirit is communicated to the entire group of disciples (Acts ii 1–3).

5. It is possible that *name of Jacob* and *name of Israel* are surrogates
for the divine name; such surrogates (the Name, the Presence, the Holy,
etc.) were commonly used in Judaism when the divine name was no
longer pronounced. D. N. Freedman has suggested that in this interpretation the emendation (see textual note *b*) becomes unnecessary. The
emendation is retained only because the phrase translated *belonging to*
suggests ownership; and so does the phrase *called by the name of*.

6. *king of Israel*. See "king of Jacob" (xli 21) and Zeph iii 15.
first and . . . last. Repeated in xlviii 12. The reference is probably
not to creation and eschatology, but simply designates an enumeration
of which there is only one member.

8. *rock*. A title frequently applied to Yahweh in the OT. The rock was
a position of security in ancient warfare; it placed the defenders above
the attackers.

COMMENT

The tone is again reversed, and the promise is resumed—and in this passage reaches a new height in the discourses of the prophet. Since the prophet has alluded to the past of Israel, he now heaps up epithets that recall the past. Israel is addressed as Jacob/Israel, recalling its eponymous ancestor as Jeshurun, a title used only here and in the Song of Moses and the Blessing of Moses (see NOTE on vs. 2), and Yahweh is called the maker of Israel, the one who has chosen Israel. The past of Israel contains saving acts as well as judgments. The theme of the renewal of the desert recurs, but here in a slightly different sense from its previous occurrences (xxxv 6–7, xli 18–19, xliii 20); as we have noted, Second Isaiah likes to repeat phrases and themes in a slightly altered sense. Here the desert that is transformed is Israel itself; this is indicated by the parallel line, in which the spirit and the blessing of Yahweh are poured out on Israel. This is a novel conception (see NOTE on vs. 3); in Israelite tradition the charisma of the spirit is given to leaders and not to the whole people. Now it is like the blessing, which was communicated to all Israelites. The agent of renewal is the vivifying force, which comes from Yahweh. Thus vs. 4 does not refer merely to the renewal of prosperity in restored Israel, although prosperity (peace) was always conceived as the fruit of righteousness; the renewal of Israel is primarily its renewal in righteousness.

The scope of vss. 5–6 must go beyond Israel. Those who adopt the names of Yahweh and Israel can scarcely be Israelites. Although it is not inconceivable that the prophet may represent the Israelites as boasting that they are the people of Yahweh, they would hardly boast of this after ruin and exile. The prophet surely sees foreign peoples and nations so impressed by this demonstration of the saving power of Yahweh that they will take his name and the name of his people. For the challenges uttered to the nations and their gods must have the effect of demonstrating that Yahweh alone is God, and Israel is his people. This theme is expanded in the discourses that follow.

The words of Yahweh in vss. 6–8 are introduced by a quotation formula, which indicates a slight change of tone and object. The words are a summary of ideas already stated. The quotation formula echoes the title "king of Jacob" (see NOTE on vs. 6). "The first and the last" echoes xli 4. The challenge to the gods and the appeal to the fulfillment of prophecy echo xli 21–29, xliii 8–12; and the idea of Israel as Yahweh's witness comes from xliii 8–12. The new element is the title of "rock" for Yahweh, traditional in Hebrew poetry but rare in Second Isaiah. Thus the lines resume and summarize much of what has gone before; their continuation and conclusion, which leads into the development of a new theme, is found in xliv 21–23 (SEC. 18).

17. AN ESSAY ON IDOLATRY
(xliv 9–20)

XLIV ⁹ The makers of idols are all nothing; the objects of their devotion are of no value; their servants[a] do not see and do not know; therefore they are ashamed. ¹⁰ Who shapes a god or pours a molten image without intending some profit? ¹¹ See, all its worshipers are ashamed; the artisans blush[b]; let them assemble and take their stand—to tremble and be ashamed. ¹² The smith[c] works over the charcoal and with his hammer he forms it; he makes it with his strong arm, even when he is hungry and his strength leaves him, when he drinks no water and is fatigued. ¹³ The carpenter measures, traces the outline with chalk; he makes it with the chisel and executes the outline with a compass; he makes it in the image of a man with human features to be set up in a temple. ¹⁴ He cuts[d] cedar; or he takes *tirzah* wood or oak and joins with other wood; or he plants a cedar which the rain nourishes. ¹⁵ Men use the wood for fuel; they take some for heat; they kindle some and bake bread; with some they make a god before which they bend low, an image they make, before which they prostrate themselves. ¹⁶ Half of it a man burns and [e]roasts meat on the coals[f]; he eats the roast,[e] is satisfied, is warm, and says, "Ah, I am warm! I look upon the flame!" ¹⁷ The rest of it he makes into a god, his idol; he adores it, he prostrates himself before it, and prays to it, and says: "Save me, for you are

---

[a] Conjectural emendation; Heb. "witnesses." Only one consonant need be supplied (*'abdēhem* for *'ēdêhem*).
[b] Conjectural emendation; Heb. "from man."
[c] Omitting Heb. *ma'ᵃṣād* (knife?).
[d] Reading with LXX; Heb. "to cut." The initial *lamed* may be asseverative: "verily he cuts" (D. N. Freedman).
[e–e] The order of the Heb. words is transposed.
[f] Emendation suggested by 1QIs[a]; Heb. repeats "half of it."

my god." 18 They do not know, nor do they understand; their eyes are[g] shut so they cannot see, and their heart so they cannot think. 19 They do not consider; they lack knowledge and discernment enough to say, "Half of it I burned—yes, I baked bread on the coals, I roasted meat, and I ate; and of the rest of it I made an abomination; I have adored a log!" 20 The lover of ashes is led astray by his deluded mind; he will not save himself; he will not say, "Is this not a lie in my right hand?"

[g] Grammar demands the plural; Heb. singular.

NOTES

xliv 11. The word translated *worshipers* means companion or associate, more precisely a member of a group or an association. The word was used in later Judaism to designate associations formed for prayer and the study of the Torah. In this context it suggests membership in a cult group; but we know nothing of contemporary religious practices that would make this more than a loose use of the word.

12–14. The image described is a wooden core plated with metal.

20. *lie*. One of the abusive terms the Israelites applied to divine images. Here the term is put in the mouth of the worshiper.

COMMENT

Whether this passage is the work of Second Isaiah himself is an object of dispute among critics and will probably remain such. We adopt the position that it is the work of a disciple or a commentator; the reasons are persuasive but not convincing. The passage is in prose, and it is the only prose passage in the entire collection of Second Isaiah; the judgment of Torrey, Fischer, Kissane, Ziegler, and Muilenburg that the passage is metrical is not easily sustained. It is polemic against the worship of false gods, which is certainly found elsewhere in Second Isaiah; and though no critic can compel an author to maintain his highest level at all times, here the polemic seems more mechanical and negative than Second Isaiah's other defenses of the unique divinity of Yahweh.

The passage centers on the work of the smith and the carpenter, who produce a divine image of wood plated with metal. The tone throughout is one of sarcasm and ridicule, and at times it is labored. In vs. 13 the prophet seems deliberately to reverse the process of Gen i 26–27; God made man in his image and likeness, and now deluded man makes God in his image. The image was rigorously prohibited in the Decalogue (Exod xx 4; Deut v 3), for Yahweh is like nothing in heaven, on earth, or beneath the earth. The makers of images have no god.

The polemic fails somewhat of its purpose because the religions of the ancient Near East were not crass idolatry, as far as we can reconstruct them. The image was representational, though of a kind of representation foreign to our thought. The image was treated like the deity; it was served daily with food and drink and care as if it were a human king; resided in a palace, held audiences, and was carried in processions. It was the earthly counterpart of the god, as the temple was the earthly counterpart of his heavenly palace. It was the symbolic presence of the god, and in this respect was not dissimilar to the Israelite ark of the covenant, which was also the symbol and seat of the presence of Yahweh in Israel. But the worshipers of these ancient religions did not make the simple identification of the god with the image suggested in the verses here. This same simple identification is found in Isa xl 19–20, xli 6–7, which we have treated as fragments of similar polemic. Such polemic can be read in Jer x 1–9 (also doubtfully original in Jeremiah) and in Ps cxv 4–8. Actually it should be called scoffing rather than polemic. Gross superstition was widespread in the ancient world, as we can see in the literature of magic and divination that has been preserved. It is altogether likely that a large number of people took a superstitious view of the image, even though the literature distinguishes sufficiently between the celestial being and his earthly counterpart. Belief and cult do not always follow literature.

H. H. Rowley suggested that behind the scoffing was a certain Israelite inability to grasp the symbolism. The Israelites did not believe that there was anything behind the image, no reality that was represented; therefore the cult was directed to the image, since it was the only reality toward which it could be directed. This explanation may seem too subtle; but either a subtle explanation must be found of such passages, or we must conclude that their authors misunderstood completely the mentality of the religions of their contemporaries. In any case, the polemic is overenthusiastic; and it is for this and other reasons that it seems to fall below the level of Second Isaiah, whose much more profound critique of idolatry is found in such passages as ch. xlvi. In that passage also there is an identification of the god with the image, but an identification less crude than we find here.

18. A HYMN OF FORGIVENESS
(xliv 21–23)

XLIV

21 "Remember these things, Jacob, and Israel, that you are my
　　servant;

　　I have formed you, you are my servant; Israel, *do not for-
　　get me.*

22 I have blotted out your rebellion like a cloud, your sins like
　　a mist;

　　Return to me, for I am your avenger."

23 Shout for joy, heavens, for Yahweh has wrought! Cry out
　　in triumph, underworld!

　　Mountains, break out in cheers! Forests, and all trees in
　　them!

　　For Yahweh has avenged Jacob; he has displayed his glory
　　in Israel.

a–a Reading with LXX and 1QIs*a*; Heb. "you will not be forgotten by me."

NOTES

xliv 21. *I have formed you*. See xliii 1.

22. *avenger*. See xli 14 and NOTE.

23. *underworld*. Renders a phrase, literally "the lowest parts of the
earth." In almost all other cases, this phrase, is parallel to a word designating the underworld, or the context suggests this meaning. The
prophet moves, in these lines, from heaven to the underworld and then
to the earth between (mountains and forests).

COMMENT

We have called this piece "A Hymn of Forgiveness," although it actually consists in a saying of Yahweh followed by a hymnic invocation to praise. It follows, as we have noticed, on the summary found in vss. 6–8. It resumes again the themes previously used: the titles of Jacob/Israel and servant, creator and avenger of Israel, and the affirmation of forgiveness (xliii 25). The comparison of sin with clouds and mist is Palestinian; in the dry months of the year there is heavy mist almost every morning, which disappears very rapidly after the sun rises. It is unusual in the OT for sin to be treated as something so transitory and insubstantial; it is Yahweh's forgiving power which removes man's heaviest burden. Hosea used the same comparison to show how frail Israel's devotion was (vi 4). The apostrophe to nature with which the passage concludes is paralleled in xlii 10–12 (see COMMENT *ad loc.* [SEC. 10]) and elsewhere.

19. YAHWEH THE LORD OF HISTORY
(xliv 24–28)

XLIV

24 Thus says Yahweh your avenger, who formed you from the
     womb;
     "I Yahweh do all things; I alone stretched out the heavens;
     I laid out the earth; *who was with me?"*

25 He frustrates the signs of soothsayers,*b* and makes fools of
     diviners;
     He upsets sages, and makes nonsense of their wisdom.

26 He establishes the word of his servants,*c* and fulfills the
     plans of his messengers;
     He says to Jerusalem, "She shall be inhabited," and to the
     cities of Judah, "They shall be built";
     And to its ruins, "I will raise you."

27 He says to the Ocean, "Dry up; I will make your streams
     waterless."

28 He says of Cyrus, "My shepherd; he will accomplish all
     that I wish,
     Saying to Jerusalem, 'She shall be built,' and to*d* the temple,
     'You will be founded.'"

a–a Following LXX, Kethib, thirty-one manuscripts, and 1QIs*a*.
b Conjectural emendation from Akk. *baru;* Heb. "boasts."
c Reading with some LXX manuscripts and Targ.; Heb. singular.
d "To" is supplied from the preposition with the preceding noun; but see
COMMENT for conjunction of this phrase with the context.

NOTES

xliv 24. *who was with me?* A rhetorical question meaning no one was with me.

25. *soothsayers* and *diviners* designate two types of professional interpreters of omens which we cannot distinguish. The *baru* priest is known from Akkadian literature, and the text is restored from this word. The *sage* was the professional wise man, a counselor and a spokesman of traditional wisdom.

26. The *servants* and the *messengers* must be the prophets who spoke of the future restoration and glorification of Jerusalem. Such passages as Isa ii 2–4 and Mic iv 1–4 are relevant, but the date of these and similar passages is uncertain.

27. An allusion to the victory of Yahweh the creator over the monster of chaos, embodied in the Ocean; see li 10, 1 2; Ps lxxiv 15. The cosmological myth is also seen in the division of the sea in the Exodus.

28. This is the first time Cyrus is named in the prophecy. He is called "my shepherd"; shepherd is a common title of kings in the OT and in other ancient Near Eastern literature; it is also a title of Yahweh. Cyrus is thus given the title of an Israelite king.

COMMENT

After a new introductory formula Yahweh is again the speaker. The theme of creation, which has been so prominent, introduces the statement; the statement goes from creation to history, which is the topic of this poem and the poems that follow. Yahweh's lordship in creation is the base of his lordship over events. In vss. 25–26 the prophet introduces interpreters of events. Mesopotamia was an ancient home of the art of divination, which reposes on the principle that every event and phenomenon presages the future. The literature that sets forth the interpretation of signs of all types is enormous; it forms a surprisingly large part of the corpus of surviving Akkadian literature. Second Isaiah rejects the principle, which is an implicit statement of fatalism; even the gods were determined by the fates, which could be read in the omens. The course of events is governed by the sovereign will and purpose of Yahweh, and only those to whom Yahweh has revealed his counsels can interpret events. The diviners are refuted by history, which is the action of Yahweh.

Events are interpreted by the servants and messengers of Yahweh, his prophets in Israel.

In this critical moment of history Yahweh has a word, the word that Jerusalem and the cities of Judah will be rebuilt. This is a more precise word than the prophet has uttered so far; the ingathering of Israel, which he has described, has not been put in such specific terms. The modern reader does not readily understand how impossible this word appeared to Israelites transported from their own land and dwelling in Mesopotamia for so long that very few if any could remember Jerusalem and Judah. But this word is spoken by him who overcame the Ocean, the mythological monster of chaos; see NOTE on vs. 27. For the lord of nature this word is not difficult to fulfill; the prophet unites the mythological victory of Yahweh with his saving act in the Exodus.

The prophet becomes even more specific; he names Yahweh's agent of salvation, Cyrus of Persia (see INTRODUCTION, "Historical Background"). On the title given Cyrus see NOTE on vs. 28. There is little reason to question the originality of the mention of Cyrus; his name recurs in the following poem, and xli 2 is more easily referred to him than to anyone else; see on both passages the COMMENT on SECS. 20 and 5. The second line of vs. 28 does raise some critical difficulty. It is slightly too obvious a repetition of vs. 26; and it is not the practice of Second Isaiah to repeat himself mechanically in a single context.

Verse 28a also mentions the temple; and the word "temple" occurs nowhere else in Second Isaiah. The restoration of the temple is not included in his picture of restored Israel and Zion, in spite of the prominence of the Zion poems in his work; see xlix 14 – 1 3 and li 1 – lii 12 (SECS. 27 and 29). The line is somewhat clumsily attached to the proceding line, and is anti-climactic. It is possible that an early glossator added a theme of restoration, which he found missing in Second Isaiah. According to the decree of Cyrus as quoted in Ezra vi 3–5, the temple rather than the city was the object of Cyrus' benevolence. It is certainly difficult to conceive how Second Isaiah could foresee a community without a temple and cult (D. N. Freedman); but apart from this line, that is what he does foresee. Were the temple of importance to him, we should expect more than a single mention of it. In fact Second Isaiah's new Zion has none of the institutions of the historic Zion. This does not imply that he thought there would be no institutions; he simply has nothing to say about them.

20. THE CALL OF CYRUS
(xlv 1–13)

XLV

1   Thus says Yahweh to his anointed, to Cyrus, whom he[a]
    grasps by his right hand,
    That he might subdue[b] nations before him, and ungird[c]
    the loins of kings,
    To open doors before him, that gates shall not be closed:

2   "I will go before you, and I will level the roads[d];
    I will shatter gates of bronze, and I will hew bars of iron to
    pieces.

3   I will deliver buried treasures to you, and hidden riches,
    That you may know that I am Yahweh, the one who
    calls you by name, the God of Israel.

4   For the sake of my servant Jacob, and Israel my chosen
    one,
    I have called you by your name; I have ennobled you, and
    you did not know me.

5   I am Yahweh, and there is no other; besides me there is
    no god; I have armed you, and you did not know me,

6   That they may know from the east and from the west that
    there is none besides me,
    I am Yahweh, and there is no other.

[a] MT can be retained by taking all of vs. 1 after "Cyrus" as parenthetical,
spoken by Yahweh, but not to Cyrus (D. N. Freedman). The infinitives al-
ternate with the first person imperfect. Very probably the text tradition is too
complex to be explained either by the emendation accepted or by the gram-
matical explanation.
[b] The vocalization of this word is unusual but grammatically acceptable
(G.K.C. 67p). If the more usual form is read, no change in the consonantal
text is necessary (*lārōd* for *lᵉrad;* from *rādad,* "subdue").
[c] Heb. "I will ungird"; see note [a].
[d] Conjectural emendation; Heb. unintelligible; LXX and 1QIs[a] "mountains."

7   I form light, and I create darkness; I produce well-being,
     and I create evil;
     I Yahweh do all these things.

8   Drip down, heavens, from above, and clouds, pour down
     righteousness;
     Let the earth open and blossom with victory, and let right-
     eousness sprout with it;
     I Yahweh have created it.

9   Woe to him who strives with his maker—an earthenware
     vessel with the potter!
     Does the clay say to the potter, 'What are you doing?
     Your work lacks skill'?*e*

10   Woe to him who says to a father, 'What are you begetting?'
     and to a woman, 'What are you bearing?'"

11   Thus says Yahweh, the Holy One of Israel and its maker:
     "Do you*f* ask me about my sons? Do you direct me about
     the work of my hands?

12   I made the earth, and I created man upon it;
     My hands stretched out the heavens, and I direct all their
     hosts.

13   I have stirred him up in righteousness, and I will make level
     all his ways;
     He will build my city, and he will restore my exiles,
     Not for a price, and not for payment"—says Yahweh of
     hosts.

e Literally "your work has no hands" (D. N. Freedman).
f Conjectural emendation; Heb. "Ask me about the future."

NOTES

xlv 1. "The anointed of Yahweh" is the title given the Israelite king
from Saul and David onward, and in particular to kings of the dynasty
of David. The ceremony of anointing consecrated an object or a person.
The title "anointed" passes into English as Messiah, and through the
Greek as Christ. Cyrus is given the place in the history of salvation
which in pre-exilic Israel was given to the king.

grasps by his right hand. To grasp by the right hand is a sign of friendship: when done by a superior, it signifies full acceptance.

3. *calls . . . by name.* Designates power over another, or a vocation to a particular mission, as of Israel (xliii 1).

4–5. Cyrus fulfills the mission of Yahweh even though he does not know Yahweh; yet to him are spoken promises of conquest similar to those spoken to the Israelite king in Pss ii 8–10, lxxii 8–10.

7. This line has often been adduced as an allusion to Persian dualism, in which there was a perpetual conflict between the god of light, Ahura Mazda, and the god of darkness, Ahriman. Such an allusion is possible, but the line does not depart from biblical language and thought; see Gen i 3–5; Amos iii 6, v 18–20. In Israelite thought nothing, not even evil and darkness, could be removed from the dominion of Yahweh. Gen i 3–5 makes darkness the result of a work of division, not of creation in the sense in which the word is used elsewhere in Gen i; but this does not alter the thought pattern. The darkness of daily experience is not the mythological darkness of the primeval abyss, even though it remains the symbol of evil. It is like the sea which Yahweh has bound within its limits. For *šālôm,* "well-being," 1QIsᵃ reads *tôb,* "good," a more common and obvious antithesis.

9. Cf. the image of the potter in Isa xxix 16; Jer xviii 1–11; Rom ix 20–24 where the image describes the absolute sovereignty of God, but the application of the image is varied. Here God's sovereignty appears in his decision to save Israel through an unbelieving foreigner, whom he chooses as his anointed and his servant.

13. The Heb. here is so compact that it becomes obscure: *in righteousness* is adverbial; but "righteousness" is the attribute by which Yahweh fulfills his promises and vindicates his supremacy. It often suggests the idea of victory, as it does here.

COMMENT

The identity and the mission of Yahweh's agent of salvation are now disclosed clearly. J. D. Smart, reviving an opinion proposed by C. C. Torrey, believes that Cyrus has been intruded into this passage, and that the "servant" and the "anointed" is Israel. But the entire context is at variance with this opinion. This would make the passage another Servant poem and settle the question of the identity of the Servant. We have noted that the title of servant is given to more than one subject in Second Isaiah. And it may be to the point that Israel is never "the anointed." In the OT this title without

qualification designates the Jerusalem king; and Cyrus was a king.
He receives, as we point out in the NOTE on vs. 1, the titles which are
given to the agents of Yahweh in pre-exilic Israel. At the probable
date of Second Isaiah (see INTRODUCTION, "Critical Questions")
Cyrus' career of conquest was well advanced, and the terms used in
vss. 1–2 are not an exaggeration. But for the prophet, Yahweh is the
power behind the conquests of Cyrus; he grants Cyrus world supremacy in order that he may restore Israel. We have no record that
Cyrus ever recognized Yahweh (vs. 3); and it is possible that the
prophet looked to something which never happened. The profession
of faith contained in the decree of Cyrus permitting the rebuilding of
Jerusalem (Ezra i 2), even on the assumption that this is an exact
quotation, is no more than a ceremonial statement expressing respect to the gods worshiped by other peoples. For Second Isaiah such
a ceremonial statement would hardly be a genuine confession of
faith in Yahweh.

In any case, the work of Cyrus is a manifestation of the power of
Yahweh, which the whole world can see. Here Second Isaiah's appeal
to prophecy acquires particular relevance, for Second Isaiah himself
declares and interprets events which are shortly to happen (xli 1–4,
21–29, xliii 9–13, xliv 6–7). He repeats, perhaps to excess, the
affirmation that there is no other god but Yahweh who acts in the
history of Cyrus (vss. 5–6).

The prophet affirms Yahweh's supremacy in vs. 7 in terms reflecting his creative power; on some possible implications in these terms,
see the NOTE. History is a stream in which light and darkness, well-
being and evil—or what men call by these names—are constantly
mingled. It makes no difference what they are called; nothing happens which is not the work of the sovereign will of Yahweh. To
the kings whom Cyrus defeats and deposes (2–3) what happens is
darkness and evil; but it is the work of Yahweh, not of some power
independent of him. The thought of this sovereignty leads to the
exclamation of vs. 8. The verse does not simply identify the conquests of Cyrus with righteousness and victory; but the conquests
are the achievement of the will of Yahweh, for they lead to the
restoration of Israel. They initiate a new era of Yahweh's providence.

Verses 9–11 indicate that Second Isaiah's concept of salvation
met or was expected to meet incredulity among the Israelites. What
form these objections took the prophet does not tell us. His response

to the objections is a reaffirmation of the sovereignty of Yahweh in the figures of the potter (see NOTE on vs. 9) and of the father and mother. These are creative acts of men, and men do not question each other at the moment of creation. Neither should they question Yahweh, who now shows the same power he exhibited in the creation of the world. We have noticed that in Second Isaiah the ideas of creation and history are constantly intertwined. If Yahweh chooses to save Israel through Cyrus rather than in some other way, it is his to choose whether Israel shall be saved and by what means.

The prophet concludes with a reaffirmation that it is Yahweh who has stirred up Cyrus, and that the deliverance of Israel is gratuitous, with no profit either to Yahweh or to Cyrus. Yahweh does it for "his glory," which is not for profit; it is simply that he may be recognized for what he is. That an Israelite prophet should view the conquests of Cyrus purely as directed to the restoration of Israel may seem an intolerably narrow view of history. But it is a fact that the restoration of a Jewish community in Palestine has had a more lasting effect than anything else accomplished by Cyrus, who has been given in history the title of the Great. In the light of subsequent developments, the prophet does not show narrow vision; he shows an astonishing insight into the meaning of history.

21. YAHWEH'S VICTORY THROUGH ISRAEL
(xlv 14–25)

XLV

14 Thus says Yahweh:

 a"The toilers of Egypt and the merchants*a* of Kush and the men of Seba, tall of stature,

 Shall pass over to you; they shall be yours; they shall walk behind you in fetters*b*;

 They shall prostrate themselves before you; they shall pray to you:

 *c*With you only is El, and there is none besides; there is no other god.

15 In truth, El is hidden with you,*c* the God of Israel, the savior.'"

16 They are ashamed—yes, they are humiliated, all who *d*are angry with him*d*; the makers of idols walk in disgrace.

17 But Israel is saved by Yahweh with an eternal salvation; they shall not be ashamed nor humiliated forever.

18 Thus says Yahweh, the creator of the heavens—he is God—

 Who formed the earth and made it—he is its founder—

 He did not make it to be a chaos; he formed it to be inhabited—

 "I am Yahweh, and there is no other.

---

a-a The translation follows Heb., taking the abstract nouns "toil" and "merchandise" for the concrete (D. N. Freedman).

b Omitting "they shall pass" of Heb.

c-c MT can be retained by understanding the words as addressed to Yahweh (D. N. Freedman); but the context does not recommend this change in the person addressed.

d-d Reading suggested by LXX; Heb. "all of them together."

19   I did not speak in secret, in a dark region of the earth;
     I did not say to the race of Jacob, 'Look for me in[e] chaos.'
     I am Yahweh; I speak righteousness and proclaim justice.
20   Assemble and come, approach together, fugitives of the
        nations;
     They are without knowledge, those who carry their wooden
        images,
     And pray to a god who cannot save.
21   Speak out, bring your proofs; yes, take counsel together;
     Who proclaimed this long before, declared it in time
        past?
     Was it not I, Yahweh? There is no other god besides me.
     I am El, Righteous and Victorious; there is not another.
22   Turn to me and be saved, all the ends of the earth!
     For I am El, and there is no other.
23   I have sworn by myself;
     In righteousness there proceeds from my mouth a word
        which will not be recalled;
     Every knee shall bend to me, and every tongue shall swear,
24   Saying,[f] 'Truly, in Yahweh is righteousness and power.'"
     They[g] shall come to him in shame, all who were angry
        with him.
25   In Yahweh the whole race of Israel will prevail, in him they
        will boast.

[e] The missing preposition in Heb. has been lost by haplography; the preceding
word ends in *beth*.
[f] Reading with LXX and transposing "saying"; Heb. "he said to me."
[g] Text reached by different word division, transferring initial *waw* from
*w*ᵉ*yēbōšû* to preceding *yābô'*; following 1QIsᵃ and other manuscripts.

Notes

xlv 14. *Egypt*, *Kush* and *Seba*. See Note on xliii 3. All three names
come from northeast Africa, and they are probably chosen because
they represent the most remote regions known to the Israelites. These
peoples make an explicit profession of monotheism; this is the first time
in the OT that such a vision appears. The confession of Naaman (II
Kings v) is made by an individual, not by a people.

15. The received text is the base of the usual translation, "You are a hidden God." But the usage of the Hebrew word does not support this reading. Yahweh is hidden with Israel, a small and defeated nation.

18. *chaos.* Heb. *tohu,* the word used to describe the earth before Yahweh's creative word is spoken (Gen i 2), the desert and abandoned sites. The prophet may have known the word in the context of a creation poem.

19. The word *chaos* recurs here. The allusion to *secret* and *dark region of the earth* refers to the underworld, the realm of the dead, a traditional source of oracles both in Greek and in Semitic mythology; see I Sam xxviii 13.

20. *fugitives of the nations.* Does not imply an eschatological catastrophe; the nations that trust in false gods must ultimately fall.

21. This line alludes to messianic oracles in earlier prophets, but it is impossible to specify what passages may be meant.

COMMENT

In some ways this poem represents a peak both of theological and of poetic intensity in the discourses of Second Isaiah. It brings together the themes of the absolutely unique divinity of Yahweh and of the unity of mankind under the sovereignty of Yahweh. The prophet reaches a breadth of vision not attained in earlier writings of the OT. The poem is formed of two utterances of Yahweh, interrupted by a brief reflection of the prophet himself.

The same three names which occur in xliii 3 are mentioned again in 14; see the NOTE on this verse. There they are said to be exchanged for Israel; here they shall come to Jerusalem "in fetters." An overliteral understanding of this verse has troubled some interpreters. The experience of captivity in war was quite well known in the ancient Near East, and it is in terms of this captivity that the prophet describes the submission of other nations to Yahweh and to Israel, the people of Yahweh. Similar announcements of the submission of the nations are found elsewhere in Second Isaiah and in Third Isaiah. The submission to Israel is to be understood in terms of submission to Yahweh; it is not a military conquest which the prophet sees, but a religious conquest; this is clear in the lines following. It is Israel which reveals Yahweh to the nations, and it is through Israel that Yahweh receives the surrender of the nations.

The nations expressly confess that there is no God but Yahweh, the

God of Israel. This confession presupposes the great saving act of Israel's liberation, which the prophet has set forth in the preceding poems. Verse 15 is the origin of the phrase "hidden God." As the text is restored this phrase no longer appears. Yahweh could truly be said "to hide himself" with Israel; for the Israel of the moment was not even a nation. It was the remnant of a nation, displaced from its own land and deprived of political liberty of action. That the one God should have attached himself to this pitiful remnant and not to one of the great and powerful peoples of the ancient world was a wonder and a scandal not only to the nations but also to many Israelites. Here as elsewhere the prophet is addressing his fellow Israelites as well as the nations to whom the discourse is formally directed. This confession of the nations will once and for all confound those who worship false gods. For the saving act of Yahweh toward Israel will have a breadth and a permanence no other nations can match. This reflection in vss. 16–17 is more likely the speech of the prophet in his own name than a part of the utterance of Yahweh.

The prophet introduces the second saying of Yahweh with an appeal to the theme of creation, here modified by a new idea. Why did Yahweh create the earth? Surely not that it might be a chaos, a *tohu;* this word is used in Gen i 2 to designate the formless waste which the world was before the creative word of Yahweh was spoken. The word is a favorite of Second Isaiah; it describes the ruined land of Edom (xxxiv 11), and several times it designates the nothingness of the worshipers of false gods. Jeremiah (iv 23) sees the land a *tohu* after the wrath of Yahweh has scorched it. It was not for this that Yahweh created the earth; he created it to be inhabited by men. This surely reflects both creation accounts (Gen i 28, ii 4–10), even if these documents were not known to Second Isaiah in the form in which we have them. In ancient Near Eastern mythologies man lived in a world that constantly moved in a cycle from creation to chaos to a new creation and back to chaos; Israelite belief never accepted this mythology.

In vs. 19 Yahweh denies that he has ever spoken "in secret, in a dark region of the earth." The phrase is obscure and variously interpreted; but it seems most probable that it denies that Yahweh has spoken by the occult art of divination. The revelation of Yahweh to Israel was given to an entire people; they did not need to seek it from professional revealers. The content of his revelation is "righteousness and justice"; on the word translated "justice" (judgment), see (SEC. 8) NOTE on xlii 1 and COMMENT. Together with righteousness it signifies order, the order of right conduct. The nations are once more challenged to produce evidence that their gods can perform deeds comparable to the deeds of Yahweh. The word which recurs in the challenge is "save"; this is the peak of Yahweh's achievement, which demonstrates more effectively than anything else that he alone is God. On the claim of prophecy, see COMMENT on xli 21–29 (SEC. 7).

Yahweh then invites all the nations of the earth to share the salvation he alone can grant them. This invitation is not a new thought, a kind of impulse in Yahweh; the prophet has already reflected that Yahweh did not create the earth that it might become a chaos. The saving purpose of Yahweh is confirmed by his oath—which he must take by his own name, swearing by the same supreme reality by which men swear. The oath of God to the patriarchs and to Israel and to David occurs very frequently in the earlier books of the OT. Now this oath, the most solemn form of asseveration, is extended to all the nations of the world. Yahweh's will to save them is affirmed with no less vigor than his will to save Israel. That which proceeds from his mouth is "righteousness," a word rich with meaning, as we have suggested above. It is not merely that Yahweh's word is true (for which there is another Hebrew word), but that it achieves the condition of righteousness; and righteousness is not fully achieved until every man acknowledges that Yahweh alone is God. This word will have its effect. The force of the final line is that the universal confession of Yahweh is the only victory Israel can expect, and the only legitimate boast Israel can make. Their victories and their boasts are not and never will be the victories and boasts of other nations; for they are the servant of Yahweh.

22. THE FALL OF BABYLON'S GODS
(xlvi 1–13)

XLVI

1   Bel falls to his knees, Nebo stoops;
Their idols are put on animals, on beasts of burden,
Packed*a* and carried, the load of a weary beast.

2   They stoop, they kneel; they are unable to deliver their
bearer*b*;
They themselves march into captivity.

3   "Listen to me, house of Jacob, and all who are left of the
house of Israel,
You who have been a burden from your birth, carried since
your nativity:

4   Until your old age, I am the one; and when you grow gray,
I will bear you.
I have done it, and I will carry you; I will bear you, and
I will save you.

5   To whom do you liken or compare me? With whom
would you confront me, that we should be equal?

6   The spendthrifts bring gold from their purse, and lay
silver in the balance;
They hire a goldsmith to make*c* a god; they worship him
—yes, they prostrate themselves before him!

7   They lift him on their shoulders, they carry him; they set
him down in his place, where he stands, he does not
budge.
When one cries out to him, he does not answer; from his
distress he cannot save him.

---

a Conjectural emendation; Heb. "your loads."
b Conjectural emendation; Heb. "burden."
c Omitting the suffix in Heb. *weya'asēhû* with 1QIs*a*.

8   Remember this, and be confused^d; rebels, return to your
     senses!

9   Remember the ancient past—that I am El, and there is no
     other God, and there is none like me,

10   Declaring the end from the beginning, and from ancient
     times things that have not happened,
     Saying, 'My decision shall be realized, and all that I in-
     tend I will do,'

11   Calling an eagle from the east, the man of my choice from
     a distant country;
     Yes, I have spoken, and I will bring it to pass; I have
     planned it, and I will do it.

12   Listen to me, you whose heart despairs,^e you who are far
     from deliverance:

13   My deliverance is near,^f it is not far off; and my victory
     does not tarry;
     I will establish my victory in Zion, and my glory in Israel."

^d Conjectural emendation; Heb. unintelligible.
^e Reading 'ôbᵉdê for Heb. 'abbîrê, a change of one consonant.
^f Reading with 1QIs^a for Heb. "I am bringing my deliverance near"; the
emendation gives a closer parallelism.

NOTES

xlvi 1. *Bel.* Akkadian cognate of Heb. *baal,* is not a proper name but
a title, "lord." The title originally belonged to Enlil of Nippur, but after
Babylonian supremacy was established in the second millennium B.C.,
the title was transferred to Marduk of Babylon.

Nebo. The Akkadian Nabu of Borsippa, a neighboring city of Babylon,
who was a god of wisdom and the patron of scribes. The passage is a
continuous play on the words translated "bear" and "carry." Babylonian
cultic practice included the processional carrying of the divine images on
festival days.

3–4. It is Yahweh speaking from here onward. The figure of Yahweh
carrying Israel appears also in Exod xix 4; Deut i 31, xxxii 11; Isa lxiii 9.
The first line of vs. 4 illustrates the division of phrases naturally joined
to achieve parallelism; "I am the one who will bear you" is divided between the first and second cola (D. N. Freedman).

11. *eagle from the east*. That is, Cyrus. The translation "eagle" is
somewhat free; the word designates a bird of prey, and apparently included several species.

12. *deliverance*. Here translates the word usually rendered by "righteousness"; it is an attribute by which Yahweh saves. See NOTE on xlv 13.

COMMENT

The prophet uses the fall of the gods of Babylon as a text on
which he discourses on the relations of Yahweh and Israel. In
ancient Near Eastern wars the images of the gods were often displaced by the conquerors; see a representation of Assyrian soldiers
carrying away images of gods in ANEP, No. 538. Actually this did
not happen when Cyrus took Babylon, and the prophet did not here
write prophecy from the event. The prophet draws a contrast between
the divine images, which cannot move unless carried, and Yahweh,
who has carried Israel from its origins. The figure is not entirely
original with Second Isaiah; see NOTE on vss. 3–4. The conduct of
Yahweh toward Israel in the past is an assurance that he will continue
to support Israel in the future.

The play on the word "carry" is prolonged by another allusion.
Solemn religious festivals in Babylon included the processional carrying of the images of the gods, which signified the visit of one god
to honor another god in his temple on his festival. This becomes an
object of ridicule for the prophet in a tone similar to the tone of the
polemic of xliv 9–20. The gods, far from being able to help, are im-
mobile unless their worshipers lift them. On the identification of the
god and the image, see the COMMENT on xliv 9–20 (SEC. 17).

The address to Israel after this scornful jibe—for Israel must be the
"rebels" of vs. 8—hints that some of the Israelites were inclined to
take the gods of Babylon more seriously than they ought. We have
noted other instances of this indirect rebuke of Israelite faltering in
faith. The prophet motivates the Israelites by recalling themes which
have appeared in the proceding poems: the exclusive divinity of
Yahweh, the fulfillment of prophecy, and finally the emergence of
Cyrus, who will be the agent of the promised deliverance. Cyrus is a
bird of prey (see NOTE on vs. 11), "the man of my choice"; he has
the titles of election, as in xliv 28 – xlv 4. Verse 12 is directly
addressed to the doubters. The victory is not far off, the achieve-

ment of Yahweh's "righteousness"; see the NOTE. This clearly suggests a date not too much in advance of Cyrus' conquest of Babylon. But the doubters needed to be told that this event, in appearance unrelated to the destiny of Israel, was a great saving act of Yahweh.

23. THE FALL OF BABYLON
(xlvii 1–15)

XLVII

1 "Come down, sit in the dust, virgin daughter of Babylon!
Sit on the ground dethroned, daughter of the Chaldeans!
For no longer will they call you soft and dainty.

2 Take the millstones, grind the meal, take off your veil;
Strip off your skirt, bare the thigh, cross the rivers.

3 Let your nudity be displayed—yes, let your sex appear;
I will take vengeance, *a*I will not be entreated."*a*

4 Our redeemer says*b*—Yahweh of hosts is his name, the
Holy One of Israel:

5 "Sit in silence, enter into darkness, daughter of the Chaldeans;
For no longer will they call you the mistress of kingdoms.

6 I was angered with my people, I profaned my heritage;
I delivered them into your hands, but you showed them
no mercy.
On the aged you made your yoke very heavy.

7 You said, 'I shall be a queen for ages';
Still*c* you paid no attention to these things, you did not
think of the future.

8 Now hear this, you pleasure seeker, you who sit in com-
placency;
You who say to yourself, 'I am, and there is no other;
I shall never be widowed, I shall not know bereavement.'

---

a–a Passive by conjectural emendation; Heb. "I will not entreat man."
b "Says" restored from "man" in the preceding verse.
c Reading '*ôd* with 1QIs*a* for MT '*ad*.

9   These two things shall come upon you suddenly, in one
day—

Complete bereavement and widowhood, they shall come
to you,

For all your sorceries, for all your many spells.

10   You were secure in your wickedness; you said, 'No one sees
me';

It was your wisdom and your knowledge that deluded you;

You said to yourself, 'I am, and there is no other.'

11   But evil will overtake you, which you do not know how
to conjure away;

Disaster will fall upon you, which you cannot avert,

And there will arrive in an instant a calamity, which you
do not foresee.

12   Stand fast, then, with your spells, with all your sorceries,

In which you have labored from your youth;

Perhaps you can succeed, perhaps you will terrify.

13   You are weary with your many counselors*d*; let them stand
forth;

Let the astrologers deliver you—the star-gazers,

Those who reveal by the new moon what*e* will happen to
you.

14   Look, they are no more than stubble, fire consumes them;

They will not save their own lives from the flame;

It is not coals for baking, nor a fire to sit before.

15   Just so are your conjurers*f* to you, with whom you have
labored from your youth;

They wander each in his own way, and there is none to
deliver you."

---

d Conjectural emendation; Heb. "plans."

e Reading *'aŝer* for Heb. *mē'aŝer*, a correction of a dittography.

f Conjectural emendation based on Akk. *sahiru;* Heb. "your merchants."

NOTES

xlvii 1. *virgin daughter.* A pathetic title, applied usually to Jerusalem, Israel, or Judah. It is always addressed to a community that faces disaster; in the ancient world no one was a more helpless victim of war than the unmarried girl.

2–3. The figures here are so realistic that they approach crudity. In Egyptian paintings women slaves at work are sometimes represented as very scantily clad. The image also suggests the harsh fact that women prisoners were at the pleasure of their captors. The context does not indicate an allusion to the punishment of the adulterous wife described in Ezek xvi 37 and Hos ii 10, suggested by Sidney Smith (*Isaiah XL–LV* [see Selected Bibliography], p. 98).

2. *cross the rivers.* Alludes to the transportation of captives.

5. *Chaldeans.* See NOTE on xliii 14.

8. The prophet is remarkably harsh in his condemnation of pleasant living. Compare Isa iii 16–17, xxxii 9–13; Amos iv 1–3, all addressed to women.

9–15. Mesopotamia was celebrated from ancient times for its practice of magic and divination. These occult arts are scornfully designated *wisdom* and *knowledge,* and their practitioners are called "counselors."

11. *conjure.* Renders a word cognate to Akk. *sahiru,* "conjurer." The rites were intended to block the activities of a malevolent demon.

12. In the context *terrify* should have as object the demons against which the spells are directed. The prophet does not name a human agent of the calamity, nor does he present Babylon as resisting a human agent. Poetic imagination adds to the tragedy by picturing Babylon as falling from no visible cause.

COMMENT

This poem belongs to the type called oracles against the nations; see Isa xiii–xxi, xxii; Jer xlvi–li; Ezek xxv–xxxii, and several passages in the minor prophets. There is no other example of the type in Second Isaiah. It is directed at Babylon, the city and the kingdom which conquered and razed Jerusalem and transported many of the survivors to Mesopotamia. As we noted in the preceding poem, the threats uttered here are quite unhistorical; Cyrus took Babylon without violence and destruction, and the city remained large and important under the Persian Empire. The prophet would probably have said that such details are not relevant to the judgments of Yahweh. Babylon fell from her place as mistress of the world, and the period of her decay was begun. Poetically the fall of Babylon receives a treatment similar to the treatment of the restoration of Jerusalem.

Babylon is addressed in terms similar to those prophets and poets used in addressing Jerusalem when it was threatened; they personify her as the young woman, the most helpless of the captives of ancient warfare. She is enslaved, put to hard labor, or forced to submit to sexual abuse. The style of living in Babylon must have impressed the Israelites by its luxury, for the prophet alludes to it in vss. 1 and 8. Second Isaiah was not the only prophet to take a harsh view of comfortable living; see the texts cited in the NOTE on vs. 8.

Babylon was the agent of Yahweh's judgment of Israel, as Assyria had been his agent in the eighth century B.C.; see II Kings xvii 1–23; Isa x 5–6; Amos v 14. Like Assyria (Isa x 7–15), Babylon has refused to recognize that its power came from Yahweh. Effectively it has arrogated divinity to itself. Now Babylon too must experience judgment. Its false security, not unlike the false security of pre-exilic Israel (Isa xxviii 14–15; Jer vii 4–11; Mic iii 11–12), will be shattered. The prophet once again alludes to the Babylonian arts of divination (xliv 25), as well as to Mesopotamian wisdom. The words he places in Babylon's mouth in vss. 8 and 10 are blasphemous, imitating the formula of the sole divinity of Yahweh (xiv 6, 14, xlvi 9). "No one sees me"; compare the complacency of the evildoer in Job xxii 13, xxiv 15, and in Ps x 4, 11, 13. With this the prophet combines scoffing at Babylonian magic. This pathetic superstition was widely practiced in ancient Mesopotamia, and the extensive literature of magic which has survived attests to the hope placed by the Mesopotamian peoples in the ability of the sorcerer to protect them from harm. The judgment of Yahweh is compared to a fire, as it often is in the OT; with a final touch of scorn the prophet remarks that it is not a fire for cooking or warming oneself.

It can scarcely be denied that the tone of the oracle exhibits a degree of vindictiveness; see the COMMENT on xxxiv (SEC. 1).

24. YAHWEH THE REVEALER
(xlviii 1–22)

XLVIII

1　Listen to this, house of Jacob,
　　You who are called by the name of Israel,
　　And who have issued from the loins*ᵃ* of Judah,
　　Who swear by the name of Yahweh, and invoke the God
　　　of Israel,
　　Not in fidelity and not in righteousness.

2　For they call themselves by the holy city, and they lean
　　　on the God of Israel—
　　Yahweh of hosts is his name.

3　"The past I revealed long ago; it issued from my mouth,
　　　and I made it known*ᵇ*;
　　Suddenly I did it, and it came to pass.

4　For I know that you are stubborn, and your neck is an
　　　iron sinew,
　　And your forehead, bronze.

5　I told it to you long ago, and before it happened I de-
　　　clared it to you,
　　So you could not say, 'My idol did it; my graven image and
　　　my cast image commanded it.'

6　You have heard, ᶜyou have beheldᶜ all this; should you
　　　not declare it?
　　From now I will reveal to you new things, secrets that you
　　　do not know.

ᵃ Reading "loins" (*ûmimmeᵉ'ê*) for Heb. "waters" (*ûmimmê*), supplying one
missing consonant.
ᵇ Emendation based on LXX; Heb. "I will make known."
ᶜ⁻ᶜ Reading *ḥazîta* for Heb. *ḥᵃzēh*, imperative. If the imperative is taken as the
infinitive absolute, as suggested by D. N. Freedman, the translation remains.

7   Now they are created, not long ago; up to now[d] you have
not heard them;
Lest you should say, 'See, I knew it.'

8   No, you have not heard—no, you have not known; for a
long time your ear has not been open.
For I knew that you would be utterly faithless; from the
womb you have been called a rebel.

9   For my own name's sake I delay my anger, and for my
honor I restrain it from you,
So as not to cut you off.

10   See, I have tested you like silver[e]; I have tried you[f] in the
furnace of affliction.

11   For my sake, for my own sake I will act—for how shall my
name[g] be profaned?
And my glory I will not yield to another.

12   Listen to me, Jacob—and Israel whom I have called;
I am, I am the beginning—and I am also the end.

13   Surely my hand founded the earth, and my right hand
stretched out the heavens;
When I call them, they stand up together."

14   Come together, all of you, and listen! Who among them
has announced this?
Yahweh loves him, he will accomplish his purpose on
Babylon and the race[h] of the Chaldeans.

15   "I, I have spoken—yes, I have called him; I have brought
him, and I have prospered[i] his way.

[d] Conjectural emendation based on LXX; Heb. "and before the day and not."
The conjunction is omitted from Heb. w^elō', following LXX. D. N. Freedman
suggests that MT can be explained either as "its day," meaning "today," or
as the emphatic *waw*.
[e] Conjectural emendation suggested by the sense; Heb. "and not with silver."
[f] Reading with 1QIs^a; Heb. "I chose you."
[g] Conjectural emendation based on LXX; Heb. omits "my name."
[h] Following LXX, *zera'*, "seed," "race," is read for Heb. z^erō'ô, "his arm."
D. N. Freedman suggests that "his arm" may be rendered "his power," and
the necessary preposition is supplied from the preceding noun. The conjunction
of "his arm" with the verb "accomplish" seems difficult.
[i] Reading wā'aṣlîªḥ with LXX for Heb. w^ehiṣlîªḥ, "he will prosper." If the
word in MT is pointed as infinitive absolute (D. N. Freeman), the translation
remains unchanged.

16 Come near me and listen to this:
     I have never spoken in secret; from the time it happened
       I was there."
     "Now the Lord Yahweh sends me and his spirit."
17 Thus speaks Yahweh your avenger, the Holy One of Israel:
     "I am Yahweh your God, who teaches you what is profit-
       able;
     I guide you in the way in which you should walk.
18 If you had hearkened to my commandments,
       Your prosperity would have been like a river,
       And your victory like the waves of the sea;
19 Your offspring would have been like the sand,
       And your issue^j like its grains;
     Your name^k would not be cut off nor destroyed from my
       presence."
20 Go out from Babylon, flee from the Chaldeans!
     Declare it with a joyful shout, proclaim this;
     Carry it to the ends of the world;
     Say, "Yahweh has avenged his servant Jacob."
21 They did not thirst when he brought them through the
       desert;
     He made water flow from the rock for them; he cleft the
       rock, and the water streamed forth.
22 "There is no peace," says Yahweh, "for the wicked."

^j MT reads superfluously "issue of the loins"; "loins" is omitted in 1QIs^a.
^k Reading with LXX; Heb. "his name."

NOTES

xlviii 1. The titles of *Jacob* and *Israel* are common in Isa xl–xlviii,
less common in 1–lxvi. Only here are they joined with the title of
Judah, which under the monarchy designated the kingdom ruled by the
dynasty of David. Here the three titles suggest the reunion of all Israel.
  2. *call themselves.* That is, call themselves by the name of.
  the holy city. That is, Jerusalem. The phrase is rare in the OT, and
reappears in lii 1. "The holy mountain" (Zion) and "the holy place"
(the temple) are frequent phrases. Here the prophet turns parenthetically

from addressing the Israelites to talking about them in the third person.

3. It is Yahweh speaking from here to vs. 19.

4. A similar figure of the hard face is applied to Israel in Ezek iii 7, but the same figure is applied to the prophet in iii 8–9 to signify his firmness.

6–7. *new things*. The message of the restoration of Jerusalem.

8. That Israel was rebellious from its very beginnings seems to be a more recent development in OT literature; see Ezek xvi 3. The rebellion of Israel is contrasted with its early fidelity in Hos ii 17; Jer ii 2. But the theme of early rebellion is found in Jer vii 24–26.

10. The comparison of affliction to the testing of metal is common in the OT.

12. *the beginning . . . the end*. See xliv 6 and NOTE.

14–15. Cyrus is the object of Yahweh's love and vocation.

16. The first line is somewhat obscure, since not speaking in secret is matched with presence. Perhaps by ellipsis the prophet means to suggest that Yahweh was present, but he was not heard because Israel did not listen to him. The last line of the verse must be the imagined response of Cyrus to the call of Yahweh. See COMMENT on xlv 1–13 (SEC. 20) for the prophet's conception of Cyrus' faith in Yahweh.

21. The departure from Babylon is a re-enactment of the Exodus.

22. This line appears also in lvii 21, and is very probably a gloss here (Duhm).

COMMENT

In this poem there is another reversal of tone, and the prophet's rebuke becomes sharper than it was in xlii 18–25, xliii 22–28 (SECS. 11, 15). Yahweh is still the speaker. Most interpreters divide the chapter into several poems, and this is recommended to some extent by the diversity of topics and the ambiguity of the speakers. Yet there seems to be a unity of theme, a theme which is pursued through reflections on several related topics. But the unity is less well organized than it is in the other poems of Second Isaiah, and this lends probability to Duhm's theory that the poem is heavily glossed. But Duhm's identification of the glosses appears to be insufficiently founded. The prophet uses the historic titles of Jacob, Israel, and Judah to address the people; they have been used frequently in the preceding poems, and the names recall the past of Israel's election and Yahweh's saving acts and judgments. The prophet alludes to the cultic acts of swearing and solemn prayer and denies that these acts were performed with the proper dispositions of "fidelity and righteousness"; see COMMENT on xliii 22–28. The prophet sees Israel as one historical continuity; the generation he addresses is the heir of Israel's past with its saving deeds and its sins. His contemporaries could scarcely have called themselves by the name of "the holy city," and he attests that they were slow to believe in the restoration of Jerusalem from its ruins. The security which had been placed in the holy city before the Exile can be seen in Jer xxvi; Jeremiah was threatened with death because he predicted the fall of Jerusalem and the temple. This false security must have been shattered by the Babylonian wars, but the generation of Second Isaiah retained that type of shallow religion which was the root of the ancient security in the holy city, a religion that demanded no more than cultic practices and assumed Yahweh had no moral will. The closing line of vs. 2 is a common invocation of praise; it is both a prayer in the mouth of the prophet and an ironic echo of the insincere cultic praise of Israel.

There is some obscurity in vss 3–5. "The past" can only mean what it says: the history of Israel from its origins to the Exile. But the "revelation" is more than the communication of facts, even more than prediction; the revealing word of Yahweh was the operative agent of the past, bringing into being that which it uttered. It was necessary that Israel should have events revealed in this way because of its obstinate unbelief. The allusion to idols in vs. 5 very probably refers to no particular idolatrous cult; it is rather a picturesque way of describing the Israelite tendency to attribute the course of events to some other agent than Yahweh. The discourses of the pre-exilic prophets contain an ample number of threats of judgment on moral grounds, and it was in these that the revealing word of Yahweh was mostly contained. The Israelites preferred to explain their misfortunes by something else than the moral and religious breakdown of which their prophets told them. Now they should be better aware of the realities, and it is their duty to announce the truth of the revelation, confirmed and illuminated by their experience.

In spite of Israel's historic incredulity, Yahweh declares to it the new deeds he is about to perform. There is a slight inconsistency between the prophet's statement here that Israel has not heard these things and his repeated affirmations in the preceding poems that coming events have been announced. In spite of the inconsistency, it seems best to take the "new things" as they have been taken in preceding passages; they are the liberation and the restoration of Israel. Israel has not heard these things, according to vs. 8, because its ear has not been open; it has refused to listen to the word of Yahweh. This has been its habit throughout its past (see the NOTE), and it has not changed its habits now. This, the prophet implies, would be sufficient reason for delaying the saving work, as Yahweh delayed his anger in the past; but Yahweh is not governed by the conduct of Israel. Whether he judges or saves, his motivation is within his inner being, his "name"; he does not respond to emotional impulse like a man. The recognition of his name is his glory; Yahweh must be recognized for what he is. He is not a spurious or inadequate God, and he can be recognized in his acts. His anger against Israel has been the anger of testing (see NOTE on vs. 10); its purpose has been to make of Israel what covenant and election destined Israel to be. Unless his anger of judgment has an ultimately saving effect, Yahweh's "name" would be profaned.

The prophet appeals once more to the unique divinity of Yahweh as manifested in creation. This new saving act is also a work of creation. A challenge is uttered to Israel (vs. 14) as it was uttered to the nations and their gods in the preceding poems; however mighty the nations may be, they have not exhibited the gift of prophecy. There is a change of speaker in vs. 14; the words of Yahweh are resumed in vs. 15. The words of the second line of vss. 14 and 15 can refer only to Cyrus; he is again given titles which belong properly to Israel and Israel's charismatic leaders; see xliv 28 – xlv 4. The reference to Babylon and the Chaldeans is questioned by some interpreters, and with more probability here than elsewhere; for in the references to Cyrus the purpose of Yahweh is not directed to Babylon and the Chaldeans. The fall of Babylon has no significance in itself except as an exhibition of Yahweh's judgment (xlvii [SEC. 23]); it is simply a necessary step toward the liberation and the restoration of Israel. But the prophet need not be required to show that rigorous consistency which would make it impossible for him to have written this line. This has not been an occult prediction (see NOTE on xlv 19 and COMMENT [SEC. 21]); it has been occult only in the sense that the manner of Israel's liberation has not been announced. In xlv 9–13 the prophet has asserted Yahweh's freedom in liberating Israel in the manner in which he chooses, but no Israelite who knew his traditions could doubt that Yahweh was committed to deliver Israel in some way or other.

The ambiguity of the speaker becomes acute in vs. 16. It is scarcely possible to attribute vs. 15 to the prophet himself. It is not much easier to attribute the first line of vs. 16 to him; of what could he say that from the time it happened he was there? But Yahweh is not the speaker of the last line of 16. The line could be spoken by the servant of xlii 1–4 (SEC. 8), but it is gratuitous to introduce him here. It could be attributed to the prophet himself; but Second Isaiah never elsewhere claims the spirit for himself. The connection between the spirit and the person sent is loose, and the syntax is unusual; Yahweh is not said to "put" his spirit upon the one sent. It must be granted that this is not a convincing argument; but if this line be attributed to the prophet, it raises some serious questions about his conception of his own mission. For this reason we make the line the imagined response of Cyrus to the commission which has just been described. The spirit is the charismatic principle of action in men who accomplish Yahweh's purpose; and Cyrus has been given nearly every title of the charismatic agent except the spirit in preceding passages (xli 2–3, 25, xliv 28 – xlv 5, xlvi 11). To put these words in his mouth is not a violent departure from the picture of Cyrus which thus emerges. It must also be agreed that this attribution would be more certain if it were explicit in the text. Duhm thought the line a gloss. The speech of Yahweh is interrupted by an introductory formula and resumed less in a tone of rebuke than a tone of grief. Yahweh recalls his "teaching" in covenant law, a teaching which, if observed, would have assured Israel's enduring prosperity. This was the thesis of Deuteronomy (xxviii); in its present form this chapter of Deuteronomy may be more recent than Second Isaiah, but the Deuteronomic thesis was older than both Deuteronomy and Second Isaiah; see Isa i 19–20. The promise of offspring as numerous as the sand echoes the promises uttered to the patriarchs (Gen xxii 17, xxxii 13). Yahweh set Israel in the way it should walk; the same image of a father and his son appears in Hos xi 3.

The poem concludes with a violent change of tone. From rebuke and grief the prophet, speaking in his own name, turns to exultation. The hour of liberation has arrived, and he summons Israel to depart. The summons is couched in terms of a call to a new exodus and a passage through the desert, a theme used in the preceding poems. This is the glory of Yahweh which should be announced to the whole world. A similar call is repeated in lii 11–12; each call marks a division in the series of discourses. With less than complete assurance vs. 22 is judged to have wandered here by scribal work from lvii 21; it is not related to the context here, and seems rather to sound a discordant note at the end of an appeal which shows progressive emotional intensity (so also Muilenburg). The prophet concludes this section with a vision of the beginning of the process of salvation.

III. ZION POEMS

25. THE SECOND SERVANT POEM: THE LIGHT OF NATIONS
(xlix 1–6)

XLIX

1 Listen to me, you coastlands; attend to me, distant peoples:
   Yahweh has called me from birth; from the womb of my
   mother he pronounced my name.

2 He made my mouth like a sharp sword; he hid me in the
   shadow of his hand.
   He made me a chosen arrow; he concealed me in his
   quiver.

3 He said to me: "You are my servant, Israel*a*; in you I will
   win glory."

4 But I said, "I have toiled to no purpose; I have spent my
   strength for nothing, all in vain.
   But my vindication rests with Yahweh, and my reward
   with God.
   *b*I shall be honored in the sight of Yahweh, and my God is
   my strength."*b*

5 "And now," says Yahweh, who formed me from the womb
   to be his servant,
   To bring Jacob back to him, and that Israel should*c* be
   gathered to him:

6 *d*"It is too slight a thing for you to be my servant, to raise

---

a "Israel" attested by critical text, but doubtful according to the sense; see
NOTE and COMMENT.
b–b This line is transposed here from vs. 5c in Heb.
c Reading with some Heb. and LXX manuscripts and 1QIs*a*; Heb. "not."
d Omitting "And he said" of Heb., probably added after the displacement of
vs. 5c.

up the tribes of Jacob,
And to bring back the saved of Israel;
I will make you a light of nations, that my salvation may
reach to the ends of the earth."

NOTES

xlix 1. There is an echo in thought, not strictly verbal, of the call of
Jeremiah (Jer i 5).

coastlands. See Note on xl 15.

2. *sharp sword*. Means the Servant speaks with power. The figure of
the *sword* is used of the Lamb in Rev i 16, xix 15.

3. *Israel*. Although attested in all manuscripts of MT except one and
by the versions, the word is often regarded as a gloss, even by those interpreters who identify the Servant with Israel. The word overloads the
line metrically; but this argument is not convincing. The gloss could be
based on xliv 21. The word *'ᵃšer*, which follows *Israel*, may equally well
be held to be the superfluous word, since it is unnecessary and prosy.
D. N. Freedman suggests that whoever the Servant is, his name is Israel;
no other name is given him. But the name of the Servant appears only
in this one of the Servant Songs, as contrasted with other passages in
which the title of servant is given to Israel. It seems that the author
wished to avoid this obvious identification.

5–6. These verses seem to place a clear antithesis between the
Servant and Jacob/Israel.

light of nations. See xlii 6. The mission of the Servant resembles the
mission of Cyrus; see COMMENT.

COMMENT

This is the second of the Servant Songs; the Servant is the speaker.
It introduces the second part of the collection of Second Isaiah, which
consists entirely of three Servant Songs and a series of Zion poems;
see INTRODUCTION, "Literary Form and Structure."

The Song begins with an apostrophe to the coastlands and the
nations, similar to xli 1; it is to them that the Servant identifies
himself. He is a chosen one; his vocation is not unlike that of
Jeremiah (see NOTE on vs. 1). The phrase "pronounce my name"
is also used of Cyrus in the first part of Second Isaiah (see xlv 4),

and is a common phrase to indicate vocation to a mission. The mission of the Servant is to be accomplished by speech, but his word is the prophetic word; it is the word of Yahweh, accomplishing what it utters. The prophet piles up phrases to indicate that the relation of Yahweh to his Servant is altogether unlike any other relationship of Yahweh to men, even unlike the relation of Yahweh to Israel. The figures used are new.

The presence of the word "Israel" in vs. 3 must be judged doubtful; but the arguments for treating it as a gloss are not entirely convincing (See NOTE on vs. 3). It appears that the presence or absence of the word is not decisive in interpreting the identity of the Servant; see INTRODUCTION, "The Servant Songs." The Servant is a means through which Yahweh will win the glory that he acquires through his saving acts toward Israel. The musing of the Servant, who is the speaker in vs. 4, is a puzzling response to the preceding lines. If the Servant is historical Israel personified, it is difficult to find the basis of the allusion to wasted toil. This is not an obvious word to designate Israel's afflictions under the judgments of Yahweh. It seems more suitable to see in the line an allusion to the prophetic speech of the past, which failed to divert Israel from the course which led to judgment. Yet there is still a "vindication" of the prophetic word coming, for Yahweh will effect the salvation the prophets promised, just as he effected the judgment they threatened. These remarks are not intended to identify the Servant simply with the prophets viewed as a single person, nor with any individual prophet, nor with the prophetic word personified, but simply to search for some clear reference behind the obscure allusion of Second Isaiah. In a very proper sense it is wrong to polarize "Israel" and "the prophets" as if they excluded each other. The prophetic word was spoken in Israel and by Israel.

In any case, the mission of the Servant is clear in vss. 5–6: it is to restore Israel, but this is said to be the lesser part of the mission. The servant is a means of light and salvation to the nations; the phrase "light of nations" appears in the response to the first Servant Song (xlii 6). In our interpretation the mission must be derived from this passage. The prophetic character of the Servant appears here as it is implied in the preceding lines, vss. 1–4—and as we have seen in xlii 1–4. The prophetic word accomplishes the restoration of Israel by renewing the faith which Israel must have before it can be saved. The allusion to "the tribes" designates that the restored Israel is not a fragment, but the structural Israel of history. The Israel restored by Cyrus was indeed a fragment, but the horizons of the prophet are not limited to the contemporary historical scene, even though he mentions it several times. The fullness of Israel and the fullness of the nations both lie beyond the historical present, and it is to this fullness that the Servant's mission must look.

26. RESPONSE TO THE POEM
(xlix 7–13)

XLIX

7   Thus says Yahweh the avenger of Israel, its Holy One,
    To the contemptible one, the abominated of nations, the
      slave of rulers:
  "Kings shall see, and stand up—and princes, and they will
    bow to the ground,
  Because of Yahweh, who is faithful—the Holy One of
    Israel, who has chosen you."

8   Thus says Yahweh:
  "At the time of my good will I answer you; in the day of my
    victory I deliver you;
  I have kept you, I have made you a covenant for a people,
  To establish the land, to distribute ravaged properties.

9   Say to prisoners, 'Come out!,' and to those in darkness,
    'Show yourselves!'
  They shall feed along the roads*a*; they will find pasture on
    all the bare heights.

10   They shall not hunger nor thirst; neither sun nor sirocco
    will strike them;
  For he who pities them guides them; he will lead them to
    bubbling fountains of water.

11   I will turn all my mountains into a road, and my highways
    will be raised up.

12   See, these come from afar; see, these from the north and
    the west, and these from the land of Syene."*b*

a 1QIs*a* reads "all the mountains," which is more closely parallel to "bare
heights," but not better for that reason.
b Heb. *Sînîm* unintelligible; conjectural emendation.

13   Heavens, shout for joy! Earth, exult! Let° the mountains
      break out in cries of gladness!
      For Yahweh has comforted his people, and he has had
      compassion on his afflicted.

° The translation follows Kethib; Kere and 1QIsᵃ read the imperative, as in the
preceding verbs, more closely parallel but without variation.

NOTES

xlix 7. *contemptible one.* The one addressed here is Israel.

8. *covenant for a people.* See xlii 6. The distribution of the property
may be an allusion to the original tribal distribution described in Josh
xiii–xix, although there is no certainty that Second Isaiah knew this
form of the tradition. The prophet pays little attention to the land as a
whole.

9–11. The theme of the wonderful road is repeated; see xxxv 5–10,
xliii 19–20.

12. See xliii 5. *Syene,* restored by conjectural emendation, was the city
at the First Cataract of the Nile, the Greek Elephantine and the
modern Aswan, the ancient boundary point between Egypt and Nubia.

COMMENT

The speaker in this response is Yahweh, who was the speaker in
the response to the first Servant Song (xlii 5–9 [SEC. 9]). The one
described in the second line of vs. 7 is more suitably Israel than anyone else, unless one wishes to anticipate here the Servant of lii
13 – liii, and there seems to be no reason for doing this. Nor does
the address to Israel at this point imply of necessity that Israel is
addressed in the preceding poem; the Servant has a mission which
concerns Israel, and there is no reason why Israel should not be addressed in this connection. As the prophet has said several times
previously, the salvation of Israel will be a saving work which will
astonish the nations.

The further lines of the response are a chain of themes derived
from the first part of Second Isaiah, with nothing really new added.
The "covenant for a people" appears in xlii 6, where it is parallel to
"light of nations." The phrase is indeed applicable to Israel as the

medium through which Yahweh's revelation and covenant reaches other nations. The land which is to be established and the properties to be distributed are most probably the land and the properties of Israel; there is no doubt, as we have noted, that the prophet's view goes beyond the immediate historical scene, but his language is often that of contemporary events. For other passages from which the themes of vss. 9–11 are echoed see the NOTES. The passage concludes with a hymnic call to praise, similar to xlii 10–13, xliv 23.

27. THE CONSOLATION OF ZION
(xlix 14–26; l 1–3)

XLIX

14 But Zion says: "Yahweh has abandoned me, Adonai has
forgotten me."

15 "Does a woman forget her nursling, and have no compassion
on the child of her womb?
But even if these should forget, I will not forget you.

16 See, I have engraved you on my hands; your walls are
always in my sight.

17 Your builders*a* hurry; those who demolished and destroyed
you have gone away from you.

18 Raise your eyes around you and look; they all assemble,
they come to you;
As I live"—the oracle of Yahweh—"you shall put all of
them on like jewels, you shall bind them like a bride.

19 For your wasted and desolate places, and your devastated
land—
For now you are too small for your inhabitants, and those
who swallowed you are far away.

20 They shall yet speak in your hearing, the children of your
bereavement:
'The place is too small for me; make room, that I may
settle.'

21 You will say to yourself, 'Who begot these for me?
I was bereft and barren, exiled and removed; who has
reared these?
See, I was left all alone; whence are these?'"

a Reading with the versions and 1QIs*a*; Heb. "your sons."

22   Thus says the Lord Yahweh:

"See, I raise my hand to the nations, and I lift my standard
to the peoples;

And they will bring your sons in their bosom, and they
will bear your daughters on their shoulder.

23   Kings will be your foster fathers, and their princesses will
serve as your nurses;

They will bow down their faces to the ground before you,
and they will lick the dust of your feet.

You will know that I am Yahweh, and those who hope
in me will not be ashamed.

24   Does one seize prey from a warrior? Is booty snatched from
a tyrant*b*?"

25   For thus says Yahweh:

"Even if booty is seized from a warrior, and prey snatched
from a tyrant,

It is I who defend your cause, it is I who save your
children.

26   I will make your oppressors eat their own flesh, and they
shall become drunk on their own blood like sweet wine.

All flesh shall know that I am Yahweh, your savior, your
deliverer, the

Strong One of Jacob."

L

1   Thus says Yahweh:

"Where is your mother's bill of divorce with which I dismissed her?

Or to which of my creditors have I sold you?

See, you were sold for your iniquities, and for your rebellions your mother was dismissed.

2   Why was no one there when I came? Why did no one
answer when I called?

Is my hand so shortened that it cannot rescue? Have I no
strength to deliver?

b Reading with LXX and 1QIs*a* '*arîṣ*, as in vs. 25; Heb. *ṣaddîk*.

Look, by my rebuke I dry up the sea, I turn rivers into a
desert;
The fish in them stink for lack of water and die of thirst.
3   I clothe the heavens with blackness, I cover them with
sackcloth."

Notes

xlix 14. *Adonai.* My lord, a title applied only to Yahweh in this form.
This is the only occurrence of *Adonai* in Isa xl–lxvi; the title is common
in Isa i–xxxix.

15. The translation of the first line follows MT and the verses, but the
text is not altogether satisfactory. Something more closely parallel to
the first colon is desirable in the second. D. N. Freedman suggests the
word *rāḥām,* meaning woman, found only in Judg v 30. But this word
is generally thought to be a vulgar epithet, and such an epithet is out of
place in this context.

16. The two cola are not closely parallel, although the parallelism
need not be rigorous. The two are more closely joined if it is supposed
that it is not the name that is engraved (perhaps tattooed?) on the
hands, but a pictorial plan or representation of the city.

17. *Your builders hurry.* Refers to the swift coming of salvation.

23. The vision of the prophet goes beyond the restoration of dispersed Israel and sees the submission of nations to Israel and Yahweh.
lick the dust. The posture of licking the dust is illustrated in ANEP,
No. 355.

25. Even victorious warriors may suffer defeat, but not Yahweh.

26. The figure is extremely crude; it designates war between the nations that have conquered Israel. Cyrus as the deliverer is not present in
this poem.
Strong One of Jacob. Echoes Gen xlix 26; see "Strong One of Israel"
in Isa i 24.

l 1. Yahweh divorces Israel the adulterous wife in Hos ii 4; Jer iii 1, 8.
The question here is a denial that there has ever been a divorce. Yahweh
remains faithful to Israel.

2. An allusion to the cosmological myth; see xliv 27.

COMMENT

Here begins the series of Zion poems of which most of chs. xlix–lv (SECS. 25–32) consists. The poems are addressed to Zion (or Jerusalem) and announce its restoration, in contrast with the poems of xl–xlviii (SECS. 3–24), which are addressed to Israel (or Jacob). The prophet begins with the note of despair to which he has alluded several times in the first part (SECS. 3–24). Yahweh is the speaker, and the words of Zion form a dialogue within the poem. The despair is met by a strong affirmation of the unbroken union between Yahweh and Jerusalem. Zion was the place Yahweh had chosen for the dwelling of his name (a common phrase in Deuteronomy); but this election had not excepted Zion from the judgment of Yahweh, as was announced in oracles such as Mic iii 12; Jer vii 1–15. Yahweh's fidelity to his covenant and his promises demanded that Zion be a particular object of his saving love. The figure is not the usual figure of paternal love, but the rarer figure of maternal love. "Engraving on the hands" may mean tattooing, a symbol of permanent attachment. The walls of Jerusalem had lain in ruins for years when this poem was written; but Yahweh sees the rebuilt walls, for it is his purpose that they should be rebuilt. The city which sat abandoned will suddenly have more people than it can hold, and it will wear its population as a bride wears her jewelry. How could Jerusalem so suddenly acquire so many citizens? The figure of Jerusalem as a woman is emphatically stated; she suffers from both barrenness and widowhood, the impossible situation for a woman to bear children. It is a paradox that the barren and widowed woman should suddenly have many children for which she cannot account. But the ingathering of Israel will be so great and so sudden that no one can see it happen. The nations that have captured and enslaved Israel will bring the Israelites back all at once; more than that, they will become the servants of those who had been their slaves. Although not explicit in this passage, the liberation of the Israelites is the submission of the nations to Yahweh; see xlv 14–25. The nations return their captives when Yahweh summons them. The figure of vs. 23, somewhat crude to modern readers, indicates the conventional posture of submission before a sovereign in the ancient Near East.

The prophet adds three assurances to this promise. The first assurance is a statement of the power of Yahweh, presented without the motives which are frequent in the first part of Second Isaiah. The threat to the oppressors of Israel seems unduly harsh, but it does not go beyond conventional language; see the NOTE on vs. 26. The same phrase, the eating of flesh, is used to describe civil strife in the kingdom of Israel in Isa ix 20. The nations shall suffer the judgment fitting to those who seek power, the judgment of war. The second assurance affirms that the union of Yahweh and Israel has not been broken by the infidelity of Israel. In ancient Near Eastern law, including Israelite law, the wife could not divorce her husband; she needed written proof that she had been divorced (Deut xxiv 1). Nor has she been sold into slavery; Israelite law has no explicit provisions for this, but it seems that custom permitted a man to sell not only his children but also his wife to meet his obligations. The denial of divorce, as we point out in the NOTES on li, is entirely consistent with the image of Hos ii–iii; but rigorous consistency is not to be sought in imagery. Hosea also sees a reunion of Yahweh with the faithless woman, and this is the point of the image in both prophets.

The third assurance is another statement of the power of Yahweh; he asks incredulously why no one responded when he called— which must mean the call of the prophet to faith and hope. Here Yalweh's creative power is alleged, but the terms are mythological; see NOTE on vs. 2. This type of allusion recurs in li 9. It is paradoxical that Yahweh should appeal to his power to destroy in order to motivate faith in his power to create and to build.

28. THE THIRD SERVANT POEM:
THE CONFLICT OF THE SERVANT
(l 4–11)

L

4 "The Lord Yahweh has given me the tongue of disciples,
   That I may know how to answer*a* the weary;
   With a word he awakens in the morning,
   In the morning he awakens my ear to listen as disciples
   do.

5 The Lord Yahweh has opened my ear;
   I have not disobeyed, I have not turned back.

6 I have yielded my back to those who strike, my cheek to
   those who pluck the beard;
   I did not hide my face from insult and spitting.

7 The Lord Yahweh helps me; therefore I am not dis-
   honored;
   Therefore I have set my face like flint; I know that I shall
   not be ashamed.

8 My vindicator is near; who will bring a case against me?
   Let us stand up together!
   Who has a charge against me? Let him approach me!

9 See, the Lord Yahweh helps me; who is it that will declare
   me guilty?
   See, all of them wear out like a garment; the moth will eat
   them up."

Response to the poem

10 Who among you fears Yahweh, and hearkens to the voice
   of his servant?

―――――――――
a Reading with LXX; Heb. unintelligible.

He who walks in darkness with no brightness upon him,
Let him trust in the name of Yahweh, and lean upon his
   God.
11 Look, all of you who set fires and kindle brands,
Walk by the light of your fire and of the brands you have
   set ablaze;
From my hand this will happen to you: you shall lie down
   in the place of pain.

NOTES

1 4. *disciples*. A rare word in the OT; it means the student who commits the words of the teacher to memory. The translation of the last two lines follows a suggestion of D. N. Freedman. By ignoring both the Hebrew accents and the arrangement of lines in BH³ a much better balance as well as less strained Hebrew results.

6. *pluck the beard*. To insult.

7. The *face like flint* signifies firmness, not distinguished in Hebrew from obstinacy; see xlviii 4.

11. It is not clear what is meant by those who *set fires and kindle brands*. The figure suggests the sowing of discord in the community. In the context of the prophecy, discord would be sown by those who were skeptical about the prophetic word.

COMMENT

This is the third Servant Song; the Servant is the speaker. We take vss. 10–11 as the response to the Song; there is such a response after each of the first three Songs, but not after the fourth. With the opening line we know at once that we are still dealing with a Servant figure who accomplishes his mission by speech, and who can therefore be said to be a prophetic figure. "The tongue of disciples" (see the NOTE) is the tongue which repeats faithfully what it has learned. Another of the rare occurrences of the word "disciple" is found in Isa viii 16–indeed, it is the only incidence besides this verse which can easily be translated "disciple"; and its use suggests the existence of a school of disciples which became a tradition, a tradition of which the authors of Second Isaiah and Third Isaiah knew themselves to be continuators. Docility and fidelity are the traits of the disciple, and these the Servant has.

The second Song alluded to difficulties the Servant has in fulfilling his mission (xlix 4); the difficulties become much more concrete here, but not so great that the third Song is a bridge to the fourth, the Song of the suffering servant. What the Servant experiences (vs 6) is the vulgar insult which does no real physical harm, a type of insult common in the ancient Near East. The prophet need not be reflecting his own experience here; much in the prophetic literature suggests that this type of insult was an expected part of the prophetic vocation, and we have noted the prophetic character of the Servant. Like Jeremiah (i 18–19), the Servant is not deterred by such treatment. He utters a challenge to a legal encounter with the unbelievers (vs. 8); the image of the suit at law is used in the first part of Second Isaiah, where Yahweh is the challenger (xli 1, 21, xliii 9). Since Yahweh is his vindicator, the Servant can issue a similar challenge; but his challenge is addressed to Israelites, not to the nations; so at least the obvious sense suggests, and foreign nations can be introduced into this passage only by multiplying difficulties. If the prophet is alluding to the experience of the Israelites in Babylon, then he is careful not to say so. No small part of the difficulty of understanding the passage comes from the fact that the sufferings of the Servant here are not great. It is for this reason we can take the prophet to be alluding to Israelite unbelief, symbolized in the rejection of the spokesmen of Yahweh, the more serious sin, which merits the condemnation implied here.

The response is addressed to two classes, one which is encouraged to believe the Servant, and the other which refuses belief. Those who need encouragement are described in terms which signify despair; and despair appeared both in Babylon and in post-exilic Jerusalem (lix 1–15). They have no hope except Yahweh. The unbelievers are addressed by an obscure phrase (see NOTE on vs. 11). The phrase does not in any way suggest that these are foreign nations or oppressors of Israel. The punishment with which the prophet threatens these people is as obscure as their identity; the most obvious meaning is that they will not share in the deliverance the prophet promises.

29. THE RESTORATION OF ZION
(li 1–23; lii 1–12)

The call of Israel

LI

1 "Listen to me, you who pursue deliverance, who seek
Yahweh;
Consider the rock from which you were hewn, the quarry*a*
from which you were dug;

2 Consider Abraham your father, and Sarah who bore you.
For I called him when he was only one; I blessed*b* him and
I made*b* of him a multitude."

3 For Yahweh comforts Zion, he comforts all her ruins;
He turns her desert into an Eden, and her wastes into the
garden of Yahweh.
Glad rejoicing is found in her, praise and the sound of
singing.

Judgment and deliverance

4 "Attend to me, peoples*c*; listen to me, *c*nations;
For teaching will proceed from me, and my judgment as a
light to peoples.

5 *d*In an instant I will produce*d* my victory, my deliverance
shall come forth *e*like a light*e*;
My arms shall judge peoples; the coastlands shall wait for
me, and they shall put their hope in my arm.

a Heb. adds "pit," a gloss; omitted.
b Reading with the versions; Heb. future.
c Reading with some manuscripts; Heb. "my people," "my nation."
d–d Conjectural emendation based on LXX; Heb. at end of vs. 4 "I will do in
an instant," vs. 5 "My righteousness is near, my salvation has gone forth, and
my arms will judge peoples."
e–e Reading with LXX.

6   Lift up your eyes to the heavens, and consider the earth
        beneath;
     For the heavens will be dispersed like smoke, and the earth
        will wear out like a garment,
        And its dwellers will die like gnats;
     But my salvation shall endure forever, and my deliverance
        shall not fail.

Assurance of victory

7   "Hear me, you who know righteousness, a people with my
        teaching in their heart:
     Do not fear the contempt of men, nor be terrified by their
        insults.
8   For the worm will consume them like a garment; the moth
        will consume them like wool.
     But my victory endures forever, and my salvation for gen-
        eration after generation."

A call to Yahweh

9   Awake, awake and put on strength, arm of Yahweh!
     Awake as in days of old, generations long past!
     Was it not you who cut Rahab to pieces, who pierced the
        Dragon?
10   Was it not you who dried up the sea, the waters of the great
        deep?
     Who made the bottom of the sea a road for the redeemed
        to pass over?
11   The redeemed of Yahweh will return, they shall enter Zion
        with a joyous shout;
     Gladness without end will be on their heads; exultation
        and joy will overtake them;
        Grief and sighing will flee.

Yahweh the consoler

12 "I—it is I who comfort you, of whom[f] you should be afraid.
Of man?—he dies; of the son of man?—he is no more than
grass;

13 You have forgotten Yahweh your maker,
Who stretched out the heavens, and founded the earth,
And you have trembled all day without ceasing because of
the rage of the oppressor,
When he is determined to destroy; but where is the rage
of the oppressor?

14 The bound shall quickly be released; he shall not die in
the Pit, nor shall his bread be lacking.

15 I am Yahweh your God, who stirs up the sea so that its
billows roar"—Yahweh of hosts is his name.

16 "I will put my words in your mouth, and in the shadow of
my hand I will hide you, while I stretch[g] out the heavens
and found the earth, saying to Zion: 'You are my
people.'"

The sorrows of Jerusalem

17 Awake, awake! Arise, Jerusalem!
You who have drunk from Yahweh's hand the cup of his
anger!
The chalice[h] of reeling you have drunk, you have drained.

18 There is no one to guide her of all the sons she has borne;
There is no one to grasp her hand of all the sons she has
reared.

19 These two things have encountered you—who will condole
with you?

---

[f] The translation is based on a reconstruction suggested by D. N. Freedman.
The second masculine plural suffix in *menahemekem* clashes with the other
pronominal forms, which are second feminine singular. By transferring the
final *mem* to the following word, one has *mimmî* as the object of "fear." The
waw with "fear" is difficult, but it can be understood as emphatic.
[g] Reading with Syr. suggested by the sense; Heb. "plant."
[h] Heb. adds "cup," a gloss; omitted.

Violence and downfall, famine and the sword—who[i] will comfort you?

20 Your sons swoon, they lie at the head of every street like an antelope in a net;
They are stuffed with the anger of Yahweh, with the rage of your God.

Liberation of Jerusalem

21 So listen to this, afflicted one—drunk but not with wine;
22 Thus says your Lord Yahweh, and your God who defends the cause of his people:
"Look, I take from your hand the cup of reeling; the chalice[h] of wrath you shall not have to drink again.
23 And I will put it in the hands of those who vex you,
Who said to you, 'Bow down, that we may walk over you';
And you flattened your back like the ground, like a street for them to walk on."

A Call to deliverance

LII

1 Awake, awake! Put on your strength, Zion!
Put on your robes of honor, Jerusalem, holy city!
For the uncircumcised and the unclean shall enter you no more.
2 Shake yourself free! Up from the dust, captive[j] Jerusalem!
Throw the yoke off your neck, captive daughter of Zion! 3 For thus says Yahweh: "You were sold for nothing, and it was not for money that you were redeemed." 4 For thus says the Lord Yahweh: "My people went down to Egypt long ago to live there as aliens; and then Assyria oppressed them violently.[k] 5 And now what have I here?"—the oracle of Yahweh—"that

---

[i] Reading with the versions, supported by parallelism; Heb. first person.
[j] Conjectural emendation suggested by the sense; Heb. "sit."
[k] Reading with LXX; Heb. "for nothing."

my people is carried off for nothing? Its tyrants howl in glee"—
the oracle of Yahweh—"and my name is held in contempt all
day, every day. 6 Therefore my people shall know my name¹ in
that day, that I am Yahweh who speaks; here I am!"

The advent of peace

7   How beautiful upon the mountains are the feet of the
    messenger of good news,
  Who proclaims peace, announces happiness, proclaims
    salvation!
  Saying to Zion, "Your God reigns."

8   Hearken! Your watchmen raise their voice, they shout in
    joy together;
  For with their own eyes they see the return of Yahweh
    to Zion.

9   Break out in a joyous clamor, ruins of Jerusalem!
  For Yahweh has comforted his people, he has redeemed
    Jerusalem.

10   Yahweh has bared his holy arm in the sight of all nations;
  And all the ends of the earth shall see the saving deed of
    our God.

Invitation to depart

11   Away, away! Leave the place! Touch nothing unclean!
  Go out of its midst, keep yourselves clean, you who bear
    the vessels of Yahweh!

12   For you shall not leave in haste, nor shall you travel as
    fugitives;
  For Yahweh strides before you, and the God of Israel is
    your rear guard.

¹ Omitting "therefore" of Heb.

NOTES

li 1. *Deliverance* stands in parallelism to *Yahweh,* and may be taken as abstract for concrete, "the Righteous One," Yahweh (D. N. Freedman). But the Israelites seek Yahweh asking for deliverance.

The figure of *the rock* and *the quarry* for the ancestor is unparalleled.

2. Cf. Gen xii 2–3, xv 5, xviii 18, xxii 17–18.

called him. I.e. Abraham.

3. The myth of the Garden of *Eden* was known in several forms besides the one found in Gen ii–iii; see Ezek xxviii 13, xxxi 9, 16, 18, xxxvi 35; Joel ii 3. *Desert* and *wastes* are both topographical terms for parts of the territory of Judah.

4. *Judgment* here does not mean the rendering of a verdict but the revelation of law, parallel to *teaching.* Yahweh promises for all nations what he did for Israel.

6. The verse is not really apocalyptic; the thought is, "Though the heavens shall be dispersed, my salvation shall endure."

9–10. An allusion to the cosmological myth in which the creative deity slays the monster of chaos. *Rahab* is a mythological name found only in the OT; see Ps lxxxix 11; Job ix 13, xxvi 12. The *Dragon* appears in Job vii 12; Isa xxvii 1; Ezek xxix 3; Ps lxxiv 13. Compare the Ugaritic myth of Baal's defeat of Yamm (Sea) and Nahar (River) in ANET, pp. 130–31.

10–11. The passage of the sea in the Exodus is represented as a reenactment of the cosmological myth of Yahweh's victory over the monster of the sea. Verse 11 is a verbal repetition of xxxv 10; it is doubtfully original here.

14. *The Pit* could be the place of captivity, but more probably it is, as elsewhere, Sheol, the realm of the dead.

16. The line echoes, consciously or unconsciously, Jer i 9 (putting words in the mouth) and Isa xlix 2 (hiding in the shadow of the hand). The metrical structure of the verse nearly collapses, and possibly the line is an expansion associating Israel with the Servant Songs.

17. The cup of Yahweh's anger is a fairly common prophetic image; see Jer xiii 13, xxv 15–29, where the image is prolonged; Ezek xxiii 32–34. Possibly the figure may be based on the practice of giving the condemned criminal an intoxicating beverage, attested in both ancient and modern times; but the figure does not suggest this. It is the cup itself which is the punishment. Intoxicating beverages of unusual strength or stronger than the tolerance of the drinker cause reeling and stagger-

ing; these are the symptoms associated with the cup of wrath. The figure seems to be based on a commonly observed fact.

19. The enumeration has four members; each pair is taken as a unit.
22. See vs. 17 and NOTE, above.

lii 3. No price or profit is involved either in the fall of Jerusalem or in its restoration (see xlv 13); it is purely and simply a question of morality.

7. Whether the prophet identifies himself with *the messenger of good news* is not clear; it seems that he envisages others who will announce the event when it actually arrives. See xl 1–9.

God reigns may signify that the restoration of Jerusalem inaugurates the reign of Yahweh; possibly, however, the phrase echoes a cultic refrain, which will be renewed in the restored temple (Pss xciii 1, xcvi 10, xcvii 1, xcix 1).

11–12. The language recalls the Exodus. Different conditions obtain, however. The Israelites shall take nothing from Babylon—unclean because Yahweh has cursed it—except *the vessels of Yahweh,* the vessels of the temple (an allusion rare in Second Isaiah to the cult); their ancestors took goods from Egypt (Exod xii 31–36). The Israelites *shall not leave in haste,* as their ancestors left Egypt; the word *ḥippazôn,* translated "haste," appears only here and in Exod xii 11 and Deut xvi 3, which concern the earlier departure. But Yahweh will protect both the van and the rear of the Israelite column, as he had done before (Exod xiv 19).

COMMENT

This long poem is the great Zion poem; whether it was formed by a collection of scattered sayings or composed as a unity, it does have a unity of mood and theme which permits us to consider it as a whole. The poem is easily divided into ten parts, which we have distinguished. The division is simply for convenience, and says nothing about the division of the poem into strophes or its analysis into the separate poems from which it was possibly compiled. The divisions are marked by such obvious signs as transitional lines, change of topic, and change of person addressed. The speech alternates between Yahweh and the prophet; Zion is addressed throughout, with the probable exception of li 4–6; see the comment on these verses below.

[The call of Israel, li 1–3]: The address of the Israelites as "pursuing deliverance" and "seeking Yahweh" does not contradict the earlier references to the incredulity and despair of the Israelites; the prophet has not charged them with abandoning their faith, but with not being committed to it. The opening line could be paraphrased by "You who say that you . . ." If you mean this, then consider the rock from which you were hewn. Most of the saga of Abraham in Genesis is concerned with the difficulties of believing in the promise of a numerous offspring when his wife was infertile. Hence the names Abraham and Sarah are both meaningful here. Israel in its very origins had no more hope of becoming a great nation than Israel in its present state of defeat has of restoration. The prophet appeals to history as a motive of faith. Yahweh has uttered his promises to Israel as he did to Abraham; and his promise will issue in a transformation of the land of Judah. On the allusions see the NOTE on vs. 3. The transformation is exaggerated; Ezek xlvii 1–12 also foresees a transformation of the land by a stream that will rise at the temple and flow to the Dead Sea. It is a variation on the theme of the transformation of the desert (xxxv, SEC. 2).

[Judgment and deliverance, li 4–6]: On "peoples" and "nations," see textual note *c*. The reason for accepting the variant is that the lines are more concerned with the nations than with Zion or Israel; and an apostrophe to the nations interrupting an address to Israel is certainly not foreign to the style of Second Isaiah. The "teaching" and the "judgment" are directed to the nations, not to Israel alone; for these words, see the COMMENT on xlii 1–4 (SEC. 8). The "victory" and the "deliverance" are the liberation and the restoration of Israel, and this demands the judgment of the nations, as in ch. xlvii. The call to look at the heavens (vs. 6) echoes xl 26, but this call is addressed to the nations; they are not, however, directed to look at them as evidence of Yahweh's creative power. They are to look at them as the most permanent of visible realities; yet compared to Yahweh's saving act they are as transitory as the most fleeting objects of experience. On the explanation of the comparison, see NOTE on vs. 6.

[Assurance of victory, li 7–8]: The address returns to Zion, and Yahweh is still the speaker. Israel is addressed in terms similar to vs. 1; it is the people which has the revelation of Yahweh and the righteousness which comes from his law. This is ample reason why they should not fear any human power; they have learned from law and prophecy that there is nothing to fear except the judgment of Yahweh. The power of men cannot endure against the everlasting saving deeds of Yahweh. The first line of vs. 8 does not imply a sudden catastrophic fall of human power; this power simply collapses from its own gradual corruption.

[A call to Yahweh, li 9–11]: The prophet now becomes the speaker; he addresses Yahweh in the name of Zion and calls upon him to act. The invocation to act merges two themes, the theme of the creation myth and the theme of the crossing of the sea in the Exodus. See the NOTE on vss. 9–10 for references to other appearances of this myth in the OT. Second Isaiah has frequently employed the imagery of the Exodus. The crossing of the sea is also merged with the theme of the road of return; see xxxv 8–10. The theme of joy suddenly emerges with emphasis in vs. 11; hitherto the prophet has not attended to the joyful character of the event he announces.

[Yahweh the consoler, li 12–16]: Yahweh is again the speaker, and he identifies himself at the very beginning of the line by an unusually emphatic use of the first personal pronoun. The emotion opposed to hope is fear; and Zion must learn that it has no one to fear. Men die, but Yahweh the creator is eternal. Yahweh is ready to admit that the fear of the Israelites is not unreasonable; they have known oppression, they have known what it means to live in constant terror of a power they cannot resist. But they have been slow to admit the supreme power, which is directed to save, not to terrify. The power of Yahweh is exhibited in the theme which was employed in vs. 10, his dominion over the sea. Let Zion be assured that Yahweh will save it; in vs. 16 the prophet echoes the ancient covenant formula, "You are my people and I am your God"; see also xlix 2. He who said these things is he who created the heavens and the earth. Verse 16 conveys the idea of the mission of Israel, and implicitly presents another ground for hope: Yahweh will surely preserve Israel because it is through Israel that his word will be uttered to all the earth. The restoration of Israel is treated as a new act of creation.

[The sorrows of Jerusalem, li 17–20]: The prophet again takes up the speech and begins with another apostrophe, as he did in vs. 9; but this time he addresses Zion. "Awake" is a variant form of the same verb with which 9 began. On the intoxicating cup of Yahweh's anger, see NOTE on vs. 17. One effect of the shattering experience of Yahweh's wrath was that the people was deprived of leadership. The prophet reflects upon the disaster of Jerusalem not without sympathy; vss. 18–20 resemble Lam ii 9, 11–12, 19. Contemplation of the magnitude of the disaster will make it easier for the Israelites to see the magnitude of the deliverance; and they may also see that the wrath of Yahweh is surpassed by his compassionate love.

[Liberation of Jerusalem, li 21–23]: The prophet begins the speech, but only to introduce the words of Yahweh. His words are words of promise, although the promise is a threat to others. The cup of wrath will be handed to those who have oppressed Israel; Babylon must have her turn in judgment. The depth of the humiliation of Israel is again alluded to, in order that the contrast between the humiliation and the liberation may be perfectly clear.

[A call to deliverance, lii 1–6]: The prophet is again the speaker in the first two verses, and then he introduces Yahweh. The opening words imitate almost to the letter the opening words of li 9, and this imitation must be deliberate. When Yahweh clothes his arm with strength, he enables Jerusalem to clothe itself with strength, the strength of him who delivers her. The liberation of Jerusalem reverses the fall of Babylon in xlvii (SEC. 23); Jerusalem becomes the queen of Yahweh her king. That the uncircumcised and unclean should not enter her may be a reference to ritual cleanliness; but it is more likely that it means that they shall not enter as attackers.

Something has happened to the words of Yahweh in vss. 3–6. The line between Hebrew poetry and elevated Hebrew prose is sometimes thin, but there can be no doubt that these lines are in prose; and they form an eccentric mass in a poetic composition. Yet the content is not out of harmony with the context. It is possible to regard 4–6 as a gloss on vs. 3, which by itself may not have been understood. The thought echoes xlv 13. Yahweh has not acted for gain in the judgment of Israel, and he does not act for gain in its restoration. He acts only for his name, or for his righteousness, or for his fidelity. This was illustrated in Israel's earlier experiences with Egypt and with Assyria. Because Yahweh's motives are not recognized, the nations take an unholy glee in the success his acts of judgments give them. If his name is to be acknowledged, he must deliver his people without profit. If the passage was original with Second Isaiah, it was very probably rewritten.

[The advent of peace, lii 7–10]: In the concluding part of the poem the prophet is again the speaker, and his language reaches a high emotional intensity. Suddenly he sees the most beautiful sight in the world, the feet of a messenger running with good news,

with the greatest news in the history of Israel. The news is couched
in the language of the cult (see the Note); but the refrain has a
richness of meaning it never had in its ritual use. By a paradox
the watchmen of Jerusalem respond with a shout; it is a paradox,
because a ruined and abandoned city would have no watchmen.
What they see is not the messenger but the return of Yahweh himself. The prophet repeats his call to a joyous shout (li 11). The great
act Yahweh is doing will be seen all over the world.

[Invitation to depart, lii 11–12]: The concluding lines are a call
to depart; see xlviii 20. The Exodus is re-enacted with differences;
see the Note. Babylon must be entirely abandoned; Yahweh creates
a new Israel which will not have to remember "the former things."

30. THE FOURTH SERVANT POEM:
THE SERVANT'S VICTORY
(lii 13–15; liii 1–12)

LII

13 "See, my servant prospers; he is exalted, he is raised up to a very great height.

14 Just as many were appalled at him[a]—
   For[b] his disfigurement was inhuman, he no longer looked like a man—

15 So many nations will be astonished,[c] and kings will close their mouths before him;
   For what was not told them they will see, and what they have not heard they will perceive."

LIII

1 Who has believed what we reported? And to whom is the arm of Yahweh revealed?

2 He grew up before him like a fresh plant, like a root from dry ground;
   He had no beauty nor honor; we saw him, and his appearance did not attract us.

3 He was despised, the lowest of men: a man of pains, familiar with disease,
   One from whom men avert their gaze—despised, and we reckoned him as nothing.

4 But it was our diseases that he bore, our pains that he carried,
   While we counted him as one stricken, touched by God with affliction.

[a] Reading with some of the versions; Heb. "at you."
[b] Conjectural emendation suggested by the sense; Heb. "so."
[c] Conjectural emendation based on the versions; Heb. "he will sprinkle."

5   He was wounded for our rebellions, crushed for our trans-
     gressions;
     The chastisement that reconciled us fell upon him, and
     we were healed by his bruises.

6   All of us strayed like sheep, each man turned to his own
     way;
     And Yahweh brought the transgressions of all of us to
     meet upon him.

7   Oppressed he was, and afflicted, but he did not open his
     mouth;
     He was led like a sheep to slaughter; and as a ewe is
     speechless before her shearers,
     He did not open his mouth.

8   By a perverted judgment he was taken away; and who
     was concerned with his case?*d*
     For he was cut off from the land of life; for *e*our re-
     bellions he was struck*e* dead.

9   He was given a tomb with the wicked, with evildoers*f* his
     sepulcher,
     Although he had done no violence, and there was no
     deceit in his mouth.

10   Yahweh decided to crush him *g*with pain*g*; but if he*h*
     gives himself as a guilt offering,
     He will see his offspring, he will lengthen his days;
     And the plan of Yahweh will succeed in his hand.

11   "For his toils he will see light*i* and be satisfied;

---

d Conjectural emendation reading *debārô* for Heb. *dôrô*. Neither the text nor
the emendation is free from difficulty; but it is easier to understand *dābār* as
"case" than *dôr* as "fate," particularly since "judgment" occurs in the first part
of the line.

e–e Conjectural emendation based upon LXX; Heb. "for the rebellion of my
people there was a stroke upon him." 1QIs*a* reads "his people" for "my people," which is an easier reading, but not superior to LXX.

f Conjectural emendation; Heb. "rich" ('*ôsê ra*' for '*ašîr*).

g–g Conjectural emendation based on the versions; Heb. "the pain"; 1QIs*a* "he
pierced."

h Reading with Vulg.; Heb. "you."

i Reading with LXX and 1QIs*a*; "light" missing in Heb.

By his knowledge[j] my servant[k] will deliver many, and he
will bear their transgressions.

12 Therefore I will give him a share with the great, and he
shall divide spoil with the powerful,

Because he exposed himself to death, and was counted
with the rebellious.

It was he who bore the sin of many, and who made en-
treaty for the rebellious."

[j] Reading with Heb., but several critics emend to "his suffering."
[k] Heb. adds "righteous," probably by dittography; omitted.

NOTES

lii 13–14. Yahweh is the speaker in vss. 13–15. There is a sharp break
between 13 and 14; 13 is possibly displaced. But no place for it can be
found in this poem or in the other Servant poems.

14–15. The *many* of vs. 14 are probably Israelites, contrasted with the
nations and *kings* of vs. 15. In the first and second Servant poems (xlii
1–4, xlix 1–6 [SECS. 8, 25]), the Servant has a mission to the nations.

liii 2. The following lines make it clear that the figure of the plant
does not suggest beauty; the *root from dry ground* is the scrub growth of
the desert. The absence of beauty and honor does not seem to refer to
the natural appearance of the Servant; it is a result of mistreatment or
illness.

3. To avert one's gaze from pain and misfortune is a natural reaction;
but in ancient belief it was dangerous to look at one who was an
obvious object of divine anger.

8. This verse suggests that the Servant was the victim of legal injustice, and the passage alludes to violence without ever being explicit.
The *perverted judgment* could be the kind of judgment which fell upon
Job, and the words which suggest violence can all be understood of
disease. The obscurity of the passage does not permit firm statements
about the experience of the Servant.

who was concerned with his case? A translation based on conjecture.
The thought suits the first member of the verse, but it must be conceded
that the translation is uncertain. Volz suggested that the Servant is "personified suffering," with no particular reference intended.

9. Condemned criminals did not receive honorable burial. *Sepulcher*
is obtained by a different vocalization of MT; *bamah*, usually rendered
"high place," may be a place of burial.

10. The *guilt offering* (see Lev iv) is a type of sacrifice intended to atone for involuntary ritual offenses. The use of the term here has no particular reference to the rite of the guilt offering; the Servant is compared to the victim of an atonement sacrifice.

10–12. There is an obvious inconsistency between the death of the Servant (vss. 7–9) and what is said in these verses. Certainly the prophet sees the Servant surviving in some fashion and experiencing vindication and success. It is not easy to postulate a resurrection in the thought of the prophet. The revival of the people Israel suits these verses, but there are other difficulties in this interpretation; see COMMENT.

11. Yahweh suddenly becomes the speaker in vss. 11–12. *see light.* To be joyful, successful, etc. *Knowledge* is retained from MT, although some critics doubt the reading. The knowledge is to be understood to mean something like the "knowledge of God" in Hos iv 1, 6, which is the knowledge and the observance of the revealed law of Yahweh.

12. The *many* and the *rebellious* appear to be Israelites.

COMMENT

This is the fourth Servant Song. The passage presents many difficulties for various reasons: the use of the passage in the NT to describe the mission of Jesus; it is such a notable departure from the patterns of thought of the OT in general and of Second Isaiah; and obscurities in the text itself. The central problem is the identity of the Servant; see INTRODUCTION for a discussion of this problem. The speaker does not identify himself, and nothing suggests that he is not the author of the poem. He speaks for a group, and nothing indicates any other group than Israel. But words of Yahweh are found in the opening and closing verses of the passage.

Yahweh is the speaker in lii 13–15. The first verse (see NOTE) does not fit well with what follows; the echo of lii 13 is found only in liii 11–12, if the opening verse is in its proper place. It is altogether possible in a poem containing so many cryptic elements that this line is intended to lead to the two concluding verses; but as it stands it must be judged harsh, and the possibility that it is displaced cannot be excluded. The following verse (vs. 14) introduces the theme, which runs through the entire poem as far as liii 10; the Servant suffers, and his suffering is such that he is physically disfigured. The allusion in lii 15 to kings and nations is difficult to interpret. In the preceding poems the nations and their kings are told that they will see the great saving act of Yahweh. If there is a connection between this song and the preceding poems, then the saving act of Yahweh must be the topic of this poem. The character of the saving act is such that it should astonish nations and close the mouth of kings. Whatever is meant, this revelation of the Servant is directed not only to Israel, but to the nations. The Servant has already been described as light of the nations (xlii 6, xlix 6).

The poet describes his revelation as incredible. "The arm of Yahweh," the exhibition of his saving power, has been mentioned in li 9 and lii 10 as the agent of salvation; and the echo of the phrase here can scarcely be coincidental. This is the work of salvation; and liii 1 affirms that it is a mysterious and incredible work.

The Servant grows up without any attractive features (see NOTE on liii 2). He is not in a position which wins honor from men. This is not due merely to the fact that he is of humble estate; the words of vs. 3 describe one who is afflicted beyond the ordinary affliction of the poor and lowly. He is one who has been touched by the wrath of God; cf. Job xix 1–22. The person who suffered, according to the wisdom of the sages, was disclosed as a sinner, even if his sins were secret; the fact that he suffered was a manifest judgment of God upon his wickedness. Men avoid looking at him not only from repugnance but also from fear; it was dangerous to look upon one who lay under a curse. The secret the prophet discloses is that the curse may not lie upon the person who suffers; it may be the curse which lies upon another and has been transferred to the person who suffers. Indeed, the one who is cursed may not recognize his own curse in the person who bears it. The words of vss. 4–5 do not specify whether it is the pain of illness or the pain which comes from physical violence which is meant, and it seems that the prophet did not intend to specify; he describes a person who is subject to all kinds of pain. His point is that the one who suffers bears pains which are not his own in the sense that they are punishments for his sins, in the theory of traditional Wisdom literature. The sufferer is innocent; and this by itself, like the Book of Job, is a declaration that the simplistic explanation of suffering proposed by traditional wisdom is false.

But the Servant does not suffer fruitlessly. Because he suffers the pains of others, others are released from pain. It is here that the identity of the speaker and the group he represents creates a problem. On the hypothesis that the Servant is Israel, the group whose pains he bears must be understood as the nations, as Israel would not address itself. This, however, is a violent transfer of subject and of thought. There has been no spokesman of the nations in preceding passages; and there is nothing in the context which suggests that such a spokesman has suddenly appeared here. The prophet clearly sees an innocent Israelite who rescues his fellow Israelites from suffering by bearing their suffering himself. This interpretation can claim no more than probability. The interpretation which takes the kings and Gentiles as the speakers of the entire poem seems improbable for the reasons indicated above. If they are the speakers, then the first personal pronouns referring to those whose sufferings the Servant bears must indicate the Gentiles. This identification is not clearly found in the poem.

Verses 7–9 clearly go beyond the idea of illness; yet in the conception of the judgment of Yahweh, it is not impossible that the prophet represents in figured language the judgment of Yahweh; see NOTE on vs. 8. And in fact it seems better to take the verses in this sense; the prophet employs popular language, in which the suffering of the innocent would be called a "perverted judgment" of Yahweh. That none "was concerned with his case" is closely paralleled, but not verbally, in Third Isaiah (lvii 1). To make the suffering of the Servant more specific is to introduce problems which are insoluble; it is sufficient for the prophet's purpose that the Servant be the victim of an unjust judgment, whether this be the judgment of human courts or, in popular Israelite language, a judgment of Yahweh. In either case he bears the pains which are due to others, and by bearing them relieves them.

In vss. 5–6, the prophet recalls the idea of solidarity, which is not original with him. In the Decalogue both the sins and righteousness of the parents endure in following generations (Exod xx 5–6; Deut v 9–10). Abraham proposes that Sodom may be spared for the sake of a few righteous men within the city (Gen xviii 23–32). The presentation of the prophet differs from the older view only in its admission that the righteous may suffer. If they do, then the unrighteous members of their group may be delivered from suffering because the righteous have sustained it. This was a revolutionary view, for in traditional wisdom suffering was inflicted only upon those who deserved it, the guilty. The prophet takes a higher and a more realistic view of suffering; it becomes a medium of salvation to the community. Only the suffering of the righteous could be such a medium, for the suffering of the unrighteous would be no more than the satisfaction of vindictive justice. But the suffering of the innocent righteous has a "plus" value in the community. The righteous must be the means of salvation for the unrighteous, for the unrighteous cannot be the means of salvation for themselves. The prophet shows an insight into the solidarity of the human condition which goes beyond earlier expressions of this idea in the OT.

There is at least a difference of emphasis in Ezek xviii and xxxiii; Ezekiel insists that both righteous and wicked shall live or die for their own deeds. He denies the principle of collective responsibility insofar as it supposes that the innocent member of a wicked group suffers guilt by association. Ezekiel does not say in so many words that the righteous cannot deliver the wicked; his interest lies in the opposite direction, in the problem of the righteous suffering with the wicked. The author of the Song turns to the old, though much refined, principle of collective responsibility.

Verses 8–10 leave little doubt that the sufferings of the Servant ended in his death, whether by illness or by violence. That he was buried with the wicked need be no more than another figure of speech to show the low regard in which he was held (see Note on vs. 9). That he was counted with the unrighteous in a peculiar sense seems probable; see the comment above on the Wisdom explanation of suffering. In this view his crimes must have been great because his sufferings were great. If the legal metaphor is pursued, it means not only that the Servant bore the punishment of others, but that he was charged with their crimes.

In vs. 10 there is a sudden change of tone from mourning to exultation. In some way the Servant is delivered from death and from the charge of guilt because he has made himself a "guilt offering" (see Note on vs. 10). This he has done by taking upon himself the guilt of others and accepting the treatment due to the guilty. Delivery from death is a paradoxical element in a poem which is earlier than any attested belief in the resurrection. The Psalms sometimes speak of delivery from the danger of death as if it were a return from death (xviii 4–5, lxix 1–2, 14–15, lxxxviii 3–6). But it is difficult to understand vss. 8–9 as descriptions of the danger of death. The prophet must therefore be expressing without explanation or rationalization his faith that the saving work of the Servant cannot end in the total defeat of death. Unless he is vindicated in some way and knows that he is vindicated, justice would not be achieved. It does not appear that the prophet's words are explained by supposing that the Servant lives on in the group he has saved and their descendants. Nor does it appear that this aspect of the prophet's vision is readily identified with some historical figure. The scope both of the Servant's atoning suffering and of his vindication go beyond any historical persons or events of ancient Israel known to us. The prophet's utterances are concerned with a saving act that lies in the future; the saving act is often illustrated from the past, most frequently from the Exodus, but there is no past event that can be recognized here. The atonement of the Servant is a part of the future saving act, which the author of the Songs has not related to the saving act in Second Isaiah. There is no reason to think that he is being studiously obscure.

It is by his "knowledge" that the Servant delivers many. The knowledge meant must be the knowledge mentioned in Hos iv 1, 6. The phrase is somewhat obscure in Hosea, but it seems to mean the knowledge of Yahweh's will in his revealed law. This sense suits the context here. The concluding lines enlarge upon the triumph of the Servant, using words and phrases that have already appeared. The Servant's victory is described in military language in vs. 12, but this is obviously a metaphor; the Servant is certainly not a military hero, whatever he is. But he is one who will restore Israel as an enduring reality.

31. YAHWEH'S ENDURING LOVE
(liv 1–17)

LIV

1 "Sing, barren one, who has not borne; break out in song
   with a shrill cry, who has not been in labor;
   For many are the children of the abandoned one, more
   than the children of the married"—says Yahweh.

2 Enlarge the place of your tent, stretch^a out the curtains
   of your dwelling—do not hold back;
   Lengthen your tent ropes, fasten your pegs.

3 For you will break out to the right and to the left;
   Your race will possess nations,
   They will resettle wasted cities.

4 Do not fear, for you will not be ashamed; do not be
   diffident, for you will not be abashed;
   For the shame of your youth you will forget, and the dishonor of your widowhood you will no longer remember.

5 For your spouse^b is he who made you—Yahweh of hosts is
   his name;
   And your avenger is the Holy One of Israel—he is called
   the God of all the earth.

6 For like a forsaken wife, and one grieved of spirit Yahweh
   has called you;
   Like the rejected wife of one's youth—says your God.

7 "In a brief instant I abandoned you; but in great compassion I will gather you.

8 In a flood of wrath I hid my countenance from you;
   But in eternal love I had mercy on you"—says Yahweh
   your avenger.

_a Reading with the versions; Heb. "they will stretch."
_b Conjectural emendation suggested by the sense; Heb. plural.

9   "This is like the days of Noah for me:

When I swore that the waters of Noah should not pass over the earth again,

So I swore not to be angry at you, nor to rebuke you.

10   For the mountains may move, and the hills may totter;

But my love will not move from you, and my covenant of friendship will not totter"—

Says Yahweh, who has compassion on you.

11   "Afflicted one, storm-tossed, unpitied:

See, I lay your stones in turquoise,^{c} and your foundations in sapphires.

12   I make your pinnacles of rubies, your gates of beryl, and all your walls of precious stones.

13   All your sons are instructed by Yahweh, and great is the prosperity of your sons.

14   In righteousness you shall be established;

You shall be far^d from oppression, for you shall not fear,

And from terror, for it will not approach you.

15   If anyone assails you, it is not from me^e; whoever attacks you^f will fall on your account.

16   See, I have created the smith, who blows upon the charcoal fire, and produces a weapon for its purpose;

And I have created the destroyer for ruin.

17   The weapon that will succeed against you has not been forged,

And the tongue that rises in court against you shall be proved guilty;

This is the portion of the servants of Yahweh,

And their victory is from me"—

the oracle of Yahweh.

---

^{c} Conjectural emendation; Heb. "antimony."

^{d} If MT is read *raḥōḳî*, "to be far," absolute infinitive in *i*, no emendation is necessary to secure the translation (D. N. Freedman).

^{e} Conjectural emendation suggested by the sense; Heb. unintelligible.

^{f} Conjectural emendation; Heb. "with you."

Notes

liv 1. For the figure of the abandoned wife, see l 1.

4. *shame of . . . youth.* Probably the ancient sins of Israel (see xlviii 8); *dishonor of . . . widowhood* is the recent disaster of the fall of Jerusalem to the Babylonians in 587 B.C.

5–7. The thought of these verses echoes Hos ii 4–25. The prophet toys with the idea of divorce. Yahweh has abandoned Israel, but it is only a temporary separation. The prophet boldly represents Yahweh as yielding to a fit of anger.

6. *wife of one's youth.* A Hebrew phrase which echoes polygamy; it designates the first of the wives, the one who had the privileged position, and whom one married when one was still possessed of the passions of the young.

9. An echo of Gen ix 11, 15; these verses belong to the *P* strand of the Pentateuch. But in *P* the statement is a covenant, not an oath.

10. Cf. li 6.

11–12. The walls and gates of precious stones are reworked much more elaborately in Rev xxi 18–21. *beryl.* Hard, lustrous material: emerald and aquamarine are two examples of beryl.

13. *All your sons are instructed by Yahweh.* Echoes Jer xxxi 33–34, without Jeremiah's emphasis on the immediacy of the teaching.

15. *not from me.* Not by my doing, not with my consent.

fall on your account. I.e. because of what they did to you.

16. An affirmation of the sovereign providence of Yahweh. He creates the smith who makes the weapons for the aggressor, and a destroyer to match the aggressor.

Comment

Another of the Zion poems follows the fourth Servant Song. Zion is addressed in terms similar to those already used; see the Notes. The wife, hitherto barren, must quickly enlarge her tent for her fabulously numerous children; there is a probable allusion here to Sarah, the historic nomad wife from whom Israel first sprang. The promise in vs. 3 echoes the promises to Abraham, and adds a reference to more recent events; for the wasted cities are the cities of Judah, left mostly abandoned and in ruins (as archaeology attests).

The appeal to confidence is again based on the unquenchable love of Yahweh for Israel; see xlix 14–16, 1 1. Israel should know, and the prophet tells it, that it has done everything that would quench love. By an anthropopathism reminiscent of Hosea, the prophet describes Yahweh as yielding to a fit of anger. But Yahweh's anger is momentary; his love is enduring. The permanent separation of divorce is unthinkable. Yahweh's forgiveness is as irrevocable as the covenant of Noah, more enduring than even the mountains and hills. Passages like this must have been in the mind of Paul when he wrote such lines as Rom xi 29: "For the gifts and the call of God are irrevocable."

The promises to Zion now reach a point of magnificence that goes beyond any mere historical reality of the restoration of Jerusalem. The point of the imagery is that Yahweh is founding a lasting city, one that will not again suffer the fate of the Jerusalem of the monarchy. What would the prophet have said if he were told that the restored Jerusalem would be laid in ruins in 70 A.D. by the legions of Titus? But the vision of the prophet here approaches the eschatological; the lasting city of Yahweh's good pleasure is not a material reality of walls and buildings located at a definite point of longitude and latitude; it is the community of the redeemed, of all those who are "instructed of Yahweh" and are "established in righteousness." Such a community will outlast any material structure in which it happens to be incorporated at a given moment of history. This is the indestructible Jerusalem which no enemy can harm. The righteousness of Yahweh is a foundation stronger than any material foundation, proof against any human effort, even the effort of those who dwell in Jerusalem to corrupt it.

Although this may be a highly subjective judgment, it seems that the level of expression and poetry falls in vss 15–17. They expand the statement of the security of the new Jerusalem, but the expansion is not impressive. The lines become prosy, whether they are metrically structured or not. It is possible that they are the work of a commentator who wished to add his own enlargement of a theme left lightly treated by Second Isaiah.

32. YAHWEH'S ETERNAL COVENANT
(lv 1–13)

LV

1 "Ho there, all who thirst, come to the waters! You who lack
money, come!

Buy and eat*a* without money—and without paying, wine
and milk!

2 Why do you pay out money for no food, and your wages
for no satisfaction?

Listen carefully to me and eat well, and feed yourselves
full with delicacies.

3 Incline your ears, and come to me; listen, and you will
live.

I will make an eternal covenant with you—a work of my
faithful love for David.

4 See, I have made you*b* a witness to peoples, a prince
and ruler of peoples;

5 See, you will call a nation which you do not know*c*; those
who do not know you will run to you.

Because of Yahweh your God, and because of the Holy
One of Israel who glorifies you."

6 Seek Yahweh while you may find him, and invoke him
while he is near.

7 Let the wicked abandon his ways, and the villainous his
thoughts;

And let him return to Yahweh, who is merciful—to our
God, for he is generous to forgive.

---

a Omitting "and come and buy" of Heb.; 1QIs*a* omits these words and "and eat"
also.
b Reading with Syr.; Heb. "him."
c Heb. adds "nation"; omitted.

8 "For my thoughts are not your thoughts, nor your ways
   my ways"—the oracle of Yahweh.
9 "For the heavens are high above the earth;
   So my ways are high above your ways,
   And my thoughts above your thoughts.
10 For just as the rain and the snow come down from
   heaven,
   And do not return without watering the earth—
   Making it bring forth and sprout, and give seed for the
   sower and bread for the eater—
11 So it is with my word which proceeds from me; it shall
   not return to me unfulfilled;
   No, it will accomplish all that I wish, and achieve all for
   which I send it."
12 For you will go out with joy, and you will be led in
   security;
   The mountains and the hills will break out in joyous song
   before you, and the trees of the field will applaud.
13 Instead of thorns the cypress will grow, and instead of
   nettles the myrtle;
   And there will be a memorial for Yahweh, an eternal sign
   which shall not be cut down.

NOTES

lv 1–2. Begrich calls attention to the similarity between these lines
and an image from Wisdom literature in Prov ix 1–6 (*Studien zu
Deuterojesaja*, p. 52). In both instances the call to a banquet issues in a
call to attain life.

3. *eternal covenant*. A common phrase. Only here in II Isaiah is the
covenant of Israel associated with the covenant of David. The dynasty of
David was founded on a covenant with Yahweh which gathered into
itself the covenant of Israel; see Pss lxxxix 4, 29, 35, 40, cxxxii 12; II
Sam xxiii 5 (and II Sam vii 8–16, although the word covenant does not
occur there).

4. *witness*. Designates the mission of Israel in xliii 10, xliv 8.

prince and ruler. Should be understood to mean leadership exercised
by proclaiming Yahweh and not by political domination. The titles are

the titles of David transferred to Israel with a new meaning; see
COMMENT.

8–9. These verses echo the complaint of the Israelites in Ezek xviii 25,
29–30, xxxiii 17–18, 20. The prophets do not pretend that they can
make the providence of Yahweh intelligible. The manner in which Israel
is restored is not the manner in which Israel expected to be restored.

10–11. The word of Yahweh is personified as his messenger and
agent.

13. *memorial*. Literally "name," which could be translated "fame."
But the parallel, *sign,* suggests the metaphor of a memorial stone or
tablet. The lasting memorial of Yahweh, the visible sign of his work, is
Israel itself, the people he created and restored.

COMMENT

In this poem Yahweh is the speaker except for an interruption
by the prophet (vss. 6–7) and the concluding lines. The invitation
to come and get free food and drink recalls earlier biblical themes
such as the provision of manna and water in the desert sojourn and
Hosea's insistence that it is Yahweh alone who provides food, drink,
and clothing for Israel (Hos ii 10–11). The prophet no doubt looks
beyond material provisions, but food and drink are not a mere
metaphor for such things as revelation. Food and drink provided
by the deity have a wonderful character; and the fact that they are
provided attests that the relations between Yahweh and his people
are harmonious. It is true, in the words of Deut viii 3, that man does
not live by bread alone but by everything that proceeds from the
mouth of Yahweh; and this includes his spirit and his revelation.
But to accept the food of Yahweh as sufficient, and not to seek
laboriously elsewhere for food which does not satisfy, is to commit
oneself to faith in the saving power of Yahweh. From this food
man will live truly and fully; in Israelite thought both sin and
disaster were diminutions of life.

Only in vs. 3 is Israel associated with David in Second Isaiah; and
the allusion to David here contains no suggestion that Second Isaiah
sees a restored monarchy in restored Israel. But if Second Isaiah
knew the words of the covenant of David as we have them in II Sam
vii 11–16 and Ps lxxxix 28–37, he had a statement of the eternity of
a covenant to which there is no parallel in the formulae of the
covenants of Israel. The eternity of David's covenant is transferred

to the covenant with Israel restored. The prophet applies to Israel
here ideas most of which he has used previously. Israel has not been
called a prince and ruler of nations, and this seems to be a transfer
to Israel of titles given to David; see Pss lxxii 9–11, lxxxix 24–27.
But it was called Yahweh's witnesses in xliii 9–10. The character of
Israel's rule over the nations we have already seen: it consists in
Israel's position as mediator of faith in Yahweh (see COMMENT
on Secs. 21 [xlv 14–25] and 27 [specif. xlix 22–23 *ad loc.*]), and it
is explicit in the last line of vs. 5.

The prophet interrupts the discourse of Yahweh with a call to
"seek Yahweh" and to abandon sin (vss. 6–7). He does not specify
any sin, even idolatry. But he addresses an unregenerate community
which has not learned fully its lesson of judgment. "To seek
Yahweh" in early Israel meant to visit the sanctuary or to seek an
oracular response. Second Isaiah has gone far beyond this early and
simple view, as did the pre-exilic prophets when they used the same
phrase (Amos v 6, 14). To seek Yahweh here is to seek forgiveness
and to abandon a way of life.

Verses 8–9 resemble Ezek xviii 25–29. The lines refer to a
problem mentioned earlier, the difficulty raised concerning the way
of Yahweh's salvation; see xlv 9–13. But they refer to more than
this problem. Yahweh's saving purpose can be grasped and must
be accepted; but no one should be so rash as to think that he comprehends its entire scope. Yahweh cannot communicate his whole
purpose to man, for man is too small to understand it. Man must surrender to the truth that there are dimensions to the ways of Yahweh
that lie beyond revelation. Yahweh never stoops to the level of man,
or to the lower level of human prudence.

Verses 10–11 express the theme of the dynamic word of Yahweh,
the word which created and which governs the movement of history.
It is like a messenger or an agent vested with power; it never returns
with its mission unaccomplished. The Israelites can see it illustrated
in the rain. In Hebrew "word" and "deed" are expressed by a single
word; the unity of the two ideas is most impressive when it is the
word of Yahweh, for Yahweh's word is the externalization of his
person. Yahweh's words are acts; his acts are also words, for they
are intelligible and meaningful, even if, as is stated in vss. 8–9, they
escape the comprehension of man. This is the paradox of the word
of God, that it is both the most meaningful and the most mysterious
of words.

This is the last word of Yahweh in Second Isaiah. The prophet concludes with his final invitation to depart; see xlviii 20, lii 11–12. Nature applauds the display of the saving power of its creator; see xliv 23, xlix 13. The ruin of Edom described in xxxiv 13, experienced also by Jerusalem, will be reversed, and life will spring up where death reigned. For the supreme work of the word of Yahweh is to call to life.

IV. THIRD ISAIAH

33. THE REWARDS OF FIDELITY
(lvi 1–8)

LVI

1 Thus says Yahweh:
"Preserve justice, and do righteousness;
  For my victory is about to come, and my saving act to
  be revealed.

2 Happy the man who does this, and the son of man who
  is firm in it,
  Keeping the Sabbath from profanation, and guarding his
  hand from every evil deed."

3 Let not the foreigner who is joined to Yahweh say: "Yahweh has separated me from his people";
  Let not the eunuch say: "See, I am a withered tree."

4 For thus says Yahweh:
"To the eunuchs who keep my Sabbaths and choose what
  I wish, and who hold fast to my covenant,

5 I will give them in my house and within my walls a
  memorial and a name
  Better than sons and daughters; an eternal name I will
  give them,[a] which shall not be cut off.

6 And to foreigners who adhere to Yahweh, to minister to
  him and to love the name of Yahweh,
  To become his servants—all who keep the Sabbath from
  profanation, and who hold fast to my covenant,

7 I will bring them to my holy mountains, and I will make
  them glad in my house of prayer;

[a] Reading with the versions and 1QIs[a]; Heb. "him."

Their whole burnt offerings and their sacrifices they will
offer[b] for acceptance on my altar;
For my house will be called a house of prayer for all
nations."

8   The oracle of the Lord Yahweh, who gathers the dispersed of Israel:
"I will gather yet others to it, to those who are gathered."

[b] Inserting *ya'ᵃlû* with 1QIsᵃ; Heb. is awkward without a verb.

NOTES

lvi 3. There is no Israelite law which generally prohibited the admission of foreigners into the Israelite community. Deut xxiii 2–7 places
restrictions on the admission of members of certain peoples. A rigorous
attitude toward foreigners in the post-exilic community is seen in Ezra
ix–x and Neh xiii. Deut xxiii 1 prohibits the admission of men whose
sexual organs are maimed.

joined. Heb. *hannilwāh,* may contain a play on the name Levi; the
foreigners are admitted to cultic acts (vs. 7). This would imply that it is
the "joining" that makes the genuine worshiper of Yahweh, not merely
carnal descent from Levi.

COMMENT

At this point begins the section of the book called Third Isaiah; the
question of authorship and the reasons for adopting the view that it
is from another author than Second Isaiah are set forth in INTRO-
DUCTION, "Critical Questions," as are the reasons why these discourses are located in the Jerusalem community after the restoration
in 537 B.C. and before the reforms of Ezra and Nehemiah.

This discourse begins with a recommendation which employs
some of the favorite words of Second Isaiah, such as "victory" and
"saving act." If we locate and date the prophecies in post-exilic
Jerusalem, then the prophet does not regard the restoration itself
as the "victory" and the "saving act." And since the terms are borrowed, it seems useless to look for a more specific meaning. The
coming of salvation is associated with the observance of the Sabbath.
Unless critical conclusions concerning the pre-exilic prophets are

entirely in error, no such commendation of the Sabbath observance is found in the preaching of these prophets. The Sabbath observance becomes a characteristic feature of Judaism only after the Exile; it is not mentioned in Second Isaiah.

Without too rigorous a unity in structure, the prophet passes to the question of foreigners and eunuchs within the community. The law of Deut xxiii 1–8 prohibited eunuchs and certain foreign peoples from membership in the Israelite community. The Books of Ezra and Nehemiah are ample evidence that the post-exilic community of their time attempted to preserve itself from religious and cultural assimilation by excluding foreign members. This prophet assures both classes of full membership. To the eunuch he promises perpetual memory, a hope better than the hope cherished by the ancient Israelite and promised to Abraham, the hope of a numerous progeny. To foreigners he promises full participation in the cultic worship of Yahweh; the language presupposes either that the temple has been built (515 B.C.) or that the prophet expects it to be rebuilt. In either case, the temple is a theme that does not occur in Second Isaiah; see NOTES on xliv 28 and COMMENT (SEC. 19). The words used of the foreigners may suggest more than full participation; to "minister" to Yahweh (vs. 6) is normally to perform cultic functions reserved to the priests and the Levites. Many scholars believe that the slaves of the pre-exilic temple were foreigners. This was forgotten or ignored in the post-exilic temple, and rigid genealogical standards were established for priests and Levites. The same or another writer in this collection explicitly sees foreigners becoming priests and Levites (lxvi 21). This prophet need not be saying as much when he sees the temple becoming a house of prayer for all nations; it is an echo of what Second Isaiah had said (xlii 1–4, xlv 14–25, xlix 1–6 [SECS. 8, 21, 25]) without mentioning the temple.

Verse 8 (with its own introductory formula) is very probably a fragment, but not a fragment that has simply wandered here. That the oracle is meant of the nations is not clear either from the oracle or from the introduction; but it seems probable that it refers to the ingathering of Israel. The author or editor of the preceding discourse has attached the verse here because its obscurity permits "the others" yet to be gathered to refer to the nations; and thus it confirms the preceding lines.

This brief passage illustrates the dangers of generalizing about post-exilic legalism. Certainly the recommendation of the Sabbath with no mention of any other obligation to Yahweh shows what is meant by post-exilic legalism. Yet in the same passage a breadth of outlook toward the nations is reached that is not reached in equally specific terms in Second Isaiah. Third Isaiah was a disciple and an editor; and he applies the principles of Second Isaiah less generally and in less elevated poetry to quite specific points.

34. THE FAITHLESS WATCHMEN
(lvi 9–12; lvii 1–2)

LVI

9 "All you beasts of the field, come to eat—all you beasts of
the forest.

10 Its watchmen are blind, none of them know;
All of them are dumb dogs, they cannot bark;
They dream, they lie down, they love to slumber.

11 They are greedy dogs, they cannot be filled;
And these are shepherds who understand nothing;
All of them go their own way, each after his own gain.*a*

12 'Come, let us*b* have wine; let us drink deeply of strong
drink;
And tomorrow will be like today—more! Much more!'"

LVII

1 The righteous perishes, and no one gives it a thought;
Men of good will are taken off, and no one perceives*c*
That the righteous is taken away from evil; 2 he arrives at
security.
They rest upon their beds, those who walk straight.

a Heb. adds, "to the last"; omitted with LXX.
b Reading plural with 1QIs*a*; Heb. singular.
c Omitting the preposition *beth* gives an easy sense and a parallel to the first
line. *Beth* is used with the infinitive construct in a sense that would suit the
context, but there is no example of this use with the participle.

NOTES

lvi 9. *beasts of the field*. Foreign nations who are invited to invade Israel. D. N. Freedman calls attention to archaic features of the language of this verse: *ḥayᵉtô*, "beast," and the use of the preposition *beth* in the middle of a construct chain: "beasts of the forest."

10. *They dream*. Heb. *hōzîm*, is a hapax legomenon; 1QIsª and some Hebrew manuscripts have the more common *ḥōzîm*. But "see visions" hardly suits the context, unless it be translated as we have translated MT.

12. For the callous words of the revelers (Muilenburg suggests that they are a fragment of drinking song), see Isa xxii 13, quoted in I Cor xv 32, and Wisdom of Solomon ii 6–9.

strong drink. Probably beer.

lvii 1. The lines are obscure, but the sense seems to be that the death of the righteous brings them into security. This is a paradoxical thought in most of the OT; but see Job iii 13–19.

COMMENT

There is no obvious connection between this poem and lvi 1–8; in most of Third Isaiah the pieces are simply strung together. The invitation to the wild beasts is usually taken as addressed to foreign nations. Foreign nations had been the weapons of Yahweh's judgments from the time of Israel's settlement in Canaan; the prophet sees the post-exilic community of Israel ripe for judgment once more. This is surely a decline from the high hopes and promises of Second Isaiah. The "watchmen" (vs. 10) are the religious leaders of the community, not necessarily the prophets alone; the post-exilic community lived under priestly leadership. The meager sources for the history of the post-exilic community give no information which enables us to fill out this picture. In a period which must be later than this passage, Nehemiah attacked the kind of abuse which could be meant here, and the priests were involved (Neh v 1–13, xiii 4–14). The leaders are charged with avarice and with failure to fulfill their duty of leadership; the priests do not teach the Torah, and the prophets do not speak the word of Yahweh. The greed of those who feast when their brothers are in need rouses the prophet's scorn, and he caricatures them. More than this, they are indifferent to the death of good men. Isa lvii 1 may be an echo of liii 8. The prophet does not suggest that the "righteous" and the "men of good will" perish by violence, though what we know of life in the post-exilic community in its earliest phases suggests that it was a grim and precarious existence. The leaders of this community were not only religious leaders, but administrators of local affairs. But the community was not organized on what the prophet thought was a sound religious basis; it also lacked competent and honest administration of its temporal needs. Ironically the prophet says that the righteous can find rest only in death; and any one who sees this should recognize how serious the situation is.

35. REBUKE OF SUPERSTITION
(lvii 3–13)

LVII

3 "But you, come here, sons of a sorceress, offspring of an adulterer and a prostitute!*a*

4 At whom do you jest? At whom do you open wide your mouth, stick out your tongue?
Are you not children of guilt, a lying race?

5 You who are inflamed with passion under great trees, and under every spreading leafy tree,
Who slaughter children in the stream beds, in*b* the clefts of the rocks.

6 In the smooth stones of the stream bed is your portion; yes, these are your allotment.
To these you have poured libations, you have brought offerings;
Shall I change my mind on account of these?

7 On a high and lofty mountain you have spread your couch; yes, there you have offered victims.

8 Behind the door and the doorpost you have set up your memorial;
For leaving me,*c* you have uncovered yourself, mounted your bed, and spread it wide;

a Reading with the versions; Heb. "and she fornicated."
b Reading with LXX; Heb. "under."
c "Leaving me," literally "apart from me," is unsatisfactory, but no other translation is possible, and no emendation has been suggested. D. N. Freedman, following M. Dahood, proposes a verbal form derived from *mĕ'āh*, meaning "to do a hundred times." This creation seems excessively bold, bolder than our translation of MT.

You have made a league with those whose couch you love, you have looked on the symbol.

9 You went down to the king with oil, you put on abundant ointments;

You sent your messengers a great distance, you made them go down to Sheol.

10 You were fatigued with the length of the journey, but you did not say, 'It is no use';

You found your strength, and so you did not become weak.

11 Whom did you fear, or of whom were you afraid when you were treacherous to me,

When you did not remember me, when you did not give me a thought?

Was I not silent? Did I not close my eyes?[d] And you had no fear of me.

12 I will declare your righteousness and your deeds—which did you no good.

13 When you cry out, let your abominations[e] save you; the wind will carry them all away, breath will take them off.

But he who seeks refuge in me will inherit the land; he will take possession of my holy mountain."

[d] This translation involves a different vocalization of MT, indicated by LXX.
[e] Reading *šiḳḳūṣîm* for Heb. *ḳibbūṣîm*, a non-word.

NOTES

lvii 3. The *sorceress, adulterer,* and *prostitute* must be Israel personified; it is rare in prophetic literature that so many abusive epithets are found in a single line. The epithets echo Ezek xvi and xxiii.

4. The derisive gestures are directed to the prophet, but they reach Yahweh himself.

5. The verse alludes to the fertility rites conducted on the high places, using terms found elsewhere; the phrase *leafy tree* is used in the OT only in allusions to the high places. The *slaughter* of *children* alludes to child sacrifices; see Jer vii 3, xxxii 35; Lev xviii 21, xx 2–4; II Kings xxiii 10.

6. *the smooth stones.* Probably stones chosen for their shape and size to be set up as symbols of the male fertility deity, the *maṣṣēbot.* Yahweh was the portion of Levi (Josh xiii 33); that Israel now chooses other gods as its portion is not a clear implication that the Levites are particularly implied here.

7. The allusion to the fertility couch resembles Jer ii 20, but is slightly less candid.

8. The allusions in this verse are obscure. The *memorial* must be a cultic emblem.

symbol. "Hand" literally may also signify an emblem, although some suggest that it means the phallus; but there is no other instance of this use of the word.

9. *the king.* A divine title applied to many deities in ancient Semitic religions. The context suggests a god of the underworld, and very probably Melkart of Tyre is meant or hinted at. Sending messengers to Sheol suggests the seeking of oracular responses from the gods of the underworld; see xlv 19.

13. *abominations.* A contemptuous designation of divine images.

COMMENT

This discourse does not follow in theme and content the preceding discourse. It begins with a series of abusive terms addressed to the Israelites. In the general hypothesis we accept concerning the origin of Third Isaiah, these invectives are addressed to the post-exilic community of Palestine. But the allusions to superstitious cults and rites attested for pre-exilic Judah (see the NOTES) have led many scholars to suggest that this is a piece of pre-exilic prophecy, which has found its way into a collection of more recent prophecies (Volz, *Jesaia II,* pp. 212–13). The hypothesis is not impossible; but there is no way to be sure that these superstitious rites did not persevere in post-exilic Judah, in particular in the period to which we attach Third Isaiah. That fertility rites of some kind are described seems to admit no doubt. There are also allusions to necromancy; see the NOTES. There are no explicit references to these superstitions in other post-exilic literature; but there is no difficulty in supposing that the theological and cultic condition of the early post-exilic community was primitive (Elliger, *Die Einheit des Tritojesaja,* pp. 77–85). Such rites could well have been practiced by those who lived in the land after the Babylonian wars; there seems to have been no center in the country which would have preserved genuine Yahwism. Jer xliv describes the recrudescence of the cult of the Queen of Heaven among those who had escaped the disaster of conquest. The discourse of Third Isaiah here is not substantially different from the discourse of Jeremiah reported in Jer xliv. The superstitious have no fear because Yahweh has not acted against them; it is quite possible that this is an allusion to the comparative security enjoyed in Judah after the Babylonian wars. To paraphrase: Let these unbelievers know that the land is not for them, but for those who have preserved the Israelite faith free from contamination by foreign cults. Israel is still the land of Yahweh, and it belongs to the people of Yahweh.

36. PUNISHMENT AND FORGIVENESS
(lvii 14–21)

LVII

14 One says:
    "Build it, build it, pave the way! Take every obstacle away
      from the way of my people!"

15 For thus says the Most High, the Exalted, whose dwelling
      is eternal and whose name is holy:
    "I dwell in the holy heights, but also with the oppressed
      and lowly,
    To restore spirit to the lowly, to revive the heart of the
      oppressed.

16 For I will not prosecute forever, nor will I be angry with-
      out end;
    For the spirit would grow faint before me, and the souls
      I have made.

17 Because of his violent injustice I was vexed, and I struck
      him, hiding my face in anger;
    And he went off wandering in his own way.

18 I saw his ways; I will heal him and give him rest[a];
    I will fill him with consolation,

19 Creating for his mourners the fruit of the lips.
    Peace, peace! to far and near"—says Yahweh—"and I will
      heal him."

20 But the wicked are like the raging sea, which cannot be
      quiet;
    Its waters toss up refuse and mud.

21 "There is no peace," says my God, "for the wicked."

[a] The translation is achieved by changing the vocalization of MT $w^{e'}anḥēhû$, "I will lead," to $w^{e'}anîḥēhû$; suggested by D. N. Freedman.

NOTES

lvii 14. An allusion to the wonderful road of return; see § 2 (xxxv). In spite of the ambiguous introduction, the words are best attributed to Yahweh, particularly because of the phrase *my people* (Elliger).

15. *the holy heights*. Echoes the mountain of the dwelling of the gods, Mount Saphon, known from Ugaritic mythology; see lviii 14. It is remarkable that the prophet does not allude to the dwelling of Yahweh in the temple of Jerusalem, the counterpart of the heavenly temple.

16. *spirit*. Here weaker than its older meaning, simply designates the vital force in man.

souls. Synonymous with "persons," but literally means "breaths."

17–18. Israel is the antecedent of the pronouns.

19. *his mourners*. The survivors of Israel who are saddened by the catastrophe. The *fruit of the lips* is the prayer of praise and thanksgiving for restoration. The *far* and the *near* are the Israelites scattered to other countries as a result of the disasters of war.

20–21. It is not clear whether *the wicked* are faithless Israelites or the nations hostile to Israel. Verse 21, glossed in xlviii 22 (§ 24), is in place here.

COMMENT

This poem begins with an echo of Second Isaiah (xxxv 8–10). But the poet is not thinking of the return from Babylon; he is thinking of the road by which Israel is to travel toward salvation. The answer of Yahweh to this exclamation takes a different turn; it is an affirmation that Yahweh dwells with "the oppressed and lowly" (vs. 15). This reflects what is called "the piety of the lowly," characteristic of the post-exilic community. This community recognized that it lacked even the splendor of the pre-exilic kingdom of Judah, which itself was a less important member of the nations of the ancient Near East. In the post-exilic community a difference arose between the wealthy and the poor, the lowly; and "the piety of the poor," following the teaching of the pre-exilic prophets, identified Yahweh with the cause of the poor.

The prevailing poverty of the post-exilic community was a result of the judgment of Yahweh on the monarchy of Judah; and this the prophet recalls in vss. 16–18. But should the wrath of Yahweh destroy his people, it would fail of its purpose. The issue of the wrath of Yahweh must be not destruction but healing. The purpose of the acts of Yahweh must ultimately be "peace," that state of security and well-being, both outward and inward, which was the ideal of the ancient Israelite. This prophet, however, does not look simply to the community as a whole. There is a hope of peace for the righteous, even if the wicked destroy their own opportunities for peace. The prophets of post-exilic Israel do not envisage a situation where the corruption of the major portion of the community will bring the entire community to ruin. The refrain of vs. 21 appears in xlviii 22, where it is out of place; see NOTE *ad loc.* and COMMENT (SEC. 24). Here it follows naturally on the preceding line, which speaks of peace as the work of the healing of Yahweh. This peace cannot reach others than the righteous.

37. TRUE FASTING
(lviii 1–14)

1 "Speak out with full voice, do not hold back; lift up your
   voice like a horn;
   Declare to my people their guilt, to the house of Israel
   their sins.

2 Day by day they seek me; they delight to know my
   ways,
   Like a nation that does righteousness, and has not abandoned the law of its God.
   They inquire of me for just judgments; they are happy
   that God is near."

3 "Why do we fast, and you do not see it? Why do we afflict
   ourselves, and you do not know it?"
   "Look, on your fast day you pursue your own profit, and you
   drive all your workers hard.

4 Look, you fast amid strife and contention, while you
   strike the poor^a with the fist;
   You do not fast today so as to make your voice heard on
   high.

5 Is this the fast which I will accept? When a man afflicts
   himself,
   And bows down his head like a rush, and spreads sackcloth
   and dust for his couch?
   Do you call this a fast, a day which pleases Yahweh?

6 Is not this the fast which I will accept?
   To loose the fetters of injustice, to remove the bands
   of the yoke;

^a Reading with the versions; Heb. "the guilty."

To set free the oppressed, to break every yoke?

7   Is it not to share your food with the starving, to admit to your house the homeless poor?

To clothe the naked when you see him, and not to withdraw yourself from your own kind?

8   Then your light will burst out like the dawn, and your healing will be quick;

Your righteousness will march before you, and the glory of Yahweh will march behind you.

9   Then you will cry out, and Yahweh will answer you; you will call for help, and he will say, 'Here I am.'

If you remove the yoke from among you, the pointing of the finger, and malicious speech,

10   If you give yourself to the hungry, and satisfy the desires of the afflicted,

Your light will rise in the darkness, and your gloom will become like noonday.

11   Yahweh will guide you always; he will sate you in the desert;

He will renew*b* your strength, and you will be like a well-watered garden,

Like a flowing spring whose waters are never exhausted.

12   They will build on your ancient ruins; you will raise up your age-old foundations;

You will be called the repairer of breaches, the restorer of ruined dwellings."*c*

13   "If you restrain your foot on*d* the Sabbath from doing*e* your business on my holy day,

If you call the Sabbath delightful, and Yahweh's holy day honorable,

If you honor it by refraining from business, from pursuing gain and from excessive talk,

b Conjectural emendation suggested by the sense; Heb. "he will strip off."
c Conjectural emendation suggested by the sense; Heb. "paths."
d The translation supposes no emendation; the prepositions *beth* and *min* frequently coincide in meaning, especially in poetry (D. N. Freedman).
e Conjectural emendation; Heb. "to do."

14   Then you will delight in Yahweh, and I will make you
     ride upon the heights of the earth;
     And I will feed you from the inheritance of Jacob your
     father—for the mouth of Yahweh has spoken."

NOTES

lviii 1. *horn.* The ram's horn used in ancient Israel as a summons to
war and to cultic assembly. Verse 1b imitates Mic iii 8.

2. *inquire.* A formal ritual petition.

3. In the OT, fasting is mentioned only as a sign of sorrow, as in the
ritual of mourning, and not as an ascetic practice. In Israelite cultic
law no fast is prescribed except the fast of the Day of Atonement (Lev
xvi 29–31, xxiii 27–32; Num xxix 7).

5. The wearing of *sackcloth* and the smearing of one's self with *dust*
and ashes were also parts of the ritual of mourning.

8. See lii 12.

9. *pointing of the finger.* Insulting gesture.

13. The *Sabbath* seems an afterthought, and these lines may be a
secondary addition to the original poem. The ideal of Sabbath observance proposed here is found in no other passage of the OT. In the
post-exilic period, the Sabbath became a day of genuine religious joy. It
is mentioned in rabbinical literature. The Sabbath observance was not
a burden: it liberated man for a meeting with God.

excessive talk. Renders Heb. *dabbēr dābār.* D. N. Freedman points
out that talking was not prohibited on the Sabbath, and suggests that the
phrase should be understood of legal processes. This meaning of the
phrase is without example. The phrase is difficult; and if the translation
is retained, there is probably an implication of idle talk.

14. *the heights of the earth.* Elsewhere—Deut xxxii 13; Amos iv 13;
Mic i 3—heights upon which Yahweh treads or upon which he makes
others tread. They are the mythological mountains upon which the
gods dwell. The ambiguity of the speaker becomes acute in this verse,
as the use of Yahweh and the first person shows. This ambiguity is
noticed elsewhere in Third Isaiah. 1QIs^a reads the third person, but the
ambiguity is not thereby removed. One may suppose a double recension,
which has been conflated (D. N. Freedman); but at the root of the
problem there seems to be a stylistic trait of some of the writers whom
we group as Third Isaiah.

COMMENT

This poem is constructed as a dialogue between Yahweh and the Israelites. The opening line is addressed to the prophet, but he does not speak in his own name in the course of the poem. The reproach is directed to the attitude which conceives the service of Yahweh as fulfilled by cultic observances; see SEC. 15 (xliii 22–28) and COMMENT. The Israelites "seek" (vs. 2) Yahweh by the cult of the temple; the "ways" they delight to know are not the "ways" of covenant law but the procedures of ritual cult. These stand in antithesis to "righteousness" and "law" (literally "judgment"). The "just judgments" they seek are the vindication of Israel, its prosperity and protection from harm. These are sought by the ritual of mourning, which is also the ritual of repentance; but in spite of the ritual of repentance, the community still suffers poverty and insecurity.

The prophet attacks the community in the tone of the pre-exilic prophets, and for one of the glaring faults so often mentioned by these prophets: the oppression of the poor and helpless by the rich. Even though the post-exilic community as a whole was a poor and struggling group, differences had arisen between the few who had most of the wealth and the mass of the population; see COMMENT on SEC. 34 (lvi 9; lvii 2). The prophet caricatures the ritual of the fast, which is carried on without interruption in the pursuit of gain. The prophet presents a brief ideal picture of a community in which common needs are supplied by common assistance; the passage could well serve as the original sketch from which Matt xxv 31–46 was composed. Should the community act in this way, the salvation which has been delayed will come quickly; the prophet describes its coming in terms drawn from Second Isaiah (see the NOTE on vs. 8). These allusions suggest that the prophet and others, reflecting on the poems of Second Isaiah and contrasting them with the miserable conditions of restored Jerusalem and Judah, explained the contrast by appealing to the failure of the community to exhibit the moral regeneration for which Second Isaiah called. The community seemed to have learned nothing from the preaching of the pre-exilic prophets, nor from the judgment which had fallen on Israel for its failure to create a true community. The restoration was not the fulfillment of the great saving act promised by Second Isaiah, nor could that saving act occur as long as Israel remained what it was. This theme occurs in other poems of Third Isaiah; it is his restatement of the preaching of Second Isaiah, applied to the resurgent people of Israel. Verse 12 suggests that the rebuilding of Jerusalem and the cities of Judah had not advanced very far at the time the prophet spoke—a constant visible sign that the salvation had not arrived. Muilenburg notices no mention of temple or sacrifice.

The lines on the Sabbath are probably a secondary expansion; see NOTE on vs. 13.

38. GUILT AND JUDGMENT
(lix 1–21)

LIX

1 See, the hand of Yahweh is not too short to save, nor his ear too dull to hear;

2 No, it is your wrongdoing that has divided you from your God;

   And your sins have hidden his face so that he does not hear.

3 For your hands are defiled with blood, and your fingers with guilt;

   Your lips speak lies, and your tongue mutters wickedness.

4 No one pleads justly, no one judges faithfully;

   They rely on unreality, they speak falsehood; they are pregnant with trouble and bring forth evil.

5 They hatch vipers' eggs and weave spiders' webs;

   He who eats their eggs dies, and when one is broken a snake bursts forth.

6 Their webs will not serve for clothing, nor can one use their works as covering;

   Their works are works of wickedness, and deeds of violence are in their hands.

7 Their feet run to evil; they hasten to shed innocent blood;

   Their plans are wicked plans; they leave a trail of plundered ruins.

8 The way of peace they do not know; there is no justice in their course;

   They travel on crooked paths; he who walks on it knows no peace.

9 Therefore justice is remote from us, and righteousness has
    not overtaken us;
    We wait for the light, but look! it is dark—for bright-
    ness, but we walk in obscurity.

10 We feel our way along the wall like blind men; we grope
    like the sightless;
    We stumble at high noon as if it were dusk; *we live in
    darkness* like the dead.

11 We groan like bears, all of us; we moan mournfully like
    doves;
    We look for justice, but there is none—for deliverance, but
    it is far from us.

12 For our crimes are many before you, and our sins bear
    witness against us;
    For our crimes are with us, and we know our wrongdoing:

13 Rebellion and denial of Yahweh—and we have been faith-
    less to our God;
    Speaking perfidy*b* and treachery, and*c* muttering lying
    words in the heart.

14 Justice is driven back, and righteousness stands off at a
    distance;
    For fidelity stumbles in the street, and sincerity cannot
    enter.

15 Justice is found missing, and he who turns from evil is
    plundered.
    And Yahweh saw, and it was evil in his sight that there
    was no justice.

16 He saw that there was no man, and he was astonished
    that there was no one to make entreaty;
    His own arm brought him victory, and his own righteous-
    ness sustained him.

17 He put on righteousness like a coat of mail, and the
    helmet of salvation was on his head;

---

a–a Conjectural emendation; Heb. unintelligible.
b Conjectural emendation based on Targ.; Heb. "oppression."
c Heb. adds "conceiving"; omitted.

Garments[d] of vengeance are his dress, and he wrapped
himself in jealousy like a mantle.

18 According to deeds he will repay: wrath to his adversaries,
due recompense to his enemies.[e]

19 They will see[f] the name of Yahweh in the west, and in
the east his glory.
For he will come like a rushing river, which the wind of
Yahweh drives.

20 And he will come as an avenger to Zion, to those who
turn from sin in Jacob—the oracle of Yahweh.

21 "But as for me, this is my convenant with them,"[g] says
Yahweh: "my spirit which is upon you, and my words
which I have put in your mouth shall not depart from
your mouth nor from the mouth of your children nor
from the mouth of your children's children"—says
Yahweh—"now and forever."

[d] The text is commonly emended by the omission of *tilbōšet*, "garment," a
hapax legomenon, as a gloss. D. N. Freedman suggests that a rare word is
probably not used as a gloss; and that the omission of *wayyilbaš*, "he put on"
at the beginning of the line as a dittography from the preceding line gives an
almost perfect chiastic structure for the four cola of this verse. This reading
is unquestionably superior.
[e] Heb. adds, "He will repay the isles"; omitted.
[f] Reading with some manuscripts; Heb. "fear."
[g] Reading *'ittām* with 1QIs[a] for MT *'ôtām*, "them" (accusative).

NOTES

lix 1. An echo of l 2.

4. *pregnant*, and *bring forth*. Refer to the female; but this is the only
instance in the entire OT in which *hôlîd*, "beget (children)," is used of
the female. Were the two sexes meant by the two verbs, one would expect an inversion of the order.

5–6. The "nothingness" of evil deeds is a common theme in prophetic
and Wisdom literature. This description of the sinners can be compared
to Prov i 10–19.

10. For the figure of darkness and blindness as symbols of disaster,
see Deut xxviii 29; Jer xiii 16; Amos v 18, 20.

11. The metaphors used in this verse are unusual—in fact do not appear in any other passage of the Bible.

15–20. Elliger (*Die Einheit des Tritojesaja*, p. 19) points out that these verses correspond to the favorable oracle of Yahweh; which normally concludes the literary form of the lamentation. The phrase *the oracle of Yahweh* (vs. 20) always follows a direct speech of Yahweh. But Yahweh is not the speaker of these lines, and the literary form is not a sufficient reason to emend the text to the first person.

17. The figure of the divine attributes as a suit of armor is imitated in Wisdom of Solomon v 17–23. In the NT the Christian virtues are described as a suit of armor in Eph vi 14–17; I Thess v 8.

19. The Assyrian advance is compared to a river in flood in Isa viii 7–8.

21. This verse appears to be a secondary expansion. It introduces a different theme and comes after the concluding formula, "the oracle of Yahweh." The language echoes II Sam xxiii 2; Jer i 9; Isa li 16; Ezek xxxvi 26–27. The thought is related to Jer xxxi 33–34.

On the *spirit;* see xliv 3 and NOTE.

COMMENT

This poem, except for vs. 21, forms an obvious unity. The prophet opens as if in answer to the question, "Why is our salvation delayed?" In the preceding poems there has been a contrast between the promises of Second Isaiah and the wretched post-exilic community of Palestine. Just as Second Isaiah had to deal with those who doubted his promises, so does Third Isaiah deal with a later generation of doubters. Yahweh either does not hear the prayers of Israel and has abandoned Israel, or he is too feeble to answer prayer, and he does not deserve worship. The prophet returns to the classic answer of prophecy. Neither weakness nor hostility in Yahweh is responsible for present conditions; it is sin and only sin which delays the arrival of salvation.

The sins mentioned are of the same character as the sins mentioned in lviii 3–4, 6, 9; but the prophet describes a deeper evil. Mutual confidence has broken down in the community; no man can trust another. This is an old prophetic complaint (Jer ix 4–5). The "blood" of vs. 3 must refer to bloodshed; certainly this is meant in vs. 7. The reflections of vss. 5–6 have the tone of Wisdom literature. The prophet is not denying that sin is successful; he means that evildoing ultimately accomplishes nothing, that it creates no value. Ultimately, of course, the sinner fails; this is a maxim of Wisdom.

But in the conditions in which the prophet was living, sin was very successful. The prophet does not distinguish between the leading men of the community and others, but there is no doubt that his accusations are primarily directed against those whose power and responsibility are the greatest.

Verses 9–14 belong to the type of poem known as "community lamentation," of which several examples appear in the Psalms. The prayer is a petition for "justice" and "righteousness," which may mean deliverance or the restoration of law and order within the community. It is probably in the sense of deliverance that the words are used in the lamentation; in vss. 14–15 the sense of law and order seems to appear. The enumeration of vices in vs. 13 adds to sins against truth and honesty the sin of rebellion and denial of Yahweh. It is unlikely that this means renunciation of the cult of Yahweh for other religions, although, as we have noticed in lvii 3–9, there is evidence of the recrudescence of superstitious cults. The rebellion and the denial are here seen as being the refusal to accept the moral will of Yahweh. Thus justice, righteousness, fidelity, and sincerity, the ingredients of Yahweh's moral will and the qualities which establish a morally integral community, are excluded.

Conditions are so appalling that a divine intervention is necessary; the situation is beyond merely human remedy. The prophet sees a theophany, a coming of Yahweh in power and majesty. Here he echoes the coming of Yahweh promised in Second Isaiah, but Yahweh comes also as a judge against those elements in Israel which have resisted salvation. For the theme of judgment, see the COMMENT on SEC. 1 (xxxiv). The theophany, like the saving act of Second Isaiah, will be manifested to all the world.

We treat vs. 21 as a secondary expansion; see the NOTE.

39. THE GLORY OF THE NEW JERUSALEM
(lx 1–22)

LX

1 "Arise, shine; for your light has come; and the glory of
Yahweh has risen on you.

2 For see, darkness covers the earth, and blackness the
peoples;
But Yahweh rises upon you, and his glory will appear over
you.

3 Nations will walk to your light, and kings to your rising
brightness.

4 Lift your eyes about you, and see; all of them assemble,
they come to you;
Your sons come from afar, and your daughters are carried in the arms.

5 Then you will see, you will beam; your heart will tremble
and expand;
For the riches of the sea will be turned to you; the wealth
of nations will come to you.

6 A horde of camels will cover you, the young camels of
Midian and Ephah;
All of them will come from Sheba; they will bear gold
and incense;
And they will announce the praise of Yahweh.

7 The flocks of Kedar will all be gathered to you; the rams
of Nebaioth will be at your service;
They will be acceptable victims on my altar; and I will
glorify my glorious house.

a–a Reading *lᵉrāṣôn al* with LXX, some Heb. manuscripts, and 1QIsᵃ for Heb.
'al rāṣôn.

8   Who are these that fly like a cloud, like doves to their
    dovecotes?
9   For the *ships are assembled* for me, the vessels of
    Tarshish at their head,
    To bring your sons from afar, their silver and their gold
    with them,
    For the name of Yahweh your God, and for the Holy
    One of Israel who glorifies you.
10 Foreigners will build your walls, and their kings will serve
    you;
    For in my anger I struck you, but in my benevolence I have
    compassion on you.
11 Your gates will always be open; day and night they shall
    not be closed,
    To admit the wealth of nations to you, with their kings
    as drivers.*
12 For the nation and the kingdom that do not serve you
    will perish, and the nations shall be utterly wasted.
13 The glory of Lebanon will come to you—the juniper, the
    box tree, and the cypress together—
    For the glory of my holy place, that I may honor the
    place where I stand.
14 The sons of your oppressor shall come to you bowed down;
    all those who insulted you shall prostrate themselves
    at your feet;
    They shall call you the city of Yahweh, Zion of the Holy
    One of Israel.
15 Where you have been abandoned, unloved, and help-
    less,* I will make you grand forever, a joy from age
    to age.
16 You will suck the milk of nations, you will suck the
    breasts* of kings;

---

b–b Conjectural emendation suggested by the sense; Heb. "the isles await."
c Conjectural emendation suggested by the sense; Heb. passive.
d Conjectural emendation based on LXX; Heb. "with none passing through."
e Reading *šad* for *šōd*, "plunder."

And you will know that I Yahweh am your deliverer—
your avenger is the Strong One of Jacob.

17 For bronze I will bring gold, and for iron I will bring
silver;
And for wood, bronze; and for stones, iron.
I will establish Peace as your administration, and Righteousness as your government.

18 Violence shall no longer be heard in your land, pillage
and ruin in your territory;
But you shall call your walls Salvation, and your gates
Praise.

19 The sun shall no longer be your light by day, nor will the
brightness of the moon shine on you at night*;
But Yahweh will be your perpetual light, and your God
will be your splendor.

20 Your sun will never set, and your moon will never wane;
For Yahweh will be your perpetual light, and the days of
your mourning are finished.

21 All of your people will be righteous; they will possess their
land forever—
A shoot of Yahweh's planting,* the work of his* hands
for his ornament.

22 The little one shall become a clan, the small one a
mighty nation; I Yahweh will hasten it in its due time."

f Reading "at night" with the versions and 1QIs*; missing in MT.
g Heb. "his planting" is impossible; 1QIs* has the same impossible form, but
adds "Yahweh."
h Reading "his" with LXX and 1QIs*; Heb. "my."

Notes

lx 2. The language echoes Isa ix 1, which describes the darkness just
before the birth of the messianic prince.

3. The prophet sees the fulfillment of Isa ii 2–3; Mic iv 1–2.

4. *Your sons . . . your daughters.* Israelites in exile.

5. Hag ii 6–9 sees the wealth of nations brought to the temple of
Zerubbabel. This temple, the "Second Temple" was built in 515 B.C. It
was replaced by Herod's Temple, begun 19 B.C.

6. Camels were freight carriers; thus an abundance of camels means an abundance of wealth.

Midian. A nomadic Arabian tribe that appears in Israelite history from earliest times.

Ephah. Mentioned only in Gen xxv 4 and I Chron i 33, both times in association with Midian.

Sheba. Both a tribe and a region; the kingdom of Sheba in southwestern Arabia was a great trading center in ancient times.

7. *Kedar.* See NOTE on xlii 11.

The *Nebaioth* were also a nomadic Arabian tribe, mentioned rarely in the OT but very probably identical with a name mentioned in the records of Ashurbanipal (668–630 B.C.); they are not the Nabataeans of the Hellenistic and Roman periods. The Arabian tribes bring incense and flocks, important elements in the sacrificial ritual.

9. The "ship of Tarshish" was a large heavy vessel built for long voyages with high tonnage. *Tarshish* was not a place but an industrial installation, a metal refinery (W. F. Albright, BASOR 83 [1941], 14 ff.). On the extensive dispersion of Israelites implied here, see the NOTE on xliii 5.

10. The second line of the verse echoes liv 7.

11. Echoed in Rev xxi 25.

13. *The glory of Lebanon* is the cedar; see xxxv 2 and NOTE *the place where I stand.* I.e. Jerusalem.

14. The new Jerusalem receives a new name, as Ezekiel's new Jerusalem has (Ezek xlviii 35).

16. The metaphor is somewhat violent.

17. In the first lines of this verse, a more costly material is substituted for each of the plainer materials. This is a figure of the wealth of the new Jerusalem. *Peace* means security from external aggression, and *Righteousness* security against lawlessness within the community.

administration and *government.* The abstract for the concrete in English; it is impossible to render literally the Hebrew, which has abstract (for concrete) in the first noun and concrete "governors" in the second.

19–20. Echoed in Rev xxi 23–25.

21. *shoot of Yahweh's planting.* See lxi 3. The figure of planting is common in prophetic literature for the restoration of Israel.

22. Echoes the promises to Abraham (Gen xv 5, xvii 16, xviii 18, xxii 17).

COMMENT

There is again a change of theme, so abrupt that there can scarcely be an organic connection between this poem and the previous ch. lix. This poem and chapter lxii are very closely related in tone and theme to the Zion poems xlix 14–lii 12 (SECS. 25–29). It is possible that lx and lxii, originally associated with the Zion poems, became detached from their context and were placed here by an editor, with lxi serving as a link. But there are features in the poem suggesting that these were written in imitation of Second Isaiah for the new situation of the post-exilic community. This community, we have seen, had problems about the deferred salvation. The prophet felt the need not only of explaining the delay but also of restating the saving act which was promised.

It is more difficult to distinguish speakers in this poem than in any other portion of the book; and this is one of the features which distinguishes the poem from the writings of Second Isaiah. We have made Yahweh the speaker in the entire poem, in spite of the appearance of Yahweh in the third person in a number of verses. But an attempt to isolate these lines as interruptions of the prophet into the utterance of Yahweh is unsatisfactory. We can only note the unusual feature that Yahweh speaks of himself in this poem in a way which is not characteristic of Second Isaiah.

The prophet sees Jerusalem as the one point of light in a world of darkness; as the light grows in intensity, it illuminates the dark world and attracts the nations. Light in the OT is the element which symbolizes both the presence of Yahweh and salvation. When the nations come, they bring with them the dispersed Israelites (see xlix 22). All the wealth of the world is brought to Zion as tribute to Yahweh, the lord (vs. 11). The prophet mentions in particular the items used in the cult (vss. 6–7); for the nations come to worship Yahweh. We have noted that the temple does not appear in the new Jerusalem of Second Isaiah (see COMMENT, SECS. 19 [specif. xliv 28 *ad loc.*] and 33 [lvi 1–8]). The worship of Yahweh is submission to Israel, for it is through Israel that Yahweh is revealed to the nations, and it is in Israel that he is worshiped (see xlix 23).

The dominant theme which emerges from these images is the theme of peace and security. All hostile forces are removed, either by voluntary submission or by destruction. There is a judgment implied in this conception which does not appear in Second Isaiah. The city whose gates are always open lives with no fear of attack; and the prophet adds with a quaint imaginative touch that they must always be open because the traffic in tribute will go on for twenty-four hours each day. There is a question whether the figure of submission to Israel does not shift from its original significance and become primarily a picture of an Israelite empire. This change in Jerusalem, from the new to the old, is indicated by a new name. A new reality, whether a human person or an object, demanded a new name in order that it be recognized as new.

The prophet returns to the theme of light with which the poem began (vs. 19), and sets the new Jerusalem in a cosmic context. The light, which is the presence of Yahweh, will outshine the sun and the moon, and it will never set. Nor will the world be illuminated by any other light; those who are not illuminated by the light of the new Jerusalem will sit in perpetual darkness. This eschatological salvation comes when the obstacle mentioned in the preceding poems (lvii–lix) has been removed, when the people of Yahweh are confirmed in righteousness. This is not only a fullfillment of the promises of Second Isaiah; the prophet reaches back into the history of the patriarchs. In this new Jerusalem the fullness of the promises of Yahweh to Abraham is achieved; this is the new and the whole Israel.

40. A MESSAGE FOR ISRAEL
(lxi 1–11)

LXI

1 The spirit of the Lord Yahweh is upon me, for Yahweh
  has anointed me;
  He has sent me to bring good news to the poor, to bind
  the wounds of the brokenhearted,
  To proclaim liberty to captives, release to the imprisoned;

2 To announce a year of grace for Yahweh, a day of deliverance for our God;
  To console all who mourn;

3 ᵃTo give them a crown instead of dust, the oil of gladness
  instead of the ᵇcloak of mourning,ᵇ
  Praise instead of a hopeless spirit;
  To declare them oaks of righteousness, the planting of
  Yahweh for his ornament.

4 They shall rebuild ancient ruins, they shall raise places
  long wasted;
  They shall repair desolate cities, wasted for many generations.

5 Strangers will stand and pasture your flocks, and foreigners
  will be your plowmen and vinedressers;

6 But you will be called priests of Yahweh, and you will be
  addressed as ministers of our God;
  You will eat the wealth of nations, and their glory will
  ᶜbecome your boast.ᶜ

ᵃ Heb. adds "to place for the mourners of Zion"; omitted.
ᵇ⁻ᵇ The order of these words is inverted in Heb.
ᶜ⁻ᶜ Conjectural emendation; Heb. unintelligible.

7 Because their*d* shame was doubled, and insult *e*they had
   as*e* their portion,
   They shall have a double portion in their land; eternal
   joy will be theirs.

8 "For I am Yahweh who love justice and hate robbery *f*and
   crime*f*;
   I will give them their reward faithfully; I will make a lasting covenant with them.

9 Their descendants shall be known among the nations,
   and their offspring among the peoples;
   All who see them will recognize them as a race blessed
   by Yahweh."

10 I will joyfully exult in Yahweh; my soul will triumph in
   my God;
   For he has clad me in garments of salvation; he has spread
   over me a cloak of righteousness,
   As a bridegroom puts on a crown, and a bride decks her-
   self with jewels.

11 For as the earth brings forth its shoots, and a garden
   brings its seeds to blossom,
   So the Lord Yahweh makes righteousness sprout, and
   praise before all nations.

d Conjectural emendation suggested by the sense; Heb. "your." 1QIs*a* reads
second masculine plural throughout, which need not be original; it may be an
effort to harmonize.
e–e Reading *yāreŝû* instead of MT *yārōnnû*, "they will shout with joy," suggested
both by the sense and by the use of the same word in the second line.
f–f Reading *we'awelāh*, for *be'ôlah*, "whole burnt offering," which involves
reading *waw* for *beth* and a different vocalization of the same consonants.

NOTES

lxi 1. Like the Servant (xlii 1), the speaker has the spirit of Yahweh.
The Servant, however, is not called anointed; see xlv 1. The mission of
the speaker echoes xlii 7 and xlix 9.
    2. *grace.* Renders a word more frequently translated "good pleasure,"
"benevolence." It designates a favorable decision, an acceptance.

3. *the oil of gladness*. Anointing oneself was part of the proper preparation for festivities.

planting. See lx 21 and NOTE.

5–6. A special position as priests is given to the entire people of Israel; see Exod xix 6. The Israelites shall mediate between Yahweh and the nations.

Strangers and *foreigners*. Two synonymous words are parallel.

the wealth of nations. See lx 5–11. The *glory* of nations is their wealth; the same Hebrew word can sometimes be translated by either term.

6. *ministers of our God*. Those who serve in temple worship.

7. Echoes xl 2.

8. *crime*. An unlawful act.

lasting covenant. See lv 3 and NOTE.

9. *a race blessed by Yahweh*. Echoes the promises to Abraham (Gen xii 2, xviii 18, xxii 18).

10. The speaker is Jerusalem; the figure of the bride is echoed in the new Jerusalem of Rev xxi 2.

11. Echoes xlv 8. The messianic prince is called "the righteous shoot" in Jer xxiii 8.

COMMENT

The poem is uttered by the prophet (vss. 1–7), Yahweh (8–9), and Zion (10–11). But the echoes of the Servant Songs (see the NOTE on vs. 1) indicate that the prophet thinks of himself as fulfilling the mission of the Servant, and thus he becomes an early interpreter of the Servant Songs. He sees the mission of the Servant as directed to Israel; the mission is to declare the arrival of the promised salvation. The poor, the brokenhearted, the captives, and the imprisoned designate the Israelites of the post-exilic community. But the "poor" and the "brokenhearted" are not Israel as a whole, but the devout core of the faithful. The words imply the duality of post-exilic Israel, which is more explicit in lxv–lxvi, the concluding SECS. 44–47. Here, vs. 3, his declaration is effective, for he utters the dynamic prophetic word which brings to pass that which it declares. The terms of the promise are drawn from Second Isaiah except for the phrase "oaks of righteousness." The phrase continues the theme of Third Isaiah that the fulfillment of righteousness will bring the delayed salvation to pass. Verse 4 suggests that the resettlement of Judah had not advanced very far when the poem was uttered.

Beginning with vs. 5 a different conception of Israel and the nations which come to Zion is proposed. Israel has been presented as the mediator between Yahweh and the nations; that position is here defined as the priesthood, which in Israel had the office of offering sacrifice and prayer in the name of the people and presenting and explaining the law of Yahweh. Israel will have no concern with its material needs, as the Israelite priesthood theoretically had no concern with these needs. The nations of the world will support Israel in its mission of mediation. The words of Yahweh describe this as the reward for Israel's suffering. As his priests their covenant is eternal, and the promises made to the patriarchs are fulfilled; see COMMENT on SEC. 39 (specif. lx 21–22 *ad loc.*).

The response of Zion is a cry of gladness. The "salvation" and the "righteousness" in which Zion is clothed are the saving acts of Yahweh; "righteousness" here (vs. 10) signifies both the moral quality and the vindication which the moral quality secures. The figure of the bride, suggested in vs. 10, is amplified in the following poem. The closing verse repeats the theme that the saving act of Yahweh will be manifested throughout the world. "Righteousness" is here again both the moral quality and vindication, and the manifestation of Yahweh elicits the praise of all nations.

41. THE SALVATION OF ZION
(lxii 1–12)

LXII

1 Concerning Zion I will not keep silent, and concerning
    Jerusalem I will not remain quiet,
    Until her deliverance comes forth like a brilliant light,
    and her salvation like a *ªflaming torch.ª*

2 Nations shall see your deliverance, and all the kings
    your glory;
    And you shall be called a new name, which the mouth
    of Yahweh will designate.

3 You will be a beautiful crown in the hand of Yahweh, a
    royal turban in the hand of your God.

4 You will no longer be called Abandoned, nor will your
    land be called Desolate;
    You will be called "She is my Delight," and your land
    will be called Married;
    For Yahweh delights in you, and your land will be mar-
    ried.

5 For as*ᵇ* a young man marries a virgin, so your builder*ᶜ*
    will marry you;
    Like the joy of the groom in his bride is the joy of your
    God in you.

ª–ª 1QIsª reads *tbʿr*, for MT *yibʿār*, which would be rendered "flames like
a torch." This makes the parallelism of the two cola more rigorous (D. N.
Freedman); but parallelism is flexible enough to permit such variations as the
reading of MT.

ᵇ Reading *kibeʿōl* with 1QIsª for MT *yibeʿal*.

ᶜ Conjectural emendation suggested by the sense; Heb. "your sons." See
COMMENT.

6   On your walls, Jerusalem, I have posted watchmen; all
       day and all night they will never be silent;
     You who remind Yahweh, be not silent.
7   Give him no quiet until he establishes, until he makes
       Jerusalem a praise in the earth.
8   Yahweh has sworn by his right hand and by his strong
       arm:
     "I will never again give your grain to your enemies to eat;
     Nor will foreigners drink your new wine, at which you
       have toiled.
9   No, those who reap it will eat it and praise Yahweh;
     Those who harvest it will drink it in my holy courts."
10   Pass through, pass through the gates; level the way of the
       people;
     Raise up, raise up the highway; clear away the stones;
     Raise a banner to the nations.
11   See, Yahweh has announced it to the end of the earth:
     Say to the daughter of Zion: See, your Savior[d] comes;
     See, his reward is with him, and his achievement is before
       him.
12   They will be called the holy people, redeemed by Yahweh;
     And you will be called Sought, a city not deserted.

[d] LXX reads "your savior"; but even LXX may be a rendition of the concrete
for the abstract, a common feature of Hebrew poetry.

NOTES

lxii 1. The theme of light appears in the companion poem in lx 1.
2. For the *new name*, see lx 14.
4. *She is my Delight*. Heb. *Hephzibah*.
Married. Heb. *Beulah*. The theme of marriage appears in Hosea and
Jeremiah; see NOTE on l 1.
6. The *watchmen* here are not the watchmen of lii 8, who by a paradox
were posted on the walls of an abandoned city to announce the return
of its inhabitants. The watchmen here have no duty except perpetual
prayer, for there can be no danger of which they should give warning.
8. That others will eat and drink what the Israelites planted is a

fairly common prophetic threat; see Deut xxviii 30–33; Amos v 11; Mic vi 15.

10. The theme of the wonderful road; see xxxv 8–10 and NOTE. This road, however, is not for Israel but for the coming of Yahweh.

Raise a banner. To call attention.

11. Echoes xl 10.

COMMENT

This poem is a companion piece to ch. lx (SEC. 39); see the COMMENT *ad loc.* The prophet is the speaker except for the saying of Yahweh in vss. 8–9. The prophet's eagerness to speak refers to his continued proclamation of the message of promise in spite of the delay of salvation and the incredulity of those whom he addresses; it may also signify the speech of intercession, but this is not obvious in the text. Themes are repeated from earlier poems both in Second and in Third Isaiah. The new name was mentioned in lx 14; see the COMMENT *ad loc.* The image of the marriage of Yahweh and Zion is somewhat altered from its earlier use (see NOTE on vs. 4); there Yahweh receives the wayward spouse back into the home, here there is a remarriage. The emendation of Heb. "sons" to "builder" in vs. 5 is demanded by the context; it is not only because of the harsh mixture of metaphor, but principally because the "sons" could only be the Israelites, while the spouse elsewhere in the context is Yahweh. The watchmen posted on the walls need not signify prophets or any religious officers. The watchmen were a part of the city's system of protection, but the new Zion will need no protection (lx 11); these watchmen have no duty except that of prayer. They pray that the saving act which has been initiated will reach its fulfillment. The oath of Yahweh is the answer to the petition; it is an oath that Zion will never again suffer invasion (see lii 2 and COMMENT [SEC. 29]). Verses 10–11 are clear echoes of Second Isaiah (see the NOTES). The poem concludes with another reference to the new name (see lx 14 and COMMENT [SEC. 39]). The conferring of new names is a favorite theme of the author of these Zion poems; see lx 14, 18; and vss. 2, 4 in this chapter.

42. THE DESTRUCTION OF EDOM
(lxiii 1–6)

LXIII

1   Who is this who comes from Edom, from Bozrah in red
     garments,
     Splendidly appareled, marching[a] in his mighty strength?
     "I who speak righteousness, I who am powerful to save."

2   Why is your clothing red, and your garments like those
     of one who treads in the wine press?

3   "I have trodden the wine trough alone, and there was not
     a man of my people[b] with me;
     I trod[c] them in my anger, I trampled[c] them in my fury;
     And their gushing blood sprinkled[c] my garments; I have
     stained[c] all my clothing.

4   For I have decided on a day of retribution; my year of
     vengeance has arrived.

5   I looked,[c] but there was no helper; I was appalled[c] that
     there was no one to sustain;
     So my own arm delivered me, and my fury sustained me.

6   I trod[c] down peoples in my anger, I shattered them[d] in my
     fury;
     I made their blood run upon the earth."

[a] Reading *ṣōʿēd* with some versions for Heb. *ṣōʿeh*, "pouring wine" (?),
strangely inappropriate to this line but in harmony with the whole image.
[b] Reading with 1QIsª; MT "the peoples."
[c] The tenses in these lines are confused. Most of them are future, but the sense
of the context and two clearly past forms suggest that consistency be attained
by vocalizing the conjunctions as *waw* conversive and reading *gāʾaltî* for the
abnormal *ʾegaltî* at the end of vs. 3.
[d] Reading *ʾašabberēm* with some manuscripts for MT *ʾašakkerēm*, "I made
them drunk"; as in note [a], MT suits the general image but is unsuitable for
this line.

NOTES

lxiii 1. *Edom* and *Bozrah*. See xxxiv, § 1.

2–3. The figure of treading the grapes for the judgment of Yahweh appears also in Joel iv 13. The grapes were placed in a large box and were trodden down by men who walked back and forth barefoot. As in xxxiv 2–7, the figures used are lurid.

5. Echoes lix 16.

COMMENT

For the background of this poem, see xxxiv (SEC. 1) with NOTES and COMMENT. We have noticed that the theme of judgment is more explicitly joined to the theme of salvation in Third Isaiah. The poem is couched in dialogue. This is the theophany of Yahweh the warrior judge. The judgment is not merely a judgment on Edom. It is on Edom, which had plundered the defenseless territory of Judah, that the judgment begins. The catastrophe is merely suggested, not described; the imagery of Yahweh marching in blood-stained garments is somewhat appalling, but by a literary touch not common in Third Isaiah, one is left to imagine the scene from which Yahweh has come. As in lix 16–20 Yahweh acts alone. The poem makes Yahweh's coming to Zion as judge more concrete. In this poem we are on the verge of apocalyptic literature, which sees the nations of the world as a gigantic power which can be overthrown by no one but Yahweh; and the overthrow is a world cataclysm.

43. A PSALM OF LAMENTATION
(lxiii 7–19; lxiv 1–11)

LXIII

7 I will recount the gracious deeds of Yahweh, the praises
of Yahweh;
According to all that Yahweh has done for us—his great
goodness to the house of Israel,
Which he has displayed in his compassion and in his
many deeds.

8 He said: "Surely they are my people, sons who will not
betray";
And he became their savior.

9 In all their affliction,
It was no emissary[a] nor messenger; it was his presence
which saved them;
In his love and his compassion he avenged them;
He lifted them and carried them from time immemorial.

10 But they became rebellious and saddened his holy spirit;
And he turned hostile to them and warred against them.

11 Then they[b] remembered their past—Moses his servant[c];
Where is he that brought[d] the shepherd[e] of his flock
up from the sea,
Who put his holy spirit in him,

12 Who made his glorious arm march at Moses' right hand,

[a] Vocalizing ṣir for MT ṣār, "enemy."
[b] Conjectural emendation suggested by the sense; Heb. "he."
[c] Reading with some manuscripts; Heb. "his people."
[d] Reading hamma'aleh with 1QIsa for MT hamma'alēm, "the one who brings
them up."
[e] The singular of the versions is demanded rather than MT plural; the verse
concerns Moses.

Who cleft the waters before them, to make himself an
everlasting name,

13 Who led them through the depths?
Like a horse in the desert, they did not stumble;

14 Like cattle which go down to the valley, his holy spirit
guided*f* them;
So did you lead your people, to make for yourself a glorious
name.

15 Look down from heaven and see, from your glorious and
holy temple;
Where is your mighty zeal, your strong feelings?
*g*Do not restrain*g* your compassion!

16 For you are our father:
Abraham does not know us, Israel does not recognize us;
You, Yahweh, are our father; "our avenger" is your name
from old.

17 Why, Yahweh, do you let us wander from your ways, and
let our hearts grow too hard to fear you?
Turn for the sake of your servants, the tribes of your
heritage.

18 *h*Why have the wicked trodden on your holy place,*h* our
enemies trampled on your sanctuary?

19 We have become like those whom you have never ruled,
on whom your name has not been invoked;
Would that you would rend the heavens and come down
—in your presence the mountains would quake!

LXIV

1 As fire kindles brushwood, and causes water to boil—
To reveal your name to your adversaries; at your presence
the nations will tremble,

---

f Vocalizing *tanḥennû* for MT *tᵉnîḥennû,* "we gave them rest."
g–g MT is emended from *'ēli hiťappāḳû,* "are withheld from me," to *'al-na'*
hitappāḳ, which involves minor changes and gives much better sense.
h–h The condition of this line permits conjecture. By supplying one consonant,
changing one, and omitting one, *lamiš'ar yārᵉšû'am,* "for a little while they
possessed," of MT becomes *lammāh sa'ᵃdû rᵉšā'îm.*

2   When you do fearful things which we did not expect,[i]
    3 and of which no one has ever heard;
    No ear has heard, no eye has seen a God except you
        who acts on behalf of those who wait for him.

4   You come to meet[j] those who do righteousness, who[k] are
        mindful of your ways[k];
    See, you were angry, for we are sinners; [l]we have long
        been rebels.[l]

5   We have become like one unclean, and all our righteous
        deeds like the rag of a menstruous woman;
    We wither, all of us, like a leaf; and our evil deeds, like
        the wind, sweep us away.

6   There is no one who invokes your name, who bestirs
        himself to hold fast to you;
    For you have hidden your countenance from us, and de-
        livered us to the power of our evil deeds.

7   But now, Yahweh, you are our father;
    We are clay, and you are the potter; we are the work of
        your hands, all of us.

8   Do not be angry, Yahweh, to excess, and do not remem-
        ber crime forever;
    Take heed, we are all your people.

9   Your holy cities have become a desert, Zion has become
        a desert, Jerusalem a waste.

10 Our holy and beautiful temple, where our fathers sang
        your praises,
    Has been consumed by fire; and all our delight has become a
        ruin.

11 Can you restrain yourself at these things, Yahweh?
    Will you be silent and afflict us beyond limit?

---

[i] Hebrew repeats "would that you would come down; the mountains would
quake in your presence" from lxiii 19; omitted. (Revised Standard Version
reads lxiii 19b as lxiv 1.)

[j] Hebrew adds "the joyful"; omitted.

[k-k] Conjectural emendation based on the versions; Heb. "who remember you in
your ways."

[l-l] As in note [h-h], the condition of the line permits conjecture. Only two consonants need be changed to recover *bekā mē'ôlām wanipse'û* from MT *bahem
'ôlam weniwwāšē'a*, "in them a long time, and shall we be saved?"

NOTES

lxiii 9. In the Exodus traditions there are variations between the messenger (angel) of Yahweh who leads the Israelites (Exod xxiii 20–23) and the leadership of Yahweh himself, his *presence* (Exod xxxiii 15–17). In later OT books and in Judaism a distinction was made between various words signifying Yahweh's presence and activity, such as the angel, the presence, the dwelling, and the name. The prophet here chooses the word that signifies an immediate association, the presence (literally "face").

11. For the *spirit* here and in vs. 14, see xlii 1. In Num xi 17 some of the spirit with which Moses is endowed is communicated to the elders.

13. *Like a horse in the desert.* Signifies sureness of foot on level ground.

14. *cattle . . . valley.* The valley is the place of grass and water, to which cattle are easily led.

15. An allusion to the heavenly temple, of which the earthly temple is the counterpart.

18. The uncertain date of the passage makes it difficult to identify the allusion. No invasion of the temple by foreign enemies is known between its destruction in 587 B.C. and the seizure of the temple by Antiochus Epiphanes in 168 B.C.; but Jewish history for this period is very poorly documented. Duhm suggested that the second temple was a poor replacement for the first; and see Hag ii 2–9.

lxiii 19 – lxiv 1. The verses are ambiguous because the traditional division of chapters interrupts a sentence. lxiv 1 is to be read as the conclusion of the sentence in lxiii 19. The prophet prays for a theophany in the traditional manner (see, e.g., Ps xviii 6–17).

2–3. To paraphrase: when Yahweh comes to save Israel, he will do strange and wonderful things beyond expectation, things which no one else has ever done.

3. This verse is quoted very loosely in I Cor ii 9 in a form that follows neither MT nor LXX.

5. The somewhat crude image expresses legal uncleanness rather than filth; the menstrual flow was unclean (Lev xv 19–24). In Israelite law and thought there is a distinction between sin and legal uncleanness, and the language here is unusual.

6. The *name* of Yahweh was invoked in prayer and in oaths.

7. *father.* See lxiii 16.

For the image of the *potter* and the *clay,* see NOTE on xlv 9. Yahweh's sovereignty is seen in his judgment.

9–10. On the allusions, see NOTE on lxiii 18. In both passages it is most probable that the disaster of 587 B.C. is meant, which would place the passages not long after this event.

11. *limit.* Israelites often suppose that Yahweh puts a limit on his anger, keeps it under control.

COMMENT

We have called this poem a psalm; in form and structure it belongs with the type of psalm called "community lamentation," which contains recitals of past blessings, description of the present need, appeals for assistance, and often an assurance that the petition is answered. The prophet begins his recital of past blessings with a formal exordium. These deeds arise from the confidence of Yahweh in Israel, a confidence which was rudely broken by the Israelites; the prophet here humanizes Yahweh in a childlike manner as the innocent benefactor who was cheated by the object of his benefaction. The prophet emphasizes the personal action of Yahweh (see the NOTE on lxiii 9). It was early in Israel's history that Israel became rebellious and that Yahweh loosed his judgments upon Israel. The state of the text of vs. 11 makes it difficult to be sure of the precise meaning of the prophet here; see the textual notes. The recalling of the great deeds of the Exodus is a reason for hope in Yahweh's good will; and the prophet asks where the power, which was then displayed, is now to be seen. In the lamentation psalms Yahweh is often urged to act for the sake of his own reputation, his "name." Verse 16 is not entirely clear. Abraham and Israel (Jacob) must be the patriarchs of history. The only reason why they would disclaim Israel is because Israel is faithless to Yahweh. Verse 17 is a mild rebuke of Yahweh for not acting more urgently—as we would say, for not putting on more pressure. Verse 18 (see the NOTE) most probably refers to the destruction of the temple by the Babylonians. This suggests that the poem should be dated at a time when this disaster was still recent enough to be recalled in such terms as these. The general period in which we place Third Isaiah (see INTRODUCTION, "Critical Questions") is close enough to the event. The condition of Israel after this judgment was no better than the condition of nations which had not been in covenant with Yahweh, nations which had disappeared from the historical scene. The prophet does not now speak in the language of the Zion poems; he has swung to the opposite pole of impatient anxiety over the delay of salvation.

The prophet prays for a theophany; the prayer is found where the chapter division has been erroneously placed (see NOTE on lxiii 19 – lxiv 1). He does not ask for a specific act either of salvation or of judgment; when Yahweh acts, no man is capable of predicting what he will do. The prophet is sure that he will not come as a savior except to the righteous. The poem then leads into the confession of sin (vs. 4), which is put in general but quite vigorous language. Again there is a mild rebuke of Yahweh. The Israelites do not invoke his name because they have seen too much of his judgment and not enough of his salvation. They are discouraged with their present situation. But there is no one else to whom they can turn. On the figure of the potter, see xlv 9. The figure as usual illustrates the sovereignty of Yahweh; but here it is the absolute dependence of Israel on this sovereignty which is signified. The ultimate basis of the plea is that Israel is still the people of Yahweh whom he may punish but cannot reject.

Verses 9–10, as observed for lxiii 18, are most probably referred to the disaster of 587 B.C. We find again an allusion to the temple; and it seems unlikely that the prophet could have spoken thus about the temple if it had been rebuilt. For it was one of Yahweh's saving acts that he made his name to dwell in Zion again after the temple of Solomon had been laid in ruins. The plea ends with the suggestion that Yahweh perhaps has overstepped the due bounds of anger, righteous as his anger may have been. Such mild rebukes are found in the psalms of lamentation; they are a part of the familiar language of Israelite prayer.

44. YAHWEH'S ACCUSATION
(lxv 1–7)

LXV

1   "I could have been sought by those who did not inquire; I
      could have been found by those who did not seek me;
     I said, 'Here I am, here I am,' to a nation that did not
     invoke my name.

2   I spread out my hands all the day to a rebellious people,
     Who walk in a way that is not good, according to their
     own devices;

3   A people who perpetually vex me to my face,
     Offering sacrifice in the gardens and burning incense on
     bricks;

4   Who sit in tombs and spend the night in huts[?],
     Who eat swine's flesh and unclean meat in^a their vessels;

5   Who say, 'Keep your distance; do not come near me, I
     will sanctify^b you';
     These are a smoke in my nostrils, a fire that flames all
     day.

6   See, it is written in my sight; I will not be silent, I will
     repay^c

7   Their^d crimes and the crimes of their^d fathers together"—
     says Yahweh—
   "Because they have burnt incense upon the mountains,
     and insulted me upon the hills,
   I will measure their full reward into their bosom."

^{a} "In" supplied from Targ. and Vulg.; missing in Heb.
^{b} MT kal must be vocalized as piel.
^{c} Heb. adds "I will repay in their bosom"; omitted.
^{d} Reading third plural with the versions; MT second plural.

Notes

lxv 3. The allusions to superstitious rites are quite obscure. It is not stated that the rites are performed in honor of other gods; but they seem to have been foreign practices with unacceptable associations.

4. It was a common practice to spend the night in a temple or shrine in the hope of receiving an oracular dream (incubation).

5. In Israelite law, holiness was communicated by contact; the offensive character of this holiness is that it is acquired by participation in unholy rites.

5–7. The indignation expressed, if it is directed at cultic deviations, seems rather exaggerated.

Comment

This poem in its present position is a response to the prayer which precedes it; but this connection is very probably due to an editor rather than to the author or authors of the prophecies. Yahweh is the speaker, and he contrasts his own availability to the failure of Israel to "seek" him. Indeed, it is rather Yahweh who has sought Israel and has not found it. The interest of the poem is entirely cultic; Israel has not sought Yahweh because it has substituted superstitious cults for the rites of Yahweh. The rites mentioned are obscure and cannot be identified with any cultic practices of the period known to us; see Note on vs. 3. The eating of pork is very probably more than a violation of the dietary laws; it was the use of the pig in a sacrificial cult which was obviously foreign. The idea of ritual holiness that could be communicated by contact was not unique with the Israelites; but the use of the word "holy," a word of such religious weight in the OT, to describe superstitious rites is a kind of blasphemy which arouses indignation. Yahweh was "the Holy One of Israel" in First Isaiah and Second Isaiah. Verse 7 seems to specify "the crimes of the fathers"; it emphasizes practices mentioned in pre-exilic literature. Cultic interest is not characteristic of Second Isaiah.

45. YAHWEH'S PROMISES
(lxv 8–25)

LXV

8   Thus says Yahweh:

"Just as, when the new wine is found in the cluster,
One says, 'Do not destroy it; there is a blessing in it,'
So I will act for the sake of my servants; I will not destroy them all.

9   I will produce descendants from Jacob, and from Judah heirs of my mountains;
My elect shall possess it, and my servants shall dwell there.

10   Sharon shall be a pasture for flocks, and the Valley of Achor a place for cattle to lie—
For my people who seek me.

11   But you, who have abandoned Yahweh, who have forgotten my holy mountain,
Who set a table for Gad, and fill cups of mixed wine for Meni,

12   I will measure you for the sword, and all of you shall stoop for the slaughter,
Because I called, and you did not answer; I spoke and you did not listen;
You have done evil in my sight, and you have chosen what I did not wish."

13   Therefore thus says the Lord Yahweh:

"See, my servants will eat, but you will hunger;
See, my servants will drink, but you will thirst;
See, my servants will be glad, but you will be abashed;

14   See, my servants will shout with a joyous heart;

But you will cry out with a sad heart, and you will howl with a broken spirit.

15 You will leave your name to my elect as a curse: 'May the Lord Yahweh kill you';

But ᵃmy servants will be calledᵃ by a different name.

16 ᵇHe who blesses himself in the land shall bless himself by the God of fidelity;

And he who swears in the land shall swear by the God of fidelity;

For the old afflictions are forgotten; yes, they are hidden from my sight.

17 For look! I create a new heaven and a new earth;

The past will not be remembered, it will not enter your mind.

18 Rather be joyful, be glad forever at what I am creating;

For look! I am creating Jerusalem 'Joy,' and her people 'Gladness.'

19 I will be joyful in Jerusalem, and I will be glad in my people;

The sound of weeping will be heard in her no more, nor the sound of a cry.

20 No longer will there be in it an infant of only a few days nor an old man who does not fill out his life;

A boy who dies at the age of a hundred, and the sinner who dies at the age of a hundred will be thought accursed.

21 They will build houses and live in them; they will plant orchards and eat their fruit.

22 They will not build for another to dwell, and plant for another to eat;

For the days of my people will be like the days of a tree; and my elect will use up the work of their hands.

23 They will not toil for nothing, nor will they bear children for calamity;

ᵃ⁻ᵃ The translation is secured by moving the final *waw* of *laʿᵃbādaw,* "to his servants," to the following verb as *waw* emphatic (D. N. Freedman). The verb in MT is *qal,* but the same consonants can be vocalized as *niphal.*
ᵇ Heb. adds "which"; omitted.

For these are a race blessed by Yahweh, and their descendants with them.

24   Before they call I will answer, and while they are speaking I will hearken.

25   The wolf and the lamb will pasture together, and the lion will eat straw like the ox; and dust will be the serpent's food;
They shall do no evil and no harm in all my holy mountain"—
Says Yahweh.

NOTES

lxv 8. This saying, like most popular sayings, is obscure. The first fruits of animals (including men) and plants had a sacred character, which made them the property of Yahweh, to whom they were offered. The first appearance of life was a tangible token of the presence and activity of Yahweh. The first clusters of the grapes might contain undesirable grapes, but because they were first they contained the *blessing* of the renewed gift of life. So the restored Israel had good and bad Israelites, but Israel contains a blessing, the promises of Yahweh and those Israelites who were faithful to him. The whole Israel will not be destroyed for the sake of its loyal members. The analogy is similar to the parables of the weeds (Matt xiii 24–30) and the dragnet (Matt xiii 47–50). *One.* The speaker is indefinite.

10. *Sharon.* See NOTE on xxxv 2. Pastures of David in Sharon are mentioned in I Chron xxvii 29.

the Valley of Achor. Very probably to be located in the immediate neighborhood of Jerusalem south of the modern city.

11. *Gad* and *Meni.* Divine names otherwise unknown. Meni suggests "portion," and it is thought that they may have been deities of fate or fortune. The cult of such deities was very popular in the Hellenistic period; but this does not show that the passage is to be placed in this period.

12. *measure.* A play on the divine name Meni.

stoop for the slaughter. Bow or kneel for execution.

15. This inverts the words of Gen xii 2, xviii 18, xxii 18, in which Abraham and his descendants become a formula of blessing. The unfaithful Israelites become a formula of cursing: "May God kill you (as he killed them)." Cf. Jer xxix 22. Israel, like Jerusalem (Isa lx 14), receives a new name to designate the new reality.

16. *in the land*. The restored Israel will possess the land of Israel.

fidelity. That is, *amen,* used elsewhere only as an asseverative particle in the sense that is familiar in prayer. The translation is not altogether certain.

17. The *new heaven* and the *new earth* are echoed in lxvi 22 and in Rev xxi 1. The idea is rare in both the OT and NT.

18. *Joy* and *Gladness*. Titles of the new Jerusalem and the new Israel.

19. Echoed in Rev xxi 4.

20. In popular belief a long life was a sign of Yahweh's favor and a reward for virtue, and a premature death was a sign of Yahweh's anger and judgment. But in the new Jerusalem the normal life span will approach the span of the antediluvian. It is difficult to render the line without paraphrase and still express the thought, since both verbs seem to go with both nouns; the words are elliptical. The line means that one who dies at the age of one hundred will be considered to have died in boyhood. But no one will die such a premature death unless he is a sinner and therefore under a curse. The line is paradoxical; the new Jerusalem will have no sinners within it.

21–22. See lxii 8. Job xiv 7–9 complains that the days of a man are not like the days of a tree, which can live on even if it has been cut down. It enjoys a kind of immortality in comparison with man.

23. The blessing promised to Abraham; see lxv 15.

25. Quoted from Isa xi 6–9.

COMMENT

This poem, which again does not have a connection with the preceding poem, is another poem of promise; but this takes a different turn from the earlier promises (see below). The poem begins with what must be a proverb or popular saying; see the NOTE. The community of Israel is compared to a cluster of grapes which one might look at and throw away as unsatisfactory. But since it is among the first clusters to be harvested, it contains a blessing, the token of Yahweh's favor manifested in the harvest. So the community of Israel might deserve to be rejected as a whole, but it contains a blessing; and the blessing is clearly identified in the following lines as the group of faithful Israelites. The prophet has divided Israel into the genuine Israel and the spurious Israel; and this division remains constant in post-exilic literature. Duhm understood the unfaithful group to be the Samaritans, and the hostility expressed is in accord with the relations of the Jewish and Samaritan com-

munities. But the identification is doubtful because of the uncertainty both of the date of the poems of Third Isaiah and of the
Samaritan schism, which in any hypothesis seems to be later than
any probable date of the poem. No doubt the feelings that issued in
the schism were already present to some extent before the time of
Nehemiah (445 B.C.), but the Samaritans were not yet a distinct
non-Jewish community; and this would still not affect the interpretation of the poem as distinguishing the genuine and the spurious
Israel. But the unbelieving Israelites seem to include more than the
dissidents of Samaria, if indeed these are meant at all. Yahweh will
fulfill his promises; the promises made to the patriarchs of land
and progeny are mentioned. Yahweh's will cannot be frustrated
even by his own people. But the promises will not be fulfilled to
the whole of historic Israel. The "you" of vss. 11–15 are the
Israelites who will be excluded from the promises.

The only specific sin mentioned is superstitious worship; on the
practices, see the NOTE on vs. 11. The preceding poems in Third
Isaiah have mentioned other sins—see lvi, lviii, lix—and there is
no reason to think that this prophet did not regard these as serious.
But Israel's sin comes to a focus, a point of clarity in its cult; here
the rejection of Yahweh, implicit in their crimes, becomes formal and
explicit. Therefore, Yahweh utters a formal curse in which the unbelievers are eliminated from a share in the blessings of the salvation to come. The delay in the coming of salvation will not be removed by the regeneration of Israel as a whole; it will be removed
by removing that part of Israel which creates the obstacle. The
prophet says nothing to indicate whether the elect group is a majority
or a minority within the Israelite community. One is justified in
suspecting that the obstacle lay mostly with the leading elements
of the community, the wealthy and the priests. That the faithful
group was a minority may be indicated in the new name of vss.
15–16. The traditional formula in the phrases cited in vs. 16 was
"the God of Israel." The elect people will not use this phrase; they
will speak of "the God of Amen." They will thus attest the fidelity
of Yahweh to his promises even when it seemed impossible to fulfill
the promises; but the line may also attest that the name of Israel
is expected to stay with the larger group, the group of unbelievers.

From vs. 17 on, the poem approaches apocalyptic. The vision
now comprehends not a new Zion but a new heaven and a new
earth. The characteristic of the Zion in this new universe is joy;

"joy" and "gladness" occur six times in vss. 18–19, and they become the new names of the city. The conditions of the antediluvian patriarchs will be restored, when the normal span of human life was several centuries. The faithful will not fear that the fruit of their toil will be destroyed by war and conquest. Indeed, the new earth will be a restoration of Paradise; it is described in terms obviously borrowed from First Isaiah. Yahweh will be near and accessible; it will not be necessary to ask anything in prayer. The division of Israel into faithful and unfaithful has taken the prophet out of the realm of history; the salvation he expects can only be achieved outside history, when the judgments of Yahweh are perfectly executed, when wickedness becomes utterly powerless.

46. THE VANITY OF HYPOCRITICAL WORSHIP
(lxvi 1–4)

LXVI

1 Thus says Yahweh:
"The heavens are my throne, and the earth is my footstool;
Where is the house that you would build for me? and
where is the place for me to rest?

2 My hand has made all these things, and all these things
are mine"*a*—the oracle of Yahweh;
"But upon this one will I look: on the lowly and the
broken*b* of spirit, and the one who trembles at my word.

3 He who slaughters an ox is like one who kills a man; he
who sacrifices a lamb is like one who breaks the neck of
a dog;
He who makes a meal offering—it is like pig's blood; he
who offers incense in praise—he blesses an idol.
Yes, these have chosen their own ways, and they have
delighted in their abominations.

4 So I have chosen to mistreat them, and I will bring their
horror upon them,
Because I called, and there was no answer; I spoke, and
no one listened;
They did what is evil in my sight, and they chose what
is against my will."

a Supplied from LXX and Syr.; missing in Heb.
b Reading *neke̅'* for Heb. *neke̅h*, suggested by 1QIsᵃ (which, however, has plural).

NOTES

lxvi 1. The thought is somewhat similar to the prayer of Solomon in I Kings viii 27; but where Solomon utters a humble deprecation, this verse is more like an explicit repudiation of the temple. See II Sam vii 4–7.

2. The verse exhibits "the piety of the poor"; in post-exilic literature the devout become identified with the poor and lowly.

3. *breaks the neck of a dog.* The dog was not a sacrificial animal. The lines seem to be a repudiation of sacrifice, as vs. 1 seems to be a repudiation of the temple; see xliii 23–24.

COMMENT

This poem is not only unconnected with the preceding one, it stands by itself in the collection of Third Isaiah. We have noticed a cultic interest in Third Isaiah; this interest has been favorable or neutral. If this poem is to be treated as a unity and not as a collection of fragments, it is hostile to the cult. It can hardly be alleged that the ritual practices mentioned in vs. 3 are illegitimate forms of superstitious cult; nothing indicates that they are other than the cultic rites of the temple.

Duhm's view that the Samaritan temple is intended is difficult. The chronology of the Samaritan temple is uncertain, but in any hypothesis the building of the temple seems too late for any date which can be accepted as probable for Third Isaiah. Furthermore, the opposition to the cult expressed in this passage is not clearly directed against any form of cult in particular. "The lowly and the broken of spirit" are preferred to those who offer sacrifice; and the statement is as valid for the Jerusalem temple as it is for any temple.

The opening lines do not formally reject the temple; but they certainly do not recommend it. The prophecy is directed against the temple and the cult, and it has no parallel in Second or Third Isaiah; see xliii 23–24 and the NOTE. But the words are not directed against the cult as insincere and combined with sinful habits, as the cult is condemned in the pre-exilic prophets. It is easy to suppose that the prophet implies this. But the only thing he contrasts to the temple and the cult is "the lowly and the broken of spirit." We have an instance of "the piety of the poor," who as a class are identified with faithful Israelites. This genuine Israelite piety cannot be achieved by any temple and sacrificial system; it consists in submission to Yahweh. There is implied a kind of blanket condemnation of all who do not belong to the class of the pious poor. If we think of the restored community of Judah as a community which struggled with grinding poverty, it is easy to see how anyone who rose above the level of poverty would be regarded as a traitor to the community.

47. APOCALYPSE: DELIVERANCE AND JUDGMENT
(lxvi 5–24)

LXVI

5   Hear the word of Yahweh, you who tremble at his word:
Your brothers who hate you and who expel you for my
name's sake have said,

"May Yahweh *be glorified,*ᵃ and let us see your joy";
But they shall be confounded.

6   There is a roar from the city, a sound from the temple;
It is the sound of Yahweh, who renders his enemies their
due.

7   Before she was in labor she bore; before the pangs came to
her she brought forth a man.

8   Who ever heard the like? Who has seen anything like this?
Shall a land be*ᵇ* delivered in one day? Shall a nation be
brought forth all at once?
For Zion, scarcely in labor, has brought forth her sons.

9   "Shall I open the womb and not bring forth?" says Yahweh,
"Shall I, who bring to birth, close the womb?" says your
God,

10   *Rejoice, Jerusalem,*ᶜ and exult for her, all you who love
her;

Let your joy for her be full, all you who have mourned
over her,

---

a–a Reading with LXX and Syr.; Heb. active.
b The translation renders the sense demanded by the context, but *yûḥal,* a form occurring only here, does not agree with *'ereṣ,* "land," which is feminine. 1QIsᵃ reads *tāḥîl,* "shall she deliver," which is grammatically acceptable but harsher than the passive. Perhaps the original text was *tûḥal,* "he shall be delivered."
c–c Conjectural emendation suggested by LXX; Heb. "rejoice with Jerusalem."

11   That you may suck and be filled from her comforting
         breasts,
      That you may sip with delight from her glorious nipple.

12   For thus says Yahweh:
      "See, I spread prosperity over her like a river, and the glory
         of nations like a rushing torrent;
      Her nurslings[d] shall be carried on the hip, they shall be
         fondled on the lap.

13   As a mother consoles a man, so shall I console you;
      You shall be consoled in Jerusalem."

14   At the sight your heart will be glad; and your bones will
         bloom like grass;
      It will be known that the hand of Yahweh is with his
         servants, but his[e] anger with his enemies.

15   For look! Yahweh will come in fire, and his chariots are
         like the whirlwind:
      To pay back his anger in fury, and his indignation in
         flaming fire.

16   For Yahweh will deliver judgment in fire, and with his
         sword on all flesh;
      And many shall be those slain by Yahweh.

17   "But those who sanctify themselves and purify themselves
         in the gardens, following one in the center,
      Eating swine's flesh and reptiles[f] and mice—
      [g]Their deeds and their thoughts[g] will perish together"—
      The oracle of Yahweh.

18 "I am [h]going to assemble all nations and tongues; and they
will come and will see my glory; 19 And I will set a sign among
them; and I will send survivors from them to the nations—to
Tarshish, to Put,[i] and Lud, [j]Meshech, Rosh,[j] Tubal, Javan, to
the remote coasts that have never heard a report of me and never

---

[d] Conjectural emendation suggested by LXX; Heb. "you will nurse."
[e] "His" supplied by conjectural emendation; missing in Heb.
[f] Conjectural emendation; Heb. "abomination."
[g-g] These words are transferred here from vs. 18.
[h] Read masculine; Heb. feminine.
[i] Reading with some manuscripts; Heb. "Pul."
[j-j] Conjectural emendation suggested by LXX; Heb. "drawing the bow."

seen my glory; and they will declare my glory among the nations.
20 And they will bring all your brothers from all nations as an
offering to Yahweh—on horses, in chariots, in litters, on mules,
and on dromedaries—to my holy mountain, Jerusalem," says
Yahweh, "just as the Israelites bring the cereal offering in a clean
vessel to the temple of Yahweh. 21 And I will take some of them
for priests and for Levites," says Yahweh.

22   "For just as the new heavens and the new earth I am making
        will endure in my presence"—
      The oracle of Yahweh—
   "So your race and your name will endure.
23   And it shall be, from new moon to new moon and from
        Sabbath to Sabbath,
      All flesh will come to worship in my presence"—the oracle
        of Yahweh.
24   "And they shall go out and look at the corpses of the men
        who rebelled against me;
      For their worm will never die and their fire will never be
        extinguished;
      And they will be an abhorrence to all flesh."

NOTES

   lxvi 5. *brothers . . . expel you* suggests a deep division within the
Israelite community; such a division between the devout and the unbelievers is reflected elsewhere in post-exilic literature; cf. Zech. vii 8–14,
xi 4–17; Malachi iii 5–18; Ps. 101.
   6. Judgment is initiated by Yahweh's roar from Zion in Amos i 2,
repeated in Joel iv 16.
   7. *she.* Zion. The apocalyptic restoration of Jerusalem will come suddenly.
   9. As in Gen xxx 2, it is Yahweh who grants or withholds fecundity.
   11. The figure of the new Jerusalem as mother is pushed too far for
more moderate literary taste.
   12. The figure of the *river* is repeated from xlviii 18.
   14. *bones will bloom like grass.* A strange figure of speech, but the
author of this poem has strained metaphor elsewhere; see vss. 8 and 11.

15. *fire*. One of the elements of Yahweh in the theophany; see Ps xviii 9; Ezek i 4, 13, 27.

17. An obscure reference to superstitious rites; see lxv 3–4, 11. The *one in the center* is a priest.

18. The assembly of all nations for judgment is a feature of later apocalyptic writing; see Joel iv 21; Zech xii 3. It is suggested in Ezek xxxviii–xxxix.

19. *Tarshish*. See lx 9.

Put. Probably in the region of modern Libya.

Lud, Meshech. Probably identical with Phrygia in Asia Minor.

Rosh. Restored from Ezek xxxviii 2, xxxix 1, location unknown.

Tubal. Probably southeast of the Black Sea.

Javan. Identical with Greek *Ion*, the eponymous ancestor of the Ionians; designates the western coast of Asia Minor and the islands of the Aegean archipelago.

20. See lx 6–14.

21. The admission of Gentiles to be priests and Levites has no parallel elsewhere in the OT.

22. *the new heavens and the new earth*. See lxv 17.

24. The rebels are most probably Israelites. The verse is adapted in Mark ix 48 to Gehenna. Here the image is that of bodies lying unburied, probably in Tophet near Jerusalem; see Jer vii 30 – viii 2, which may be the source of this passage.

COMMENT

The unity of this poem is not strict, and it is possible that it has been composed as a cento of passages that had or were thought to have that unity of theme which is called apocalyptic. It has been enlarged by a prose gloss in vss. 18–21. The passage was very probably composed or added by an editor as a conclusion to the collection of Third Isaiah, or possibly to the entire collection of Isa i–lxvi. The passage contains several allusions to earlier books; see the NOTES.

Verses 5–6 are detached from the poem by some commentators. But the "roar" of Yahweh is the apocalyptic sound of judgment. The poem moves through two themes, salvation and judgment in that order. But first the prophet mentions the unfaithful Israelites. "Hate" and "expel" do not refer to any open and permanent division in the Israelite community of which we know. The preceding poem indicates a division between the wealthy, including the priests, and the pious poor. The institutional structure of the community was in the hands of those whom the prophet and the pious poor regarded as apostate Israelites. Verse 5 suggests that these apostates expressed incredulity toward the prophet's predictions of a glorious future and were contented with a realistic adjustment to life as it could be lived. Judgment begins from the temple, the seat of Yahweh's presence.

The prophet is sure that the saving act will come suddenly; it is like conception and birth in a single day. The saving act means the sudden appearance of a large number of true Israelites; this again suggests that the prophet and his followers formed a minority; see COMMENT on SEC. 45, specif. lxv 11–16. This miracle is possible to Yahweh. The children of the new Jerusalem are compared, somewhat broadly, to infants at the breast. The rare comparison of Yahweh to a mother illustrates not only his care but his tenderness.

The judgment is begun with a theophany; see the NOTES. Even here the prophet's thought turns to the faithless Israelites who practice superstitious rites which we cannot identify; see NOTE on vs. 17. It is on these rather than on the nations that the judgment falls. The gloss in 18–21 takes a favorable view of the nations, although the word "survivors" suggests the apocalyptic slaughter. But it is possible that the prose gloss preserves imperfectly some thoughts which occurred in the original form of the poem. These nations are not judged; they receive missionaries, and in response to the proclamation they bring the Israelites living abroad as a sacrificial offering to Yahweh, just as the Israelites bring cereal offerings. For this quasi-priestly act they will be rewarded with admission to the ranks of the sacred personnel of the temple. Here in a clumsily written prose gloss is one of the most spacious views of religion and mankind which is found in the entire OT. The poem resumes in vs. 22 with a promise of the eternity of Israel.

Most readers and interpreters would be happy if the book ended here; and it is quite probable that originally it did end here. But a conclusion is added, which fills out the picture of the judgment; this may come from an editor who felt that it had been left incomplete in the early lines of the poem. The faithless Israelites should not be left in obscurity. The lines describe what happened to them in vs. 16. They remain a perpetual monument to the ultimate issue of infidelity, a constant reminder that Yahweh is righteous and cannot accept the unrighteous. The lines give an impression of narrowness which is all the more noticeable because it follows the breadth of the prose gloss. But they do not depart from the prophetic idea of judgment; they are unusual in their imagery, which is less pleasing to modern readers. We are indeed at the threshold of apocalyptic, which paints the judgment in lurid colors. It was the protest of later generations against the massive evil of a godless world which they felt helpless to resist. If Yahweh had judged Israel as he did, surely his judgment of the nations would be far more grim.

INDEX OF BIBLICAL PASSAGES

INDEX OF HEBREW WORDS

INDEX OF SUBJECTS

INDEX OF PROPER NAMES

INDEX OF AUTHORS

ɔ